RIC
OUP
23¢
10.50
COMPAR-A-BUY
35.0¢ PER POUND

NEW
07/29/79

#937 GENERIC
CHICKEN NOODLE
SOUP
022 814
24

COMPAR-A-BUY
35.0¢ PER POUND

RIC
FFEE
$1.19
22OZ
COMPAR-A-BUY
86.5¢ PER POUND

NEW
07/29/79

22
#976 GENERIC
WHITE CORN MEAL
257 220
10

89¢
5LBS
COMPAR-A-BUY
17.8¢ PER POUND

ALL
ANER
69¢
32OZ
COMPAR-A-BUY
69.0¢ PER QUART

NEW
07/29/79

22
SOLO COZY REFILL
ASST. COLORS 7OZ
734 558
12

73¢
50CT
COMPAR-A-BUY
73.0¢ PER 50 COU

S
NUTS
92¢
6.5OZ
COMPAR-A-BUY
W. $2.26 PER POUND

NEW
07/29/79

22
PLANTERS DRY
ROASTED UNSALTED
PEANUTS
521 922
12 S.G.W.

$1.15
8.25OZ
COMPA
$2.23 POUND

RY
ONDS
$1.09
4OZ
COMPAR-A-BUY

NEW

22
SUN GIANT
ALMONDS HICKORY
SMOKED
522 326

$1.09
4OZ
COMPAR-A-BUY

1.

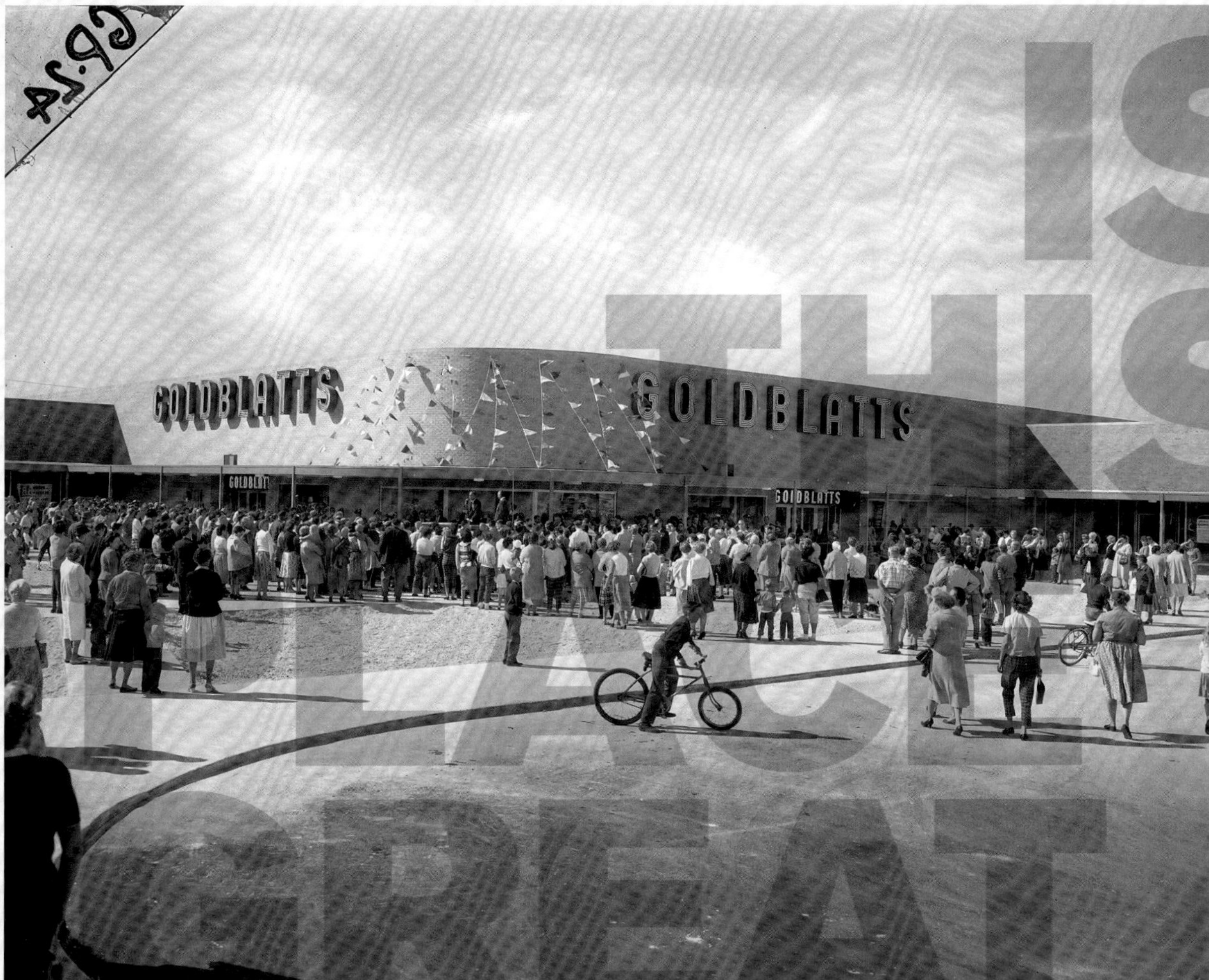

IS THIS PLACE GREAT OR WHAT

2.

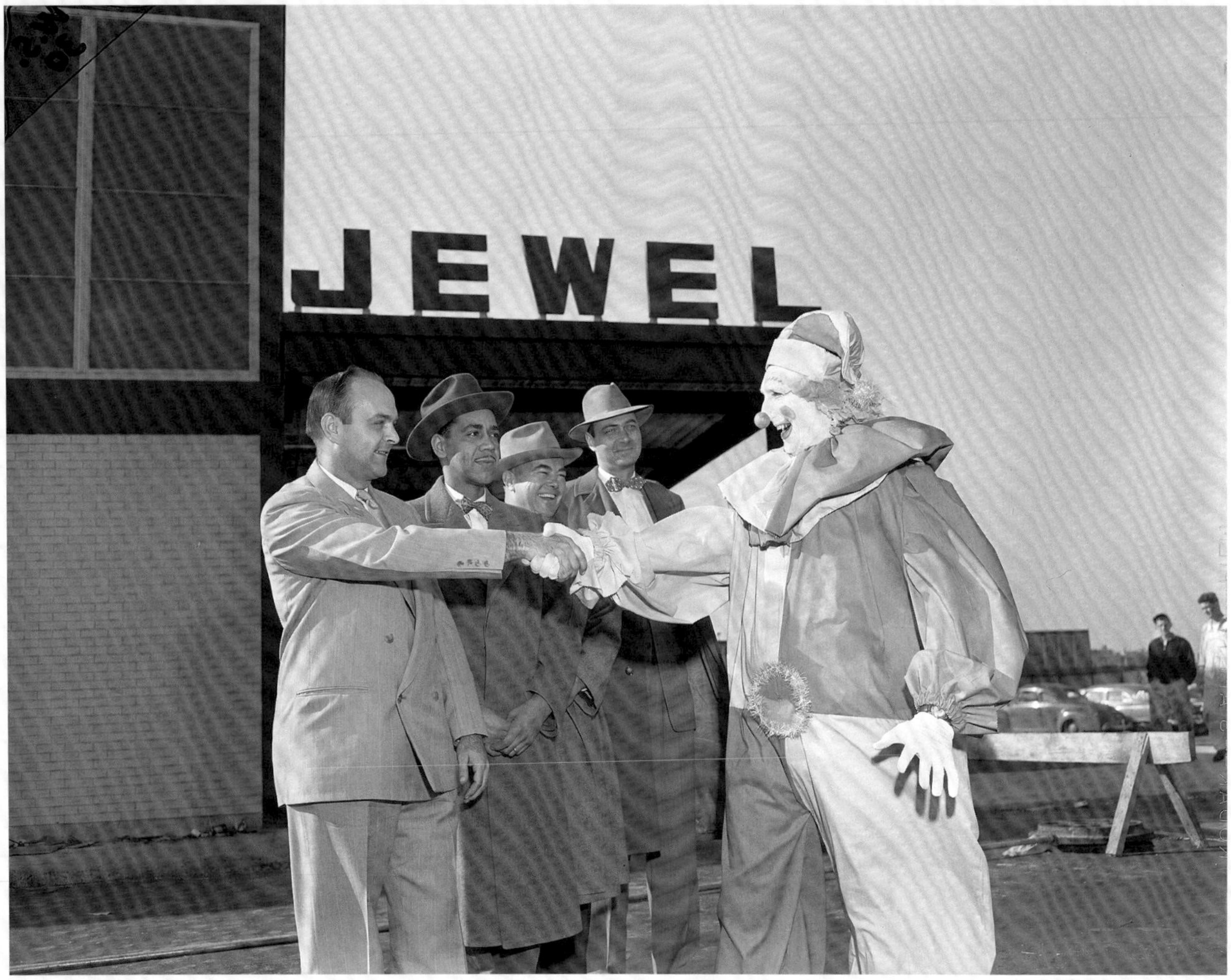

3.

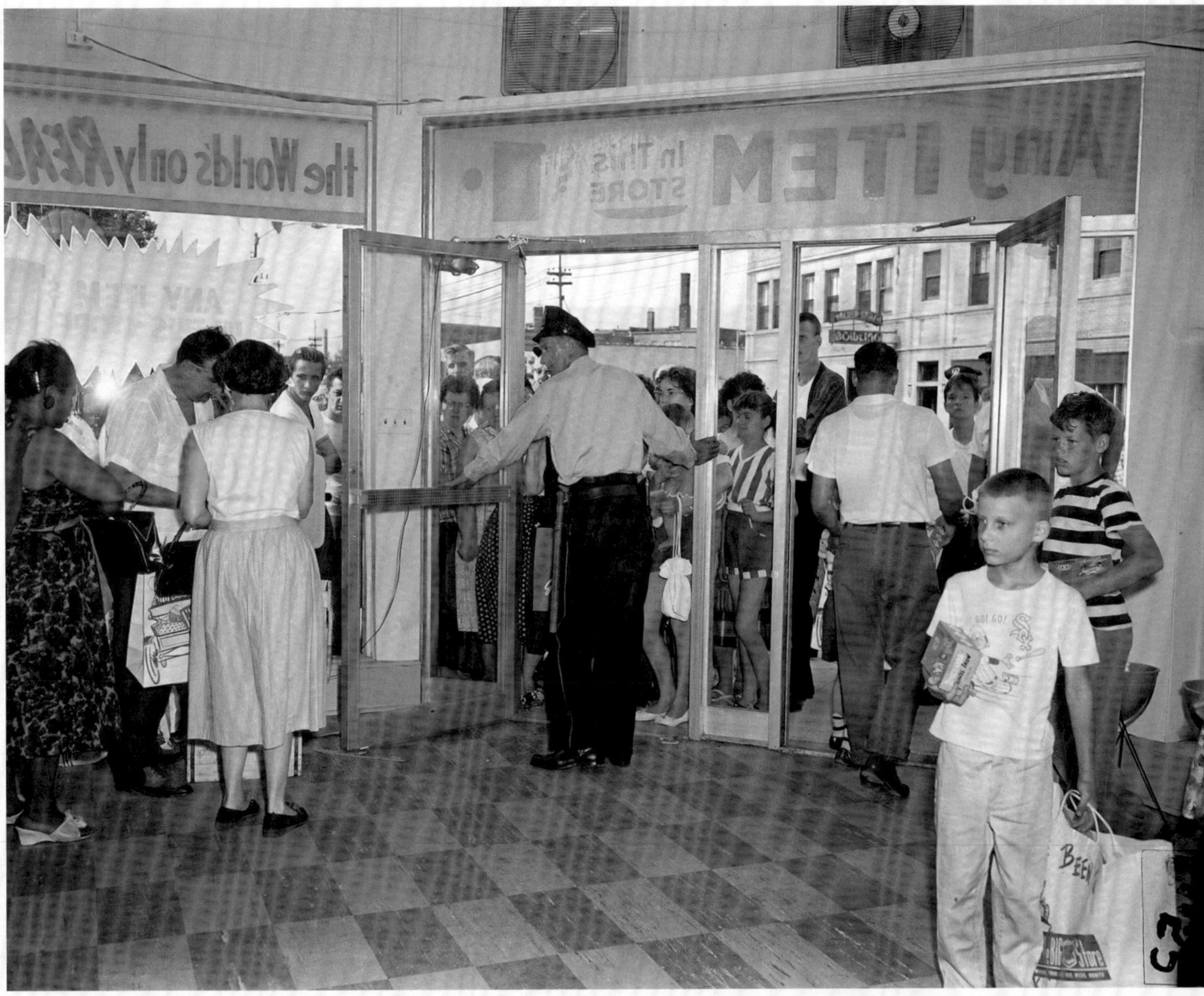

COPIA: RETAIL, THRIFT, AND DARK STORES, 2001–11

4.

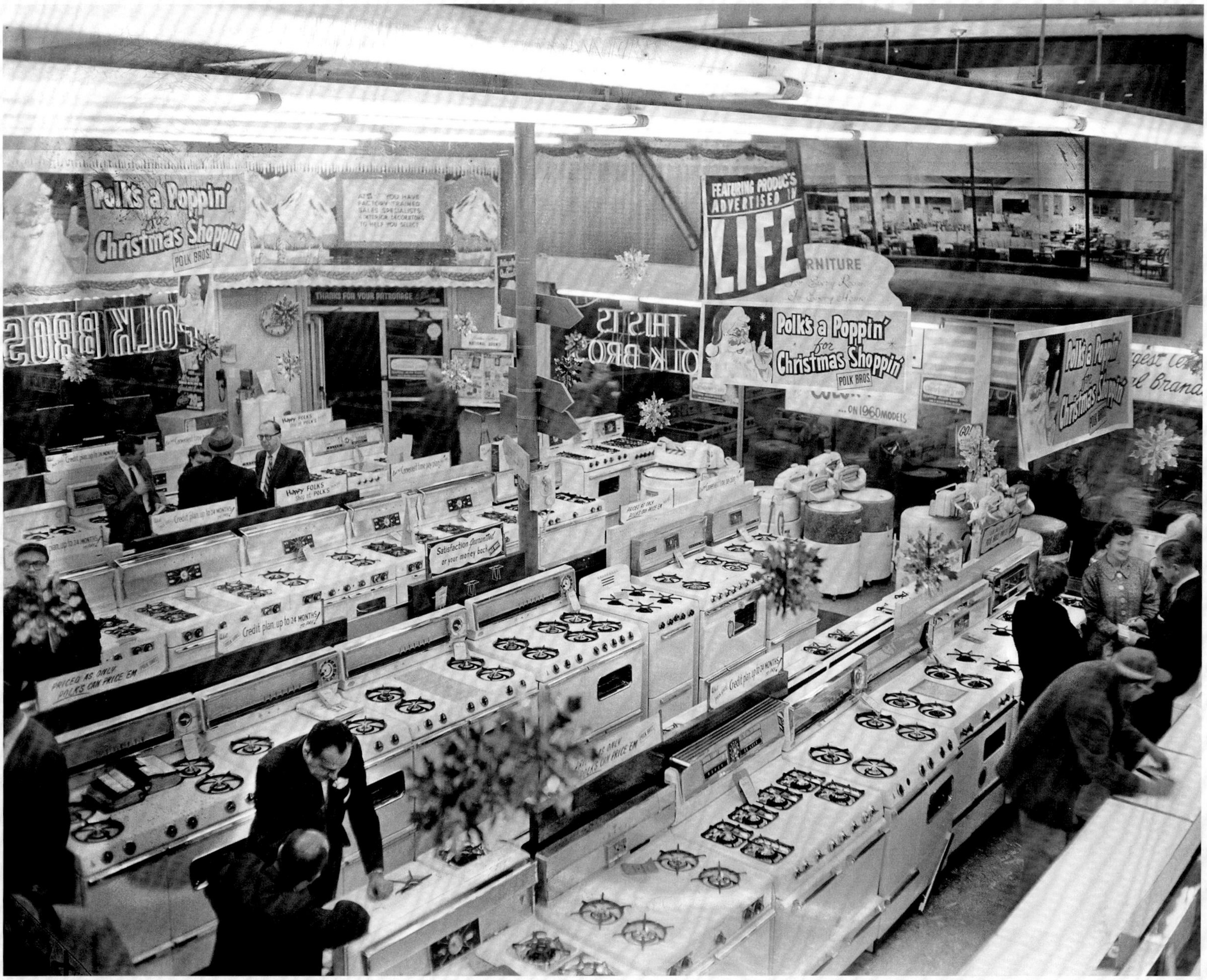

PHOTOGRAPHS BY BRIAN ULRICH

THE CLEVELAND MUSEUM OF ART

aperture

IS THIS PLACE GREAT OR WHAT

COPIA: RETAIL, THRIFT, AND DARK STORES, 2001–11

PHOTOGRAPHS BY BRIAN ULRICH

5.

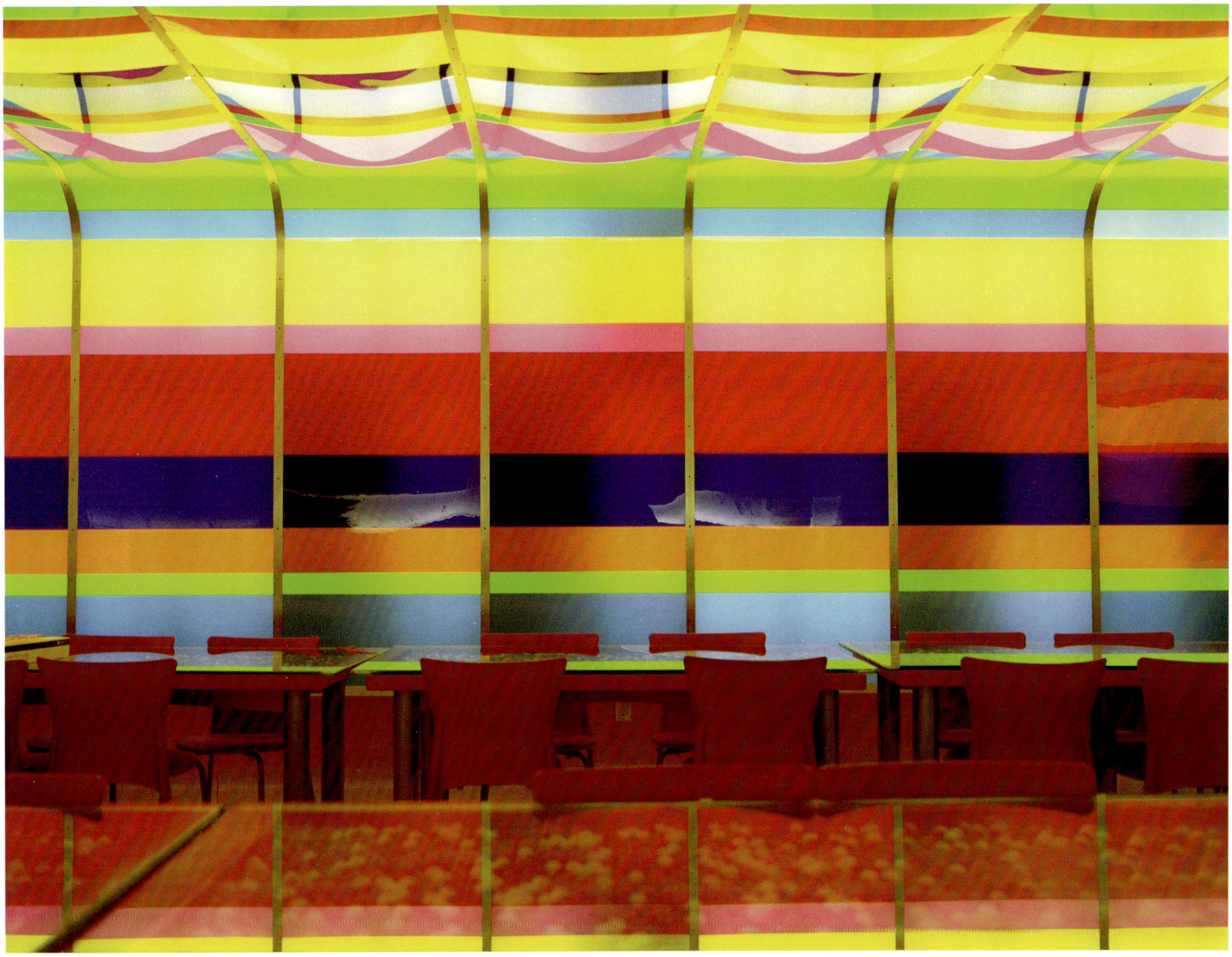

RETAIL

6.

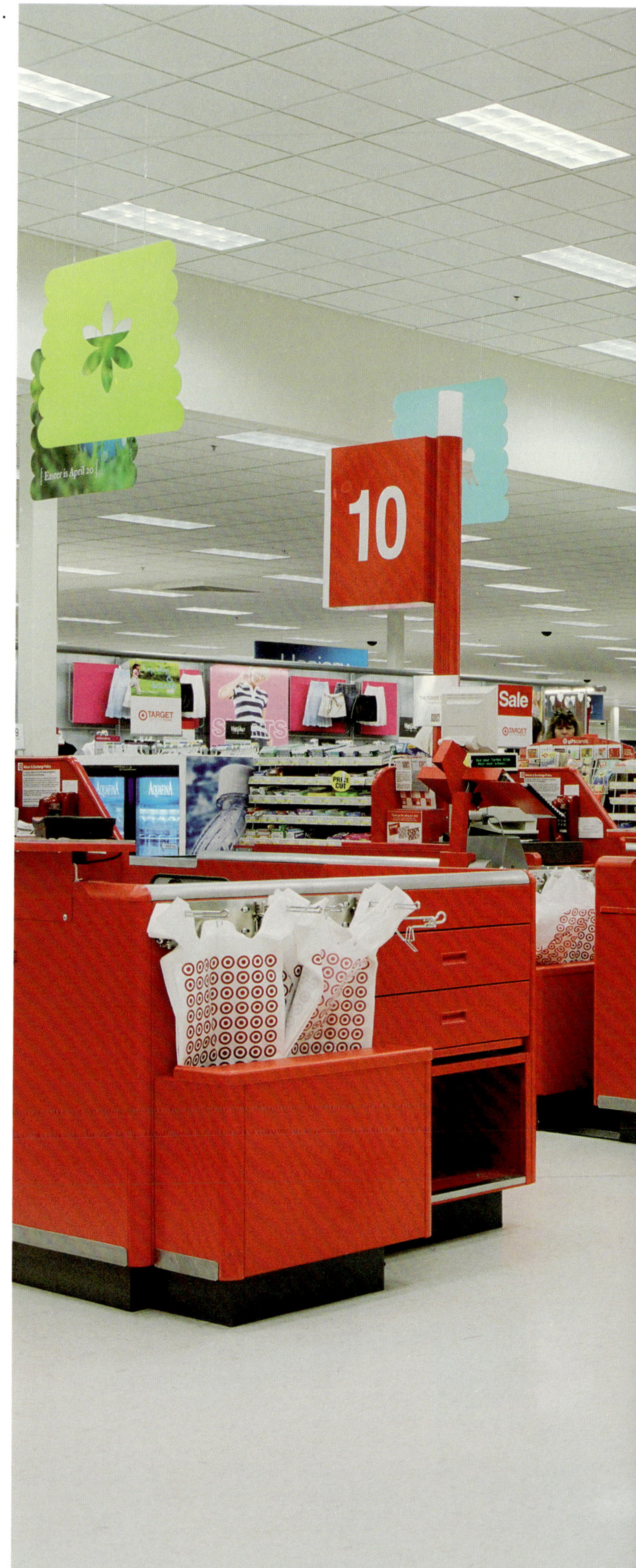

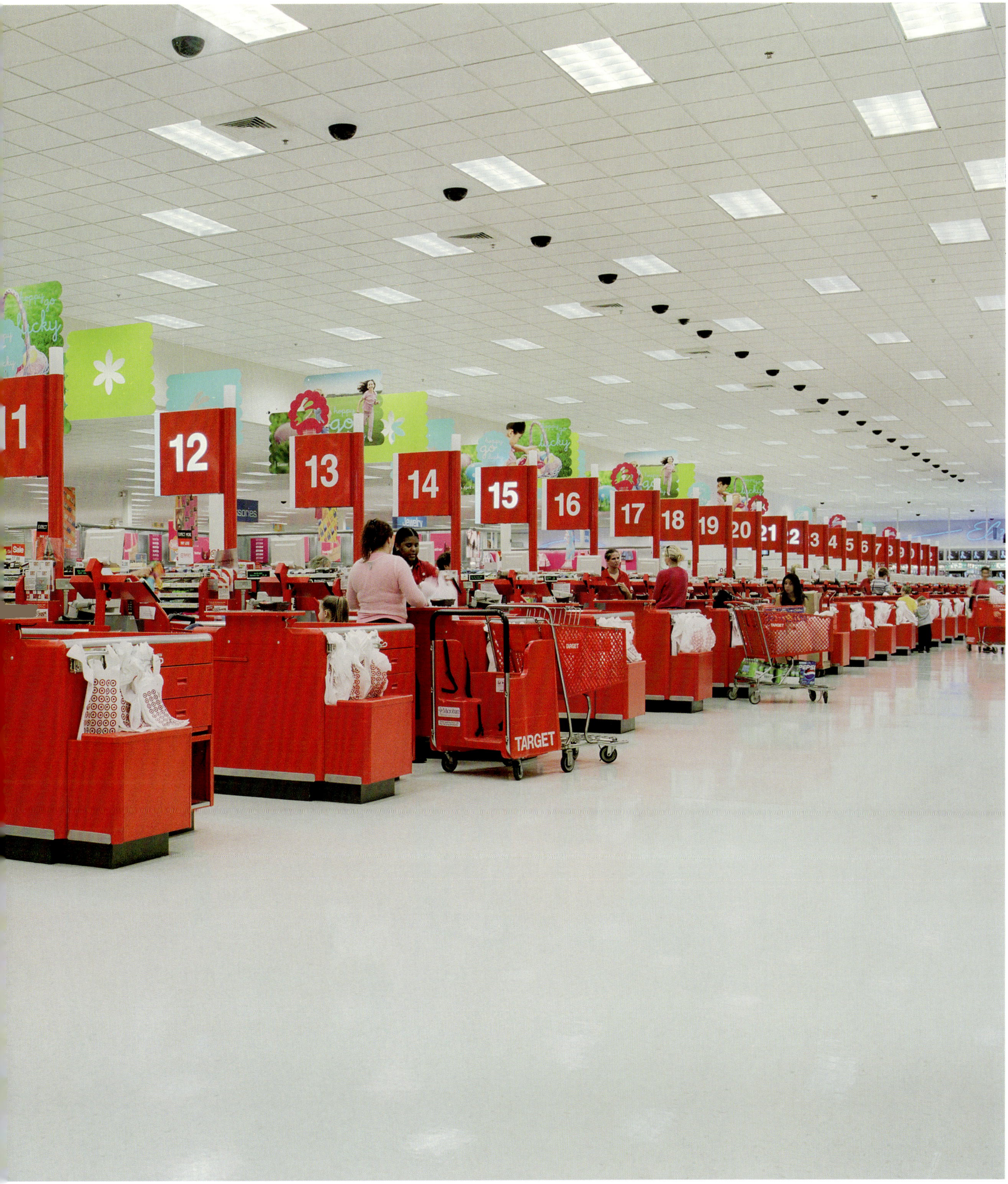
12
13
14
15
16
17
18
19
20
21
TARGET

7.

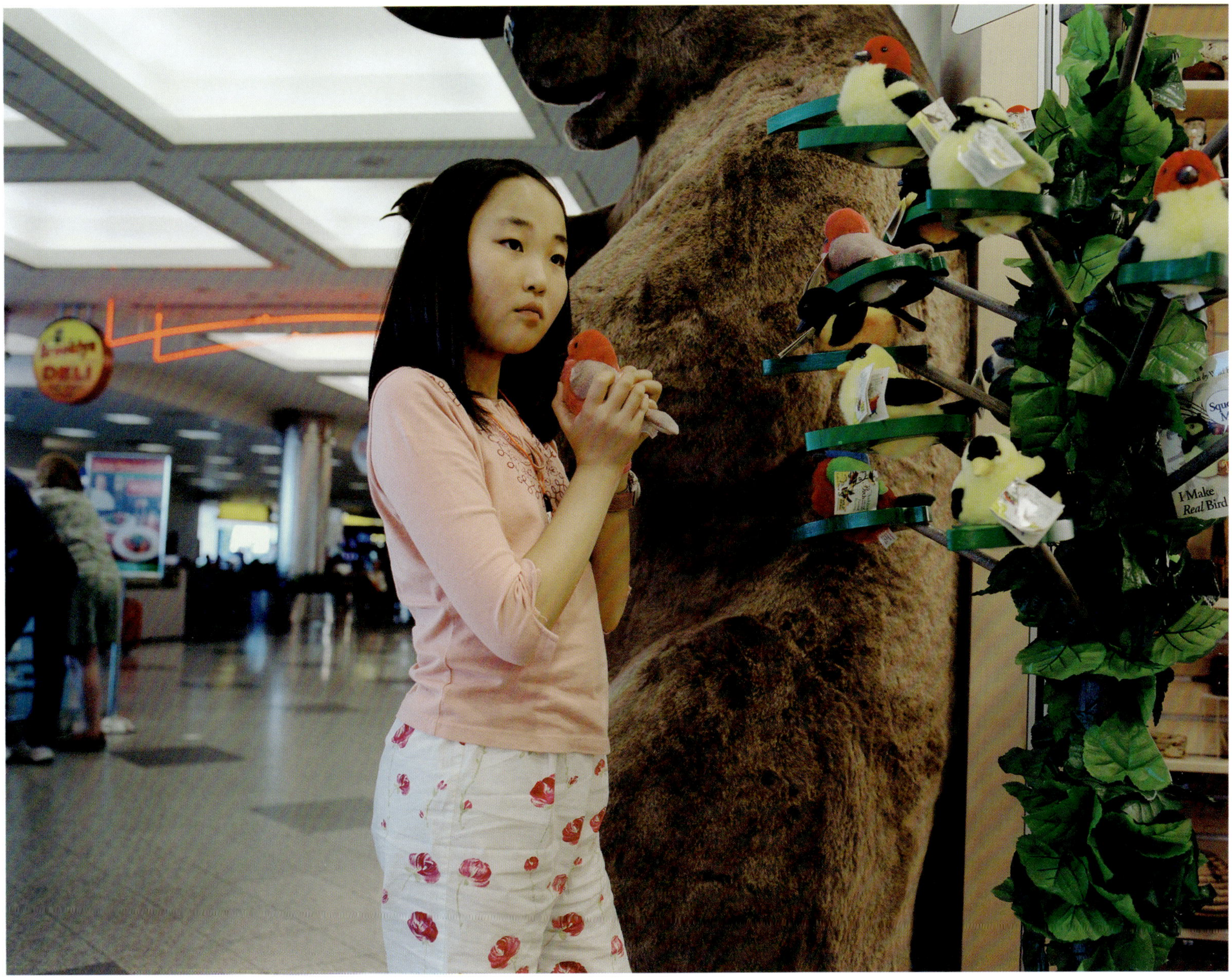

8.

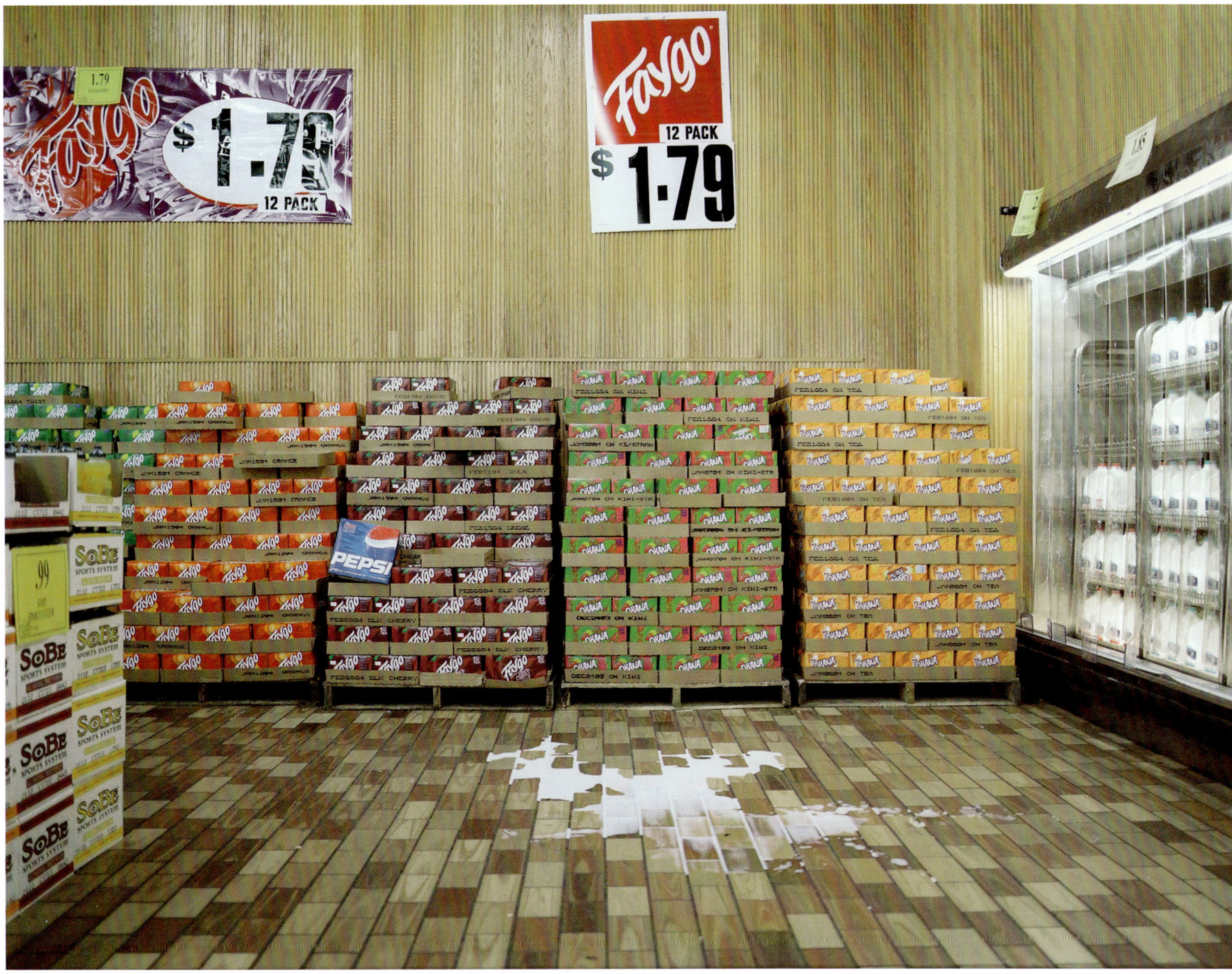

1.79
Faygo
$ 1.79
12 PACK
Faygo
12 PACK
$ 1.79
PEPSI
.99
SoBe
SPORTS SYSTEM

9.

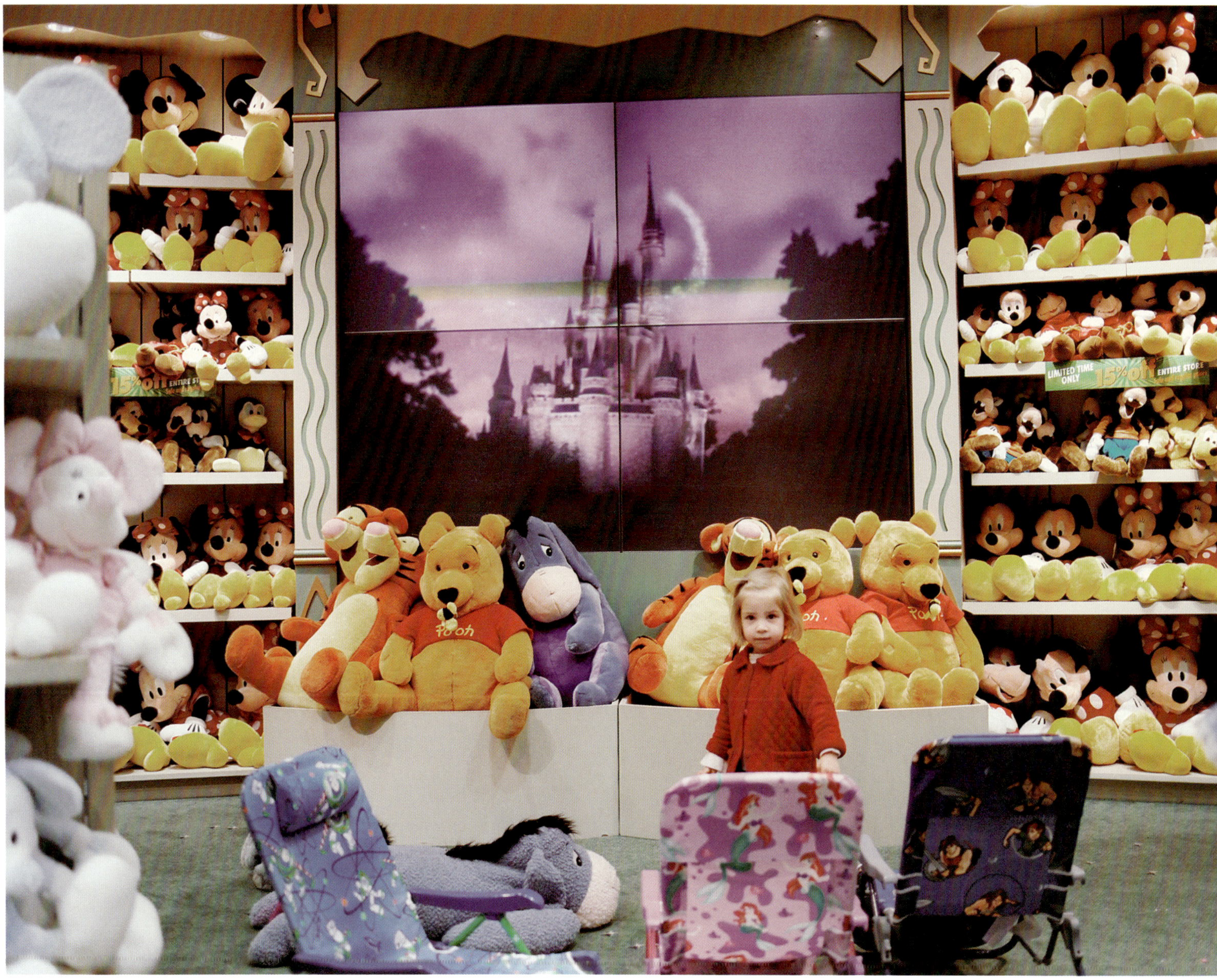

10.

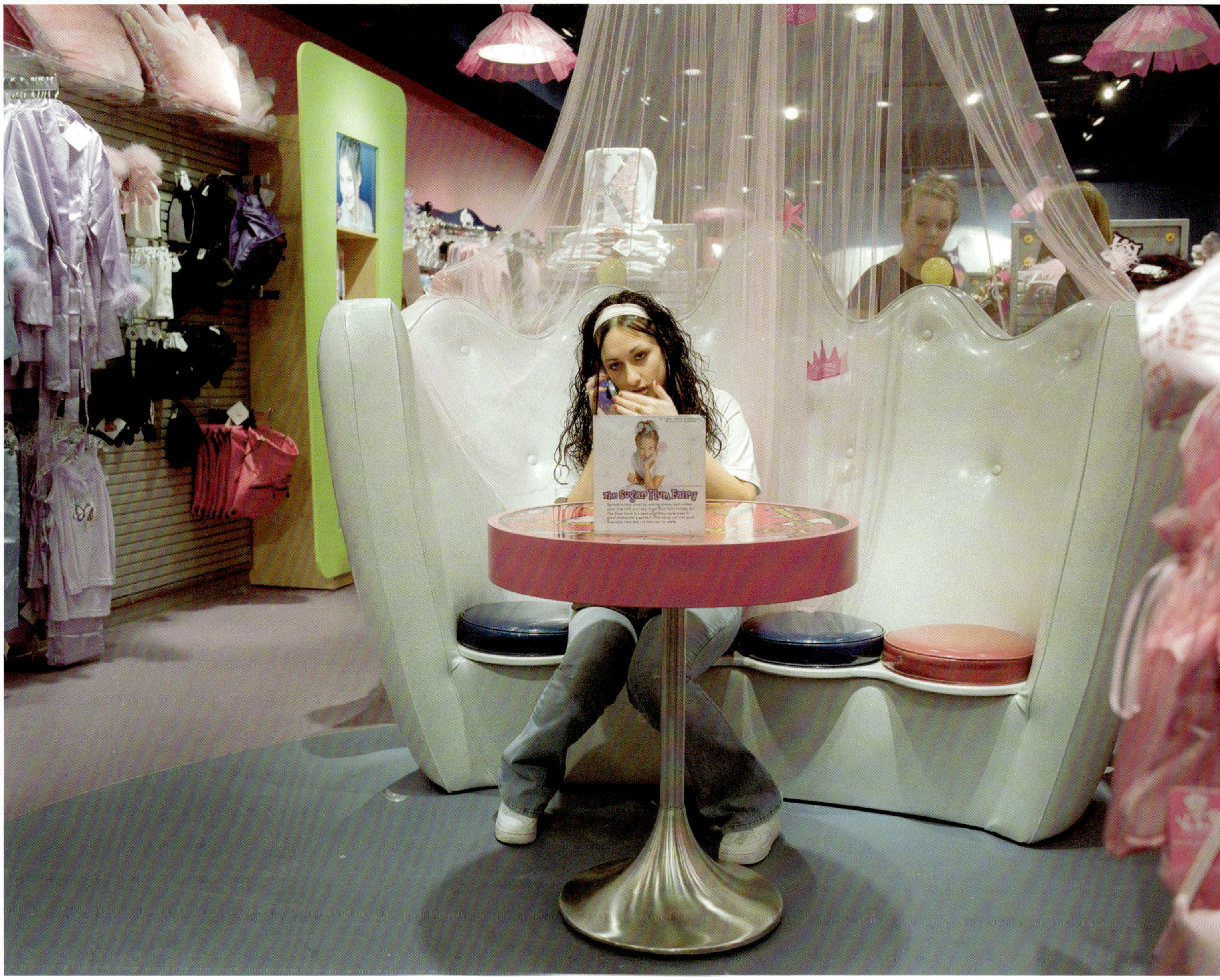

11.

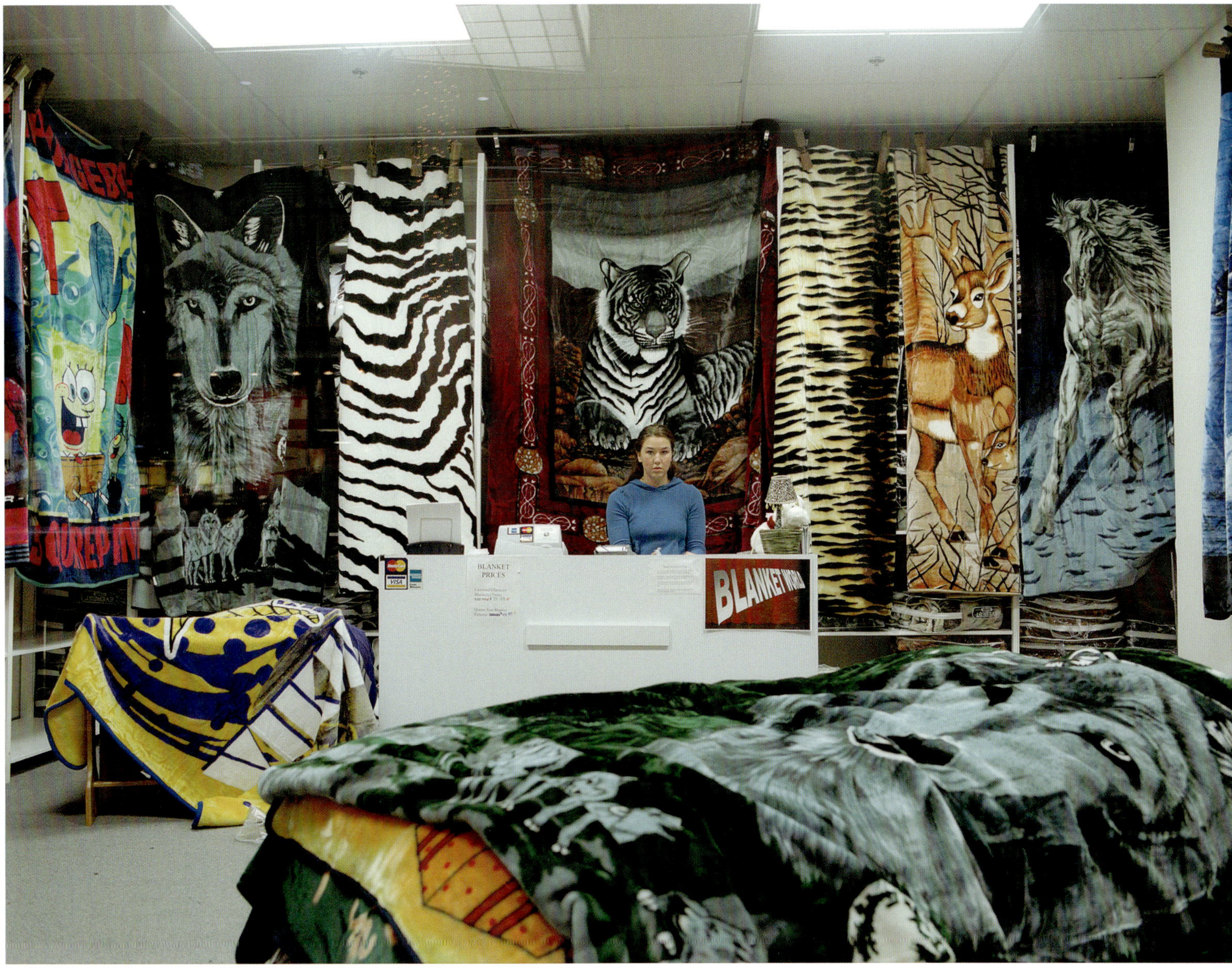

12.

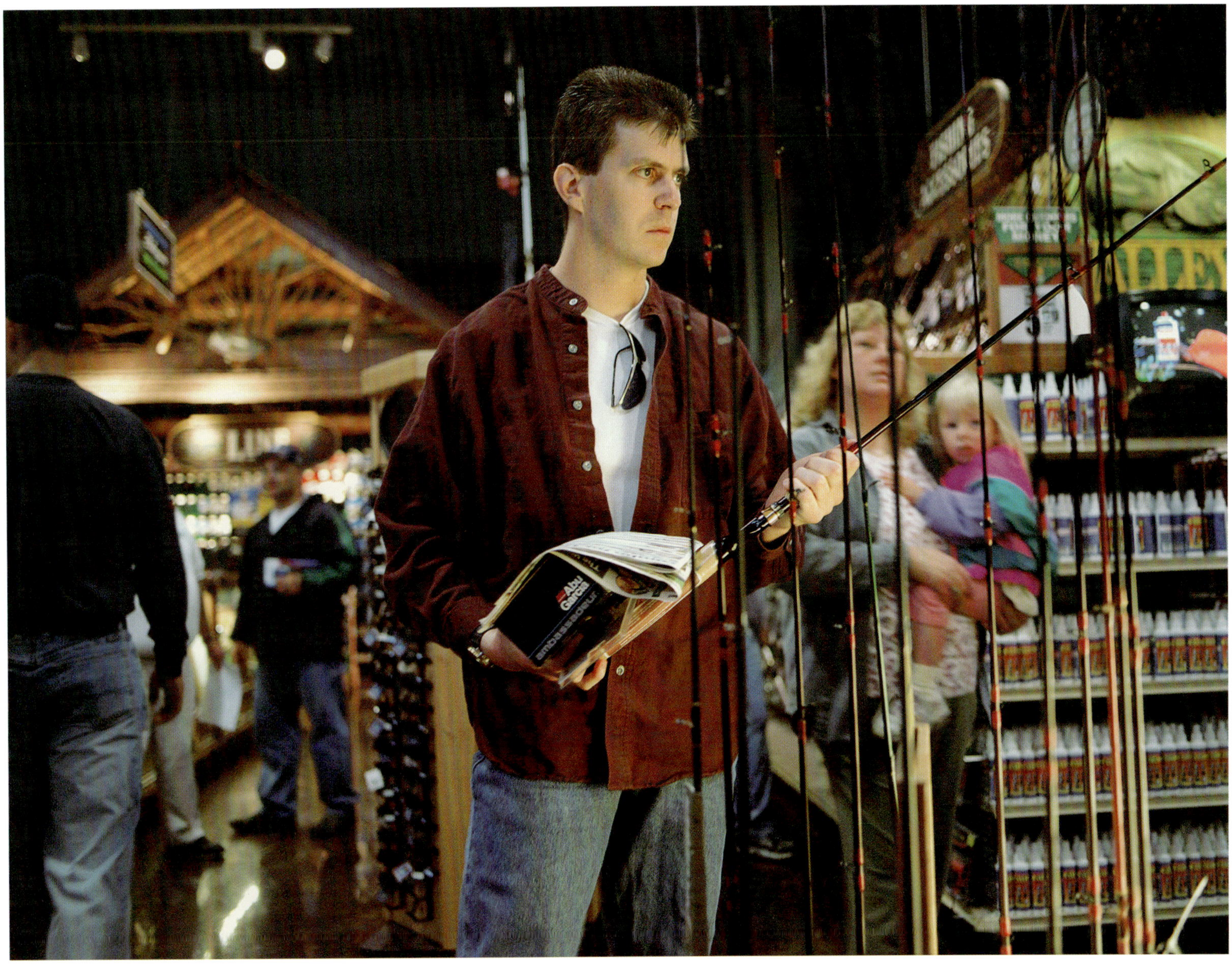

13.

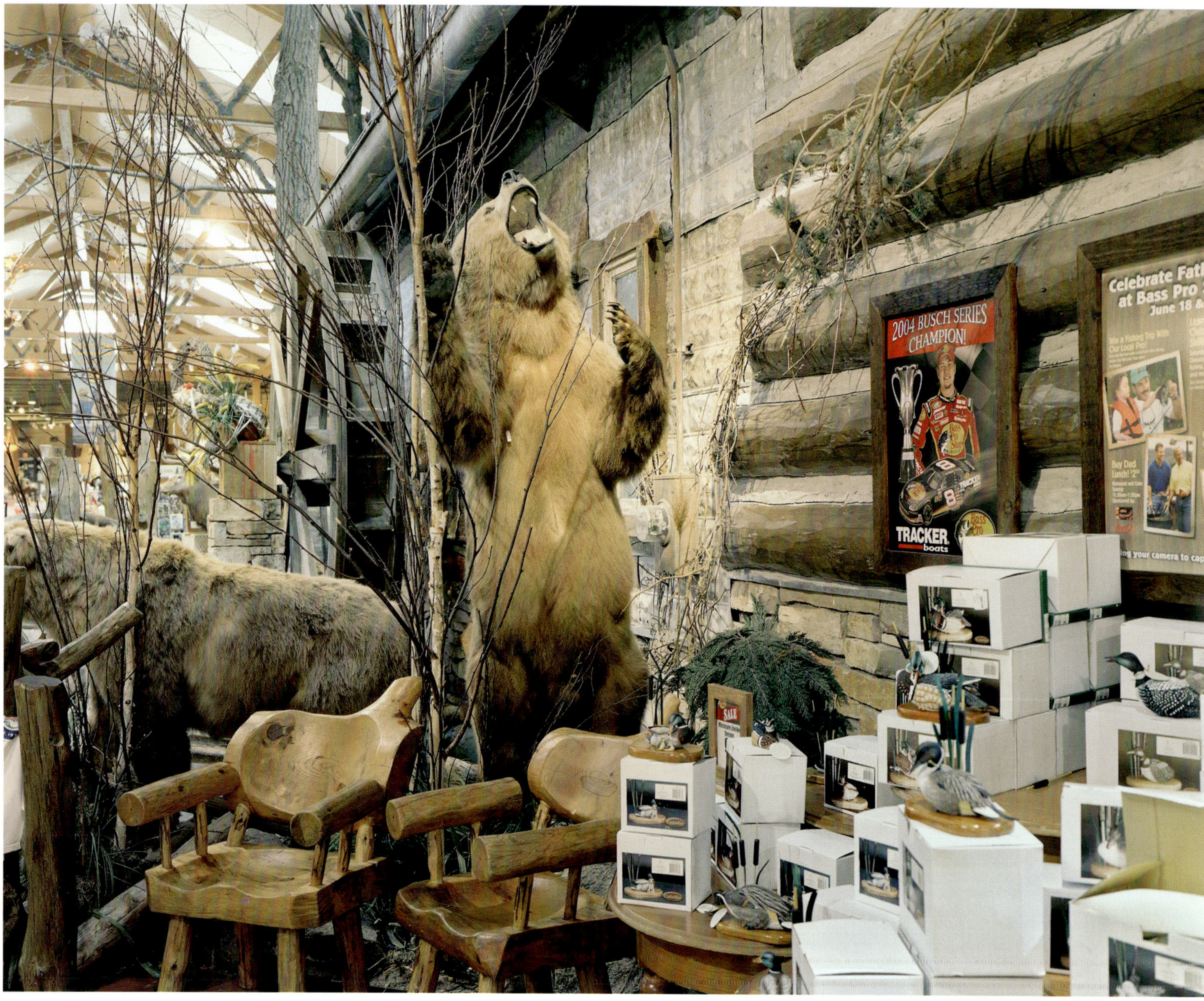

14.

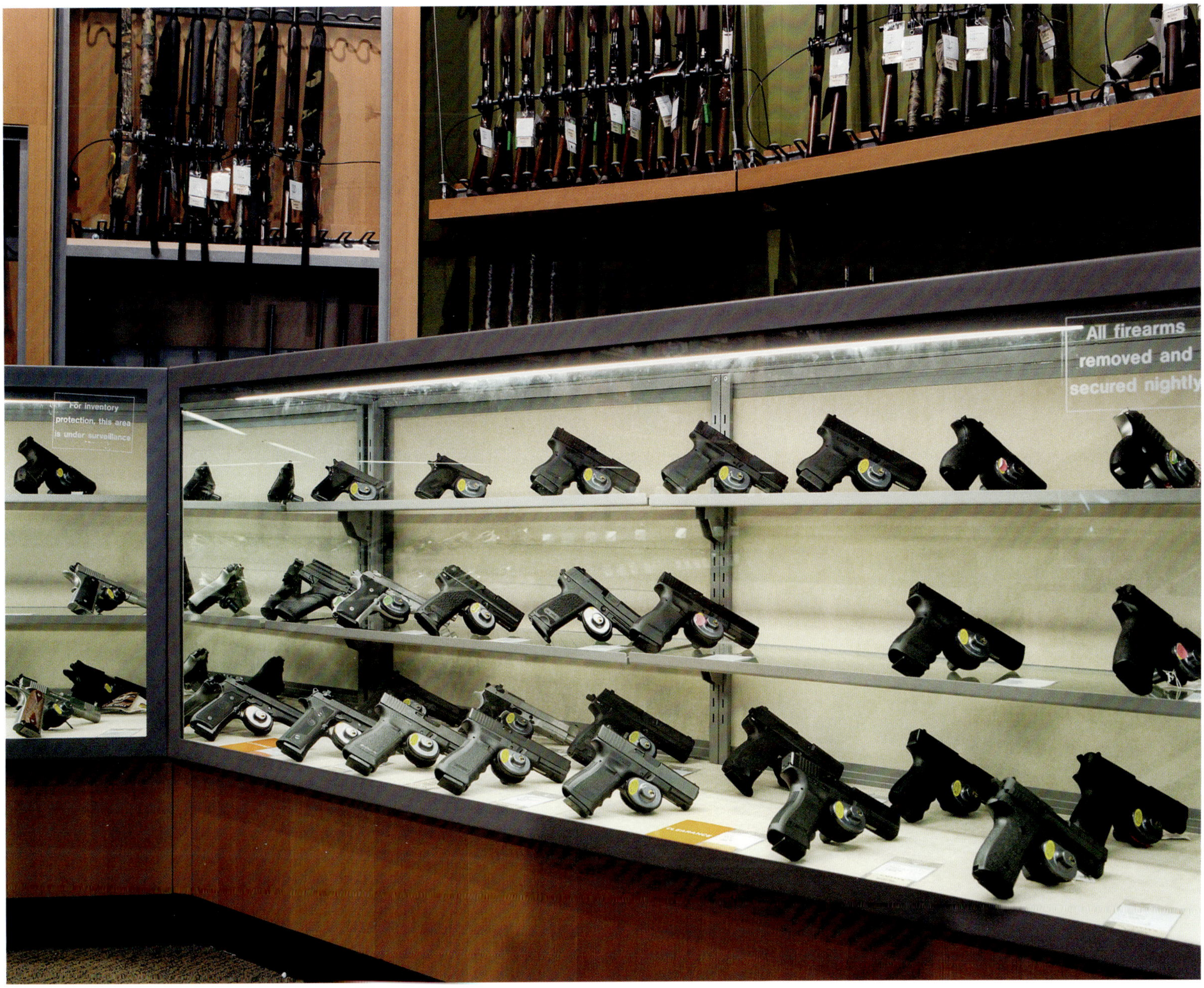
All firearms removed and secured nightly
For inventory protection, this area is under surveillance

15.

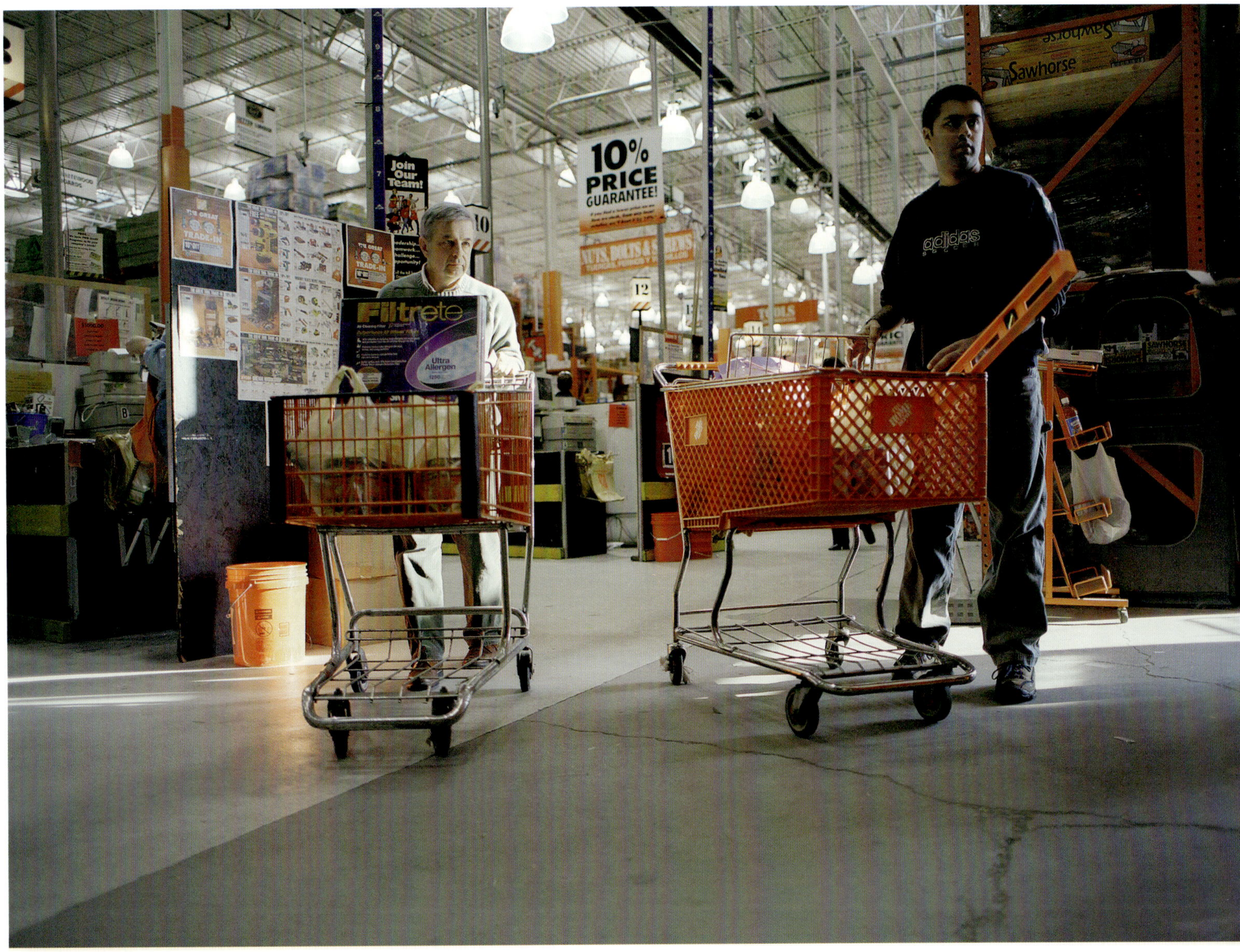
10% PRICE GUARANTEE!
Join Our Team!
Filtrete
Ultra Allergen
NUTS, BOLTS & SCREWS
Sawhorse
adidas

16.

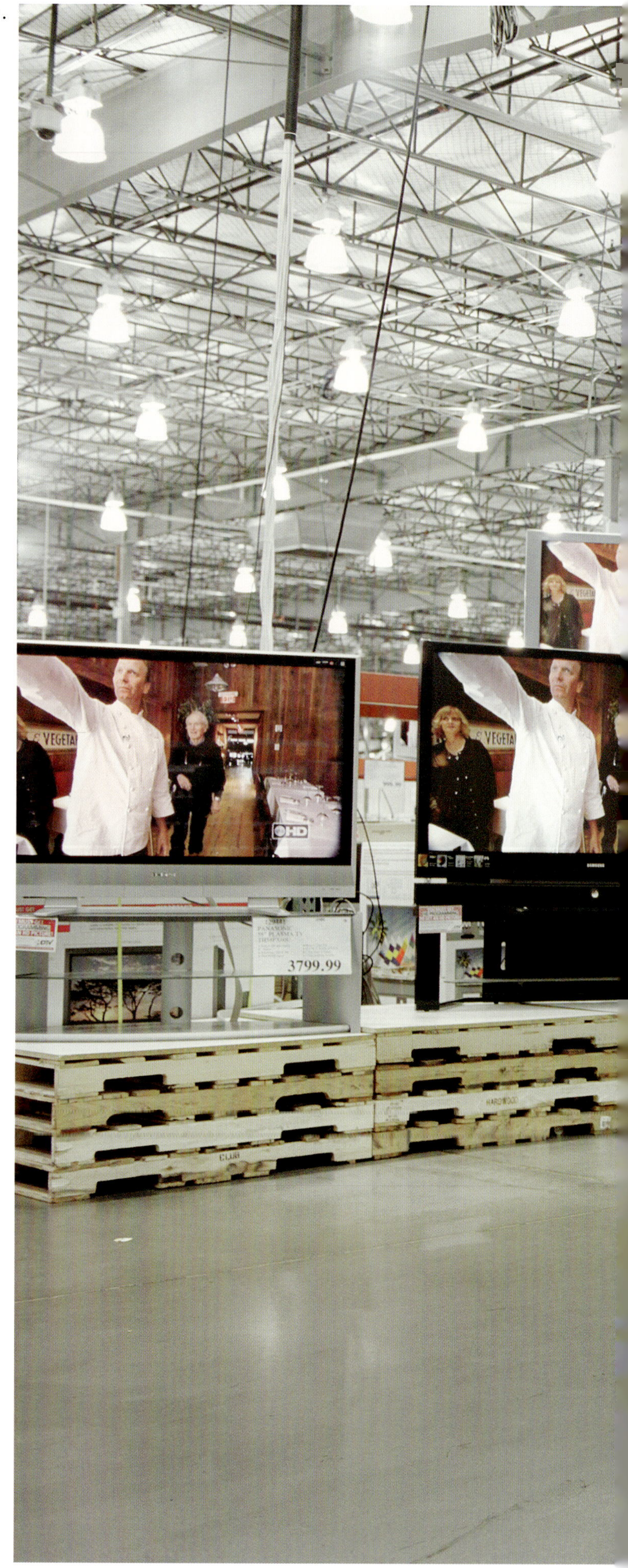

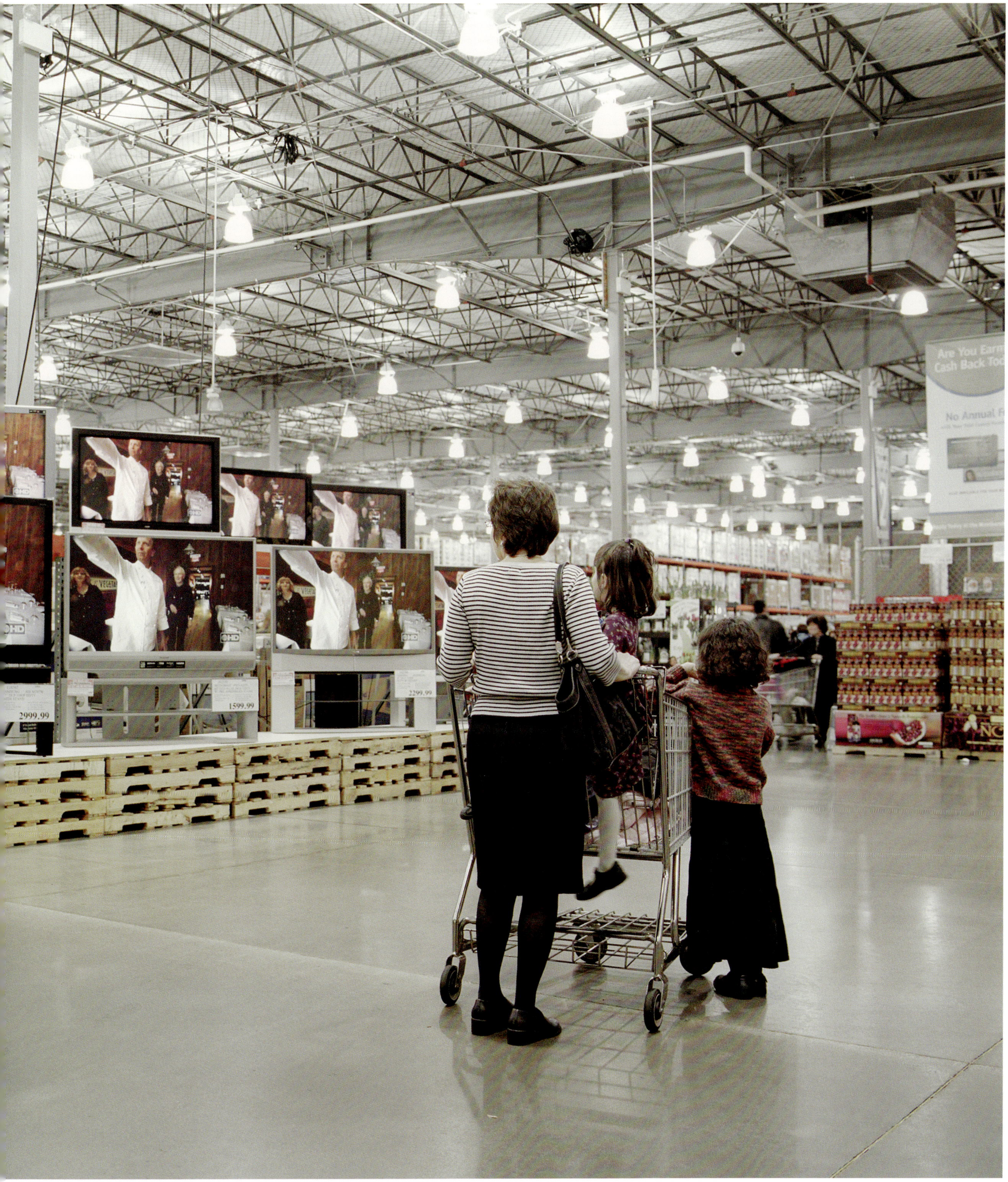
2999.99
1599.99
2299.99

17.

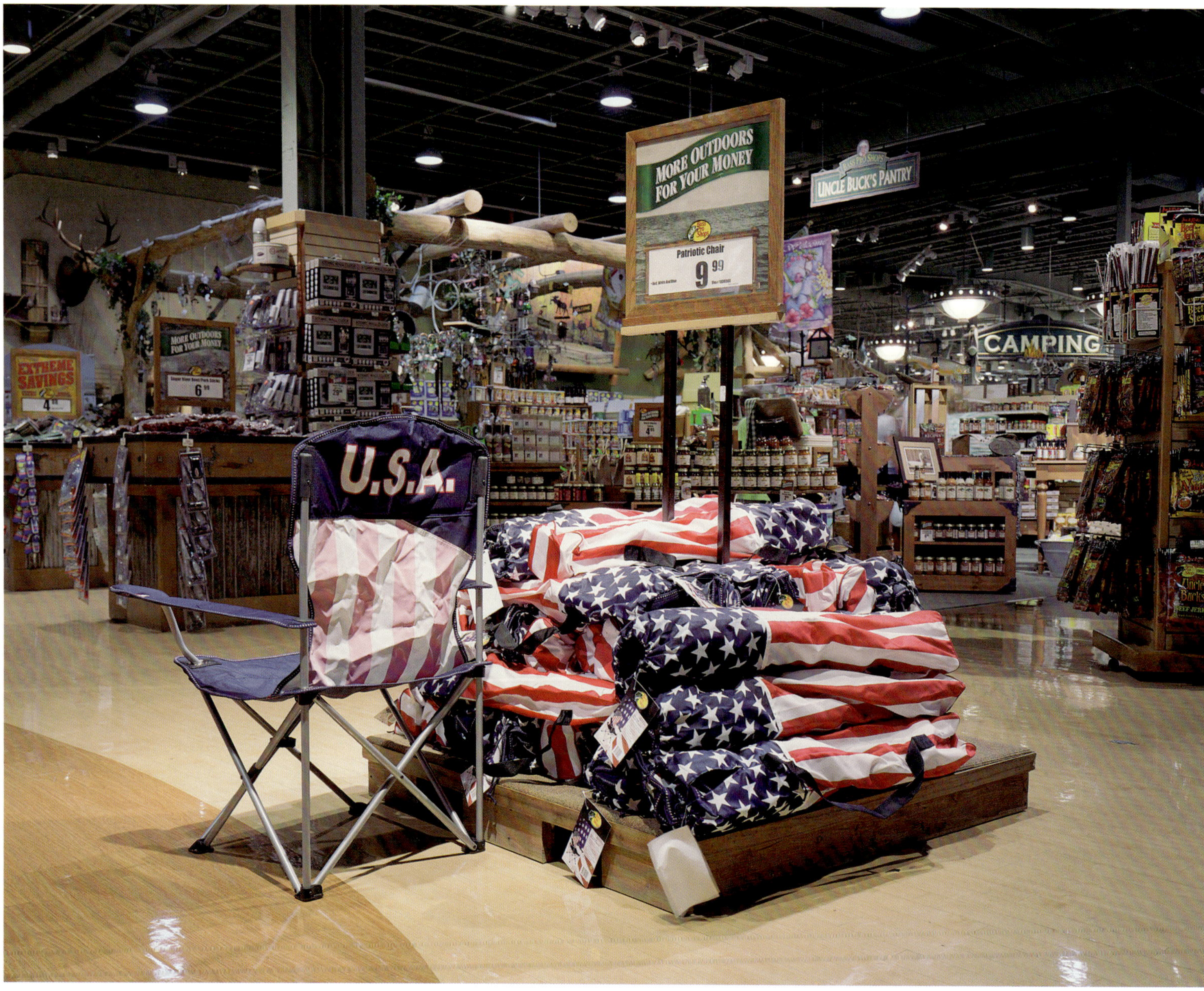

MORE OUTDOORS
FOR YOUR MONEY
Patriotic Chair
9 99
UNCLE BUCK'S PANTRY
CAMPING
EXTREME
SAVINGS
U.S.A.

18.

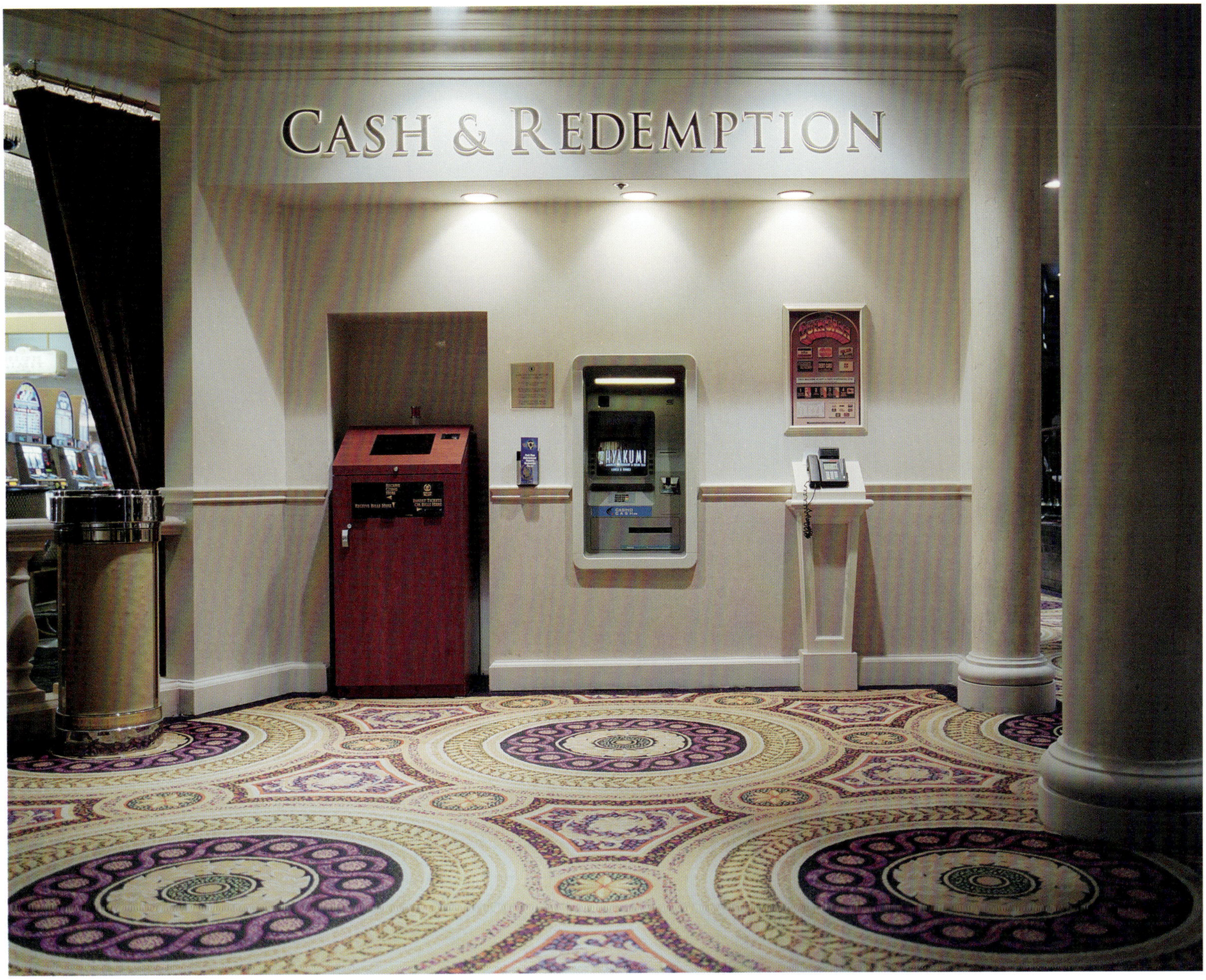

19.

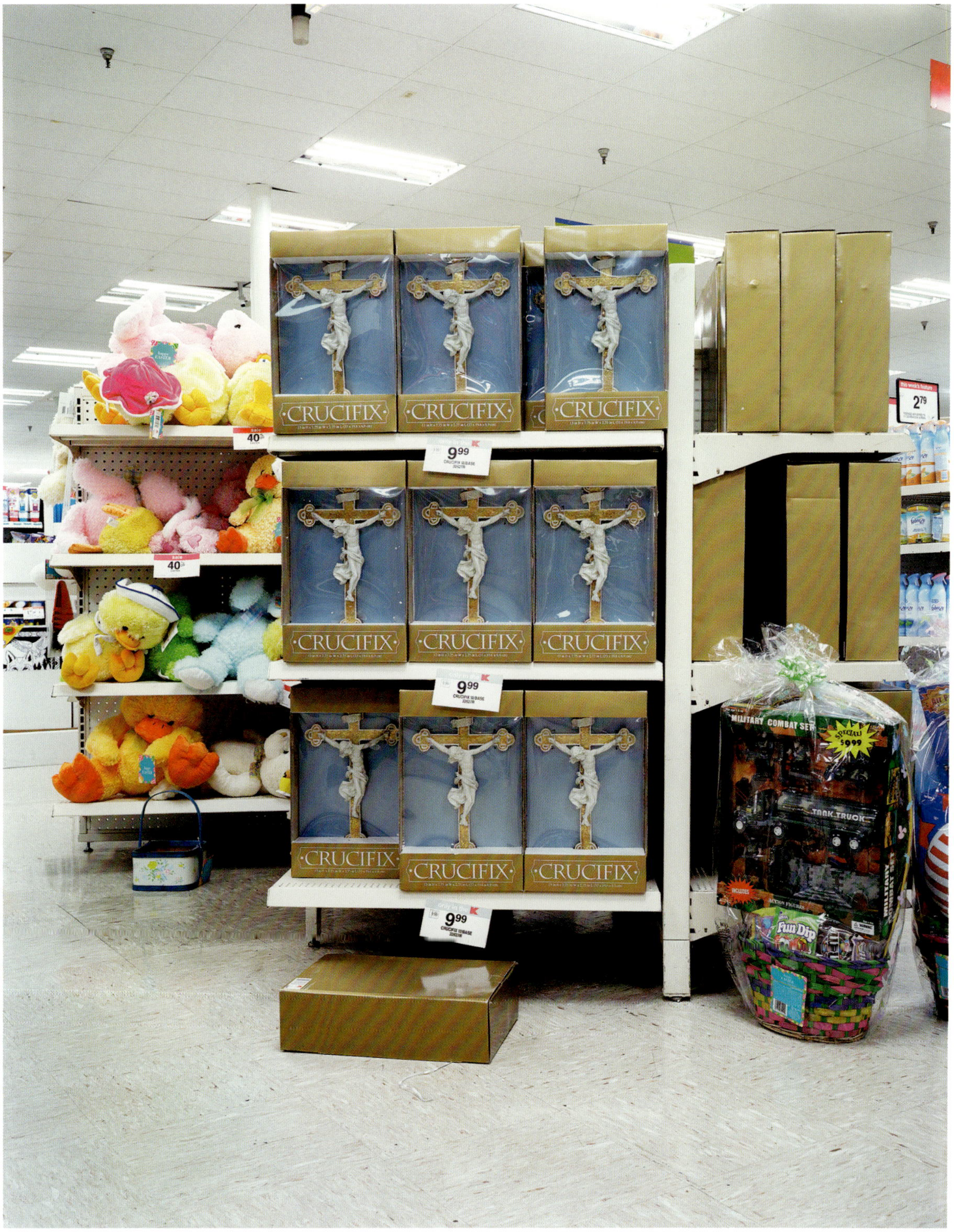
CRUCIFIX
CRUCIFIX
CRUCIFIX
CRUCIFIX
CRUCIFIX
CRUCIFIX
CRUCIFIX
CRUCIFIX
CRUCIFIX
9 99
9 99
9 99
40
40
2 79
MILITARY COMBAT SET
TANK TRUCK
Fun Dip

20.

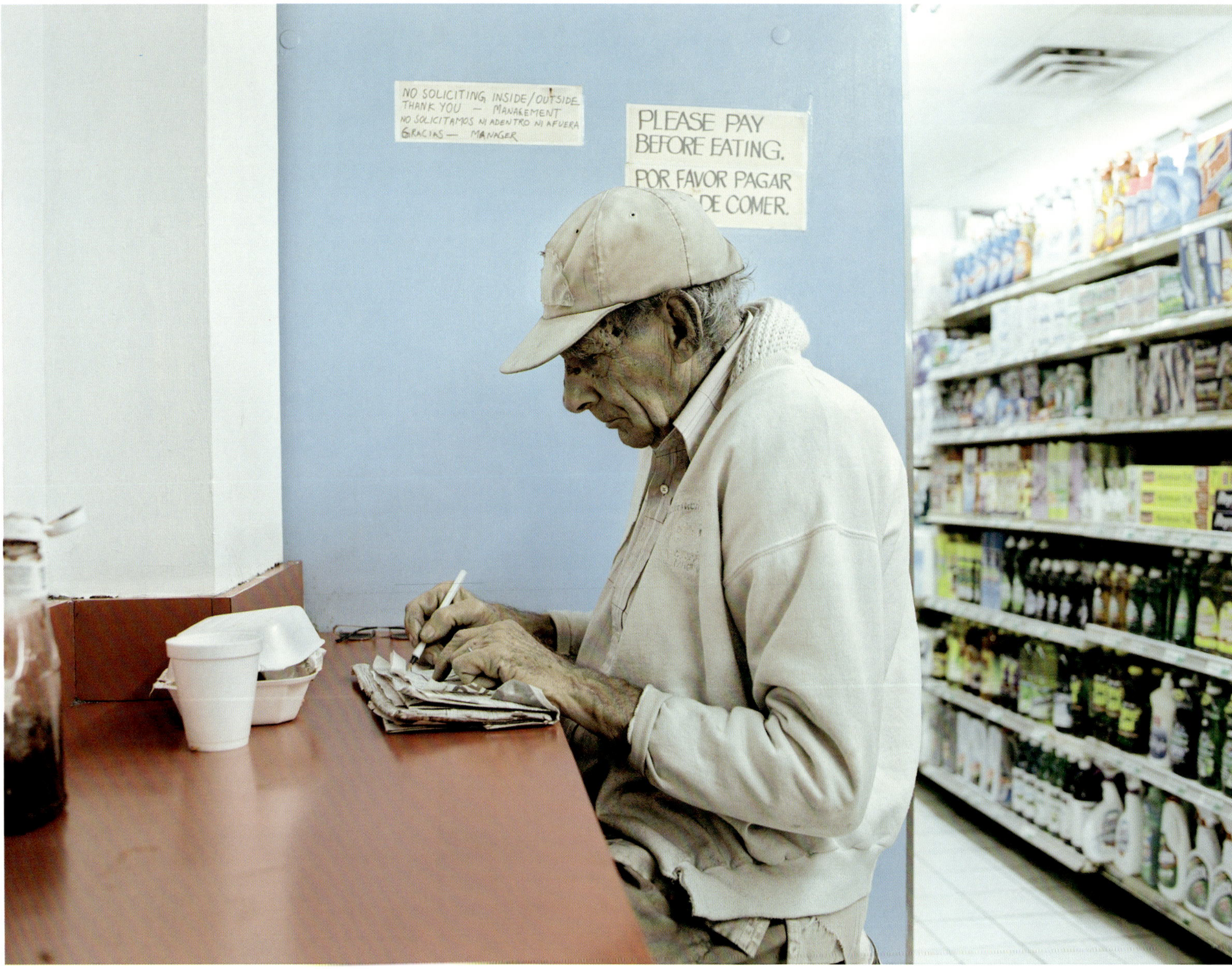
NO SOLICITING INSIDE/OUTSIDE
THANK YOU — MANAGEMENT
NO SOLICITAMOS NI ADENTRO NI AFUERA
GRACIAS — MANAGER
PLEASE PAY
BEFORE EATING.
POR FAVOR PAGAR
DE COMER.

21.

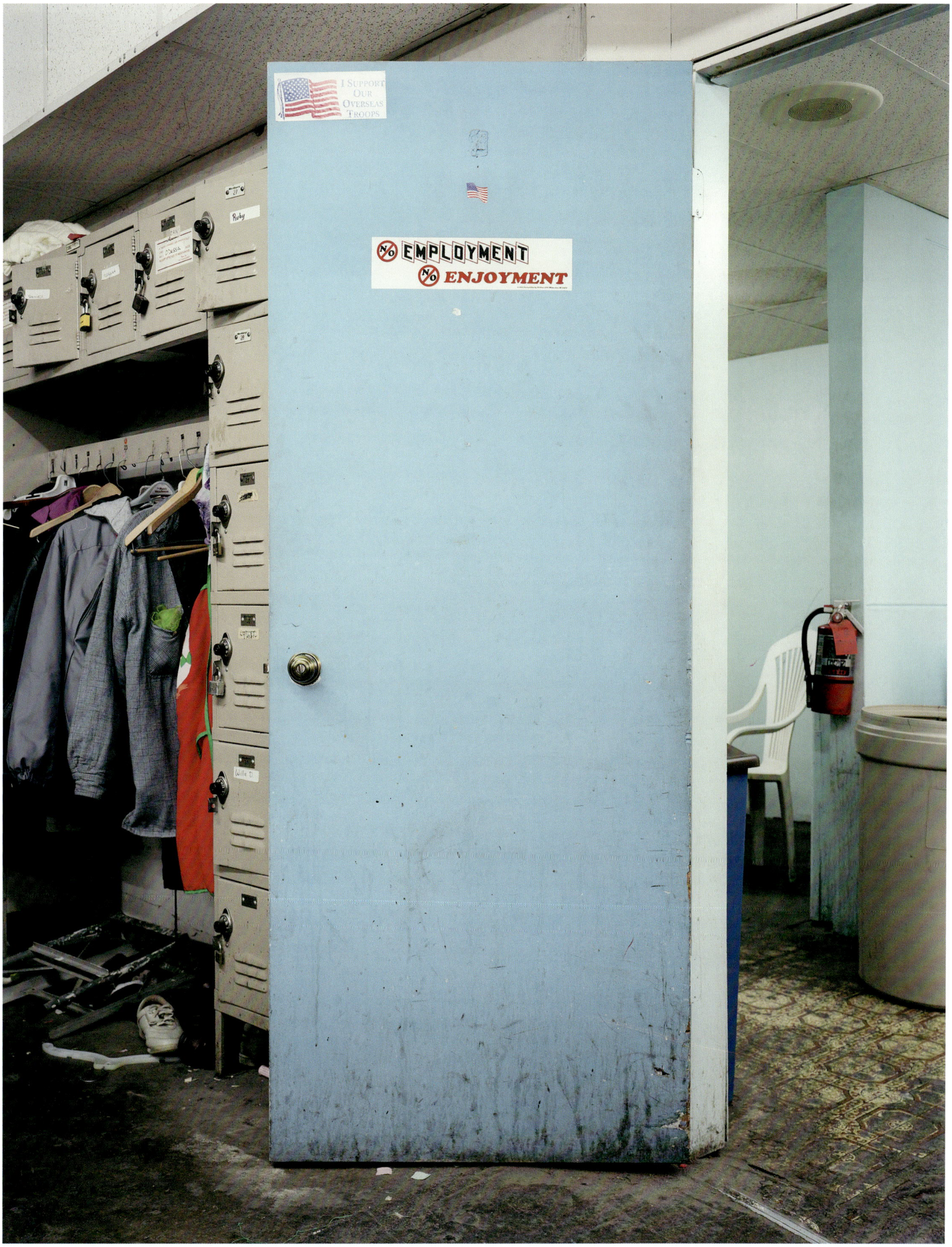

22.

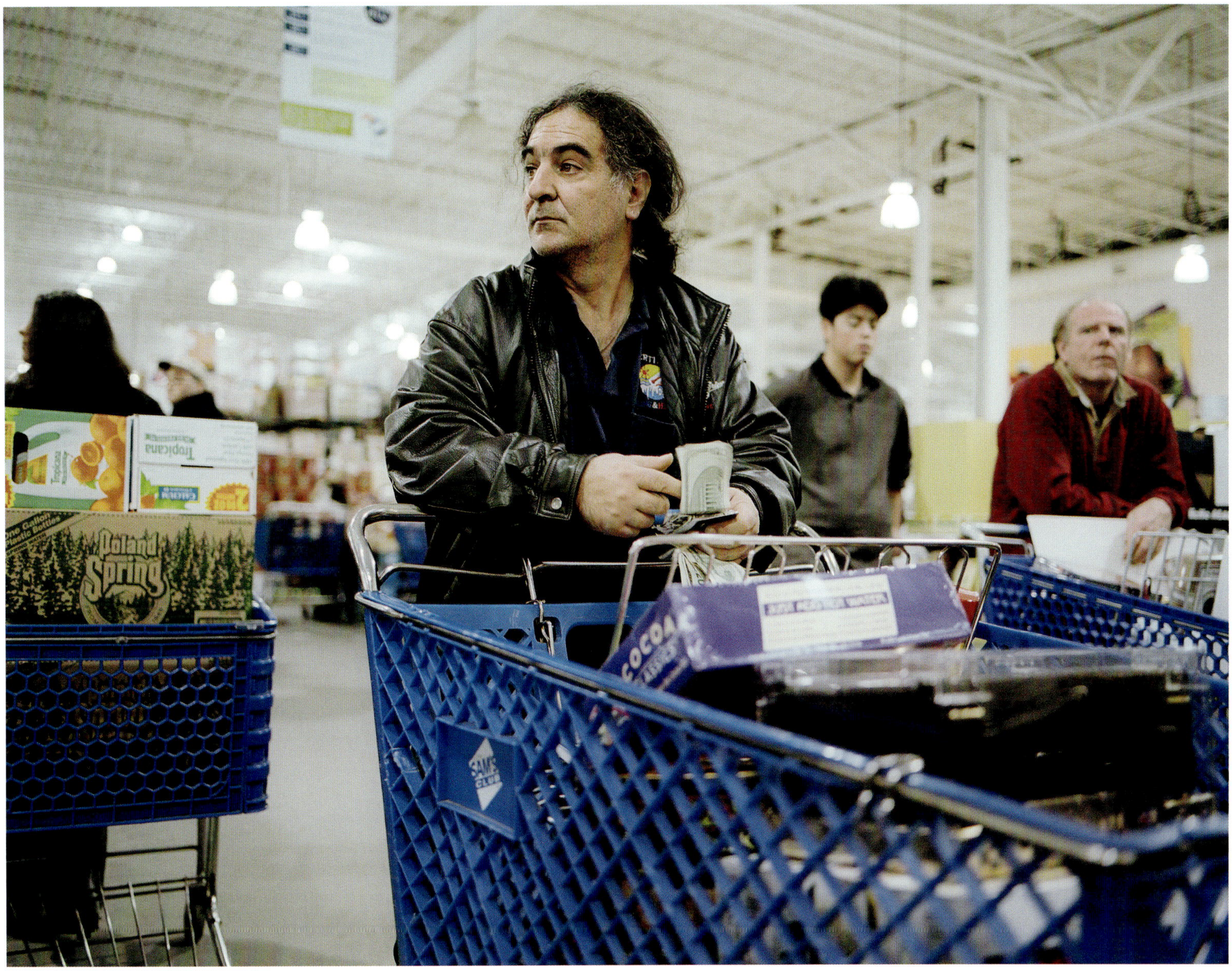

23.

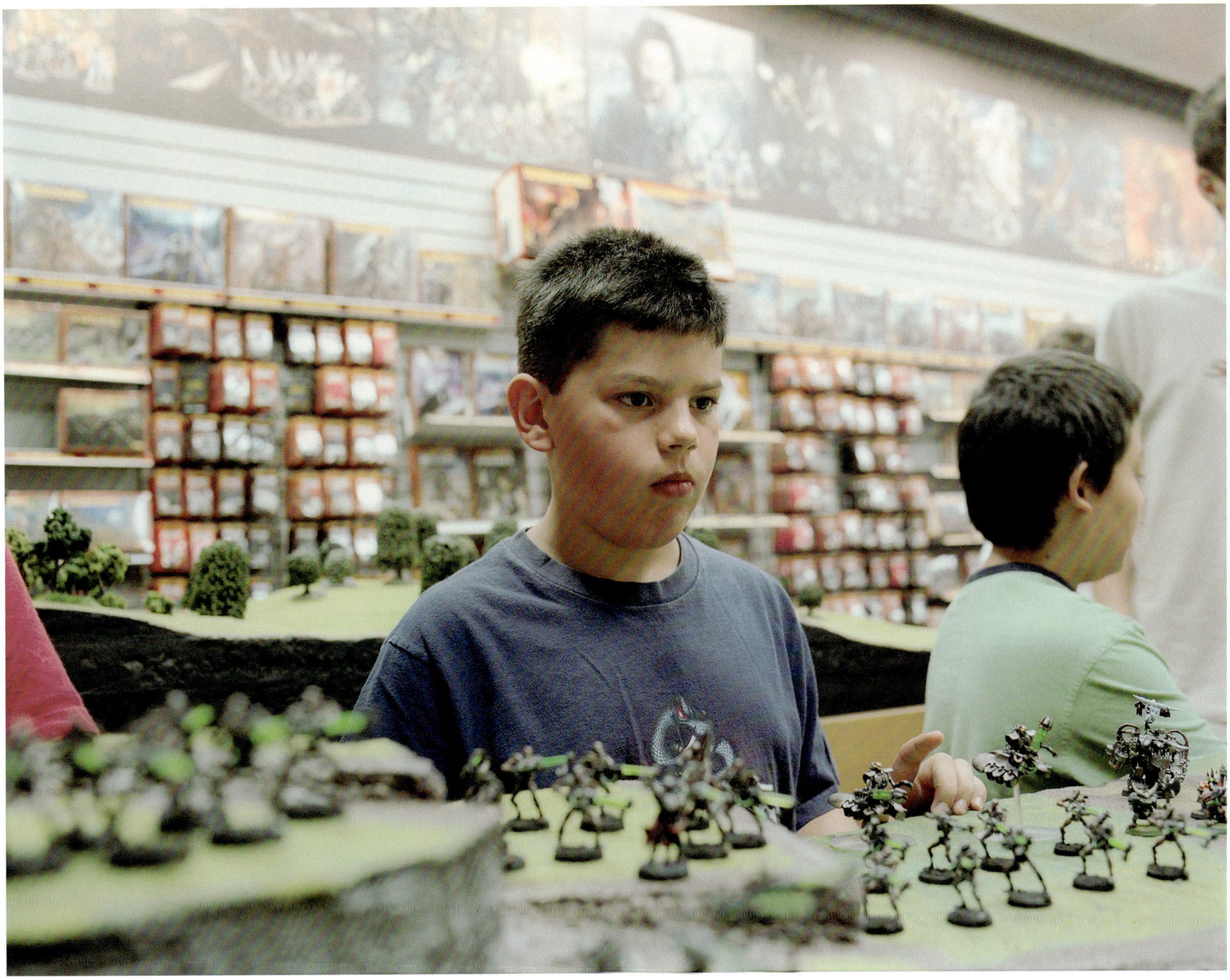

24.

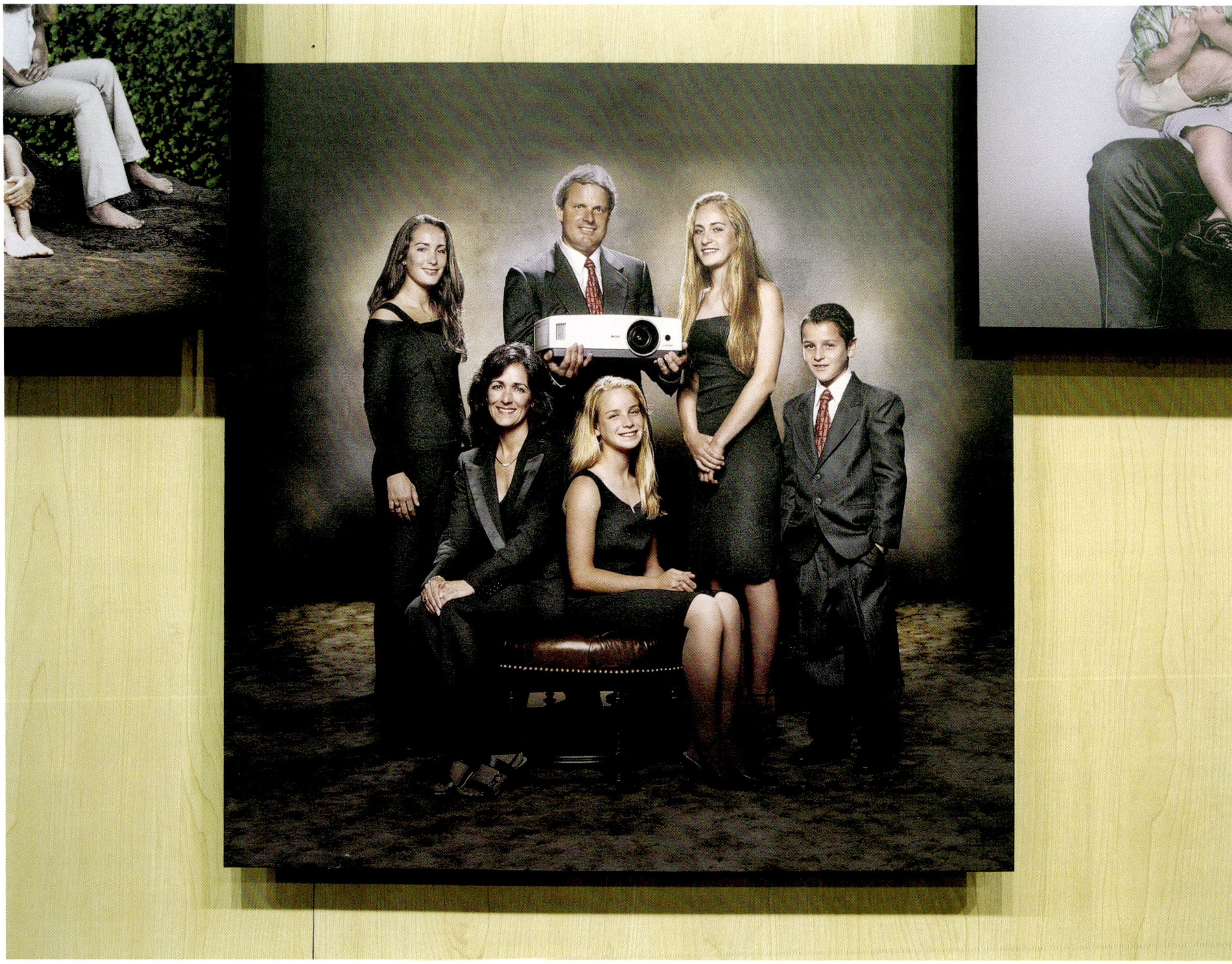

25.

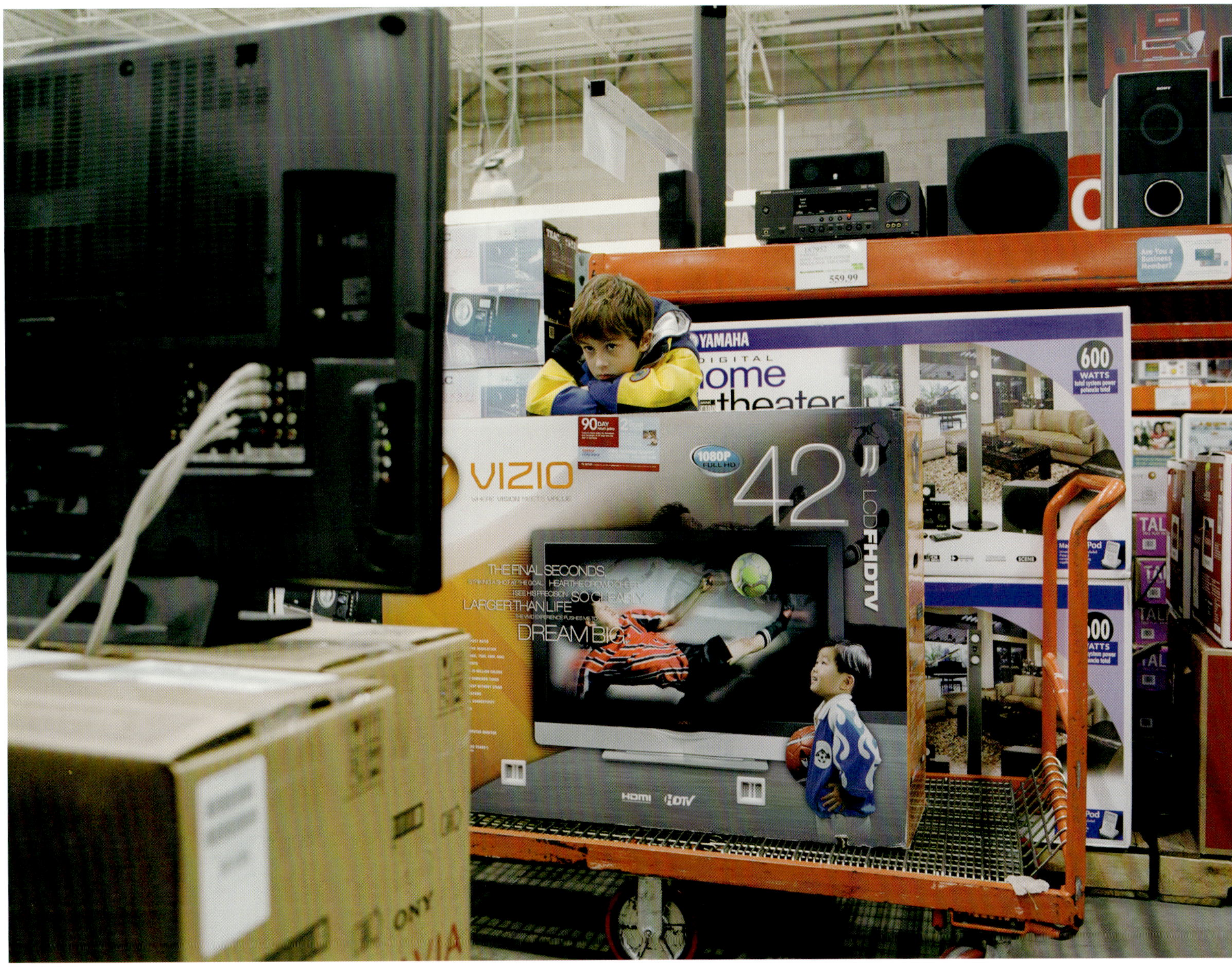
YAMAHA
DIGITAL
600 WATTS
90 DAY
VIZIO
1080P FULL HD
42
LCD FHDTV
THE FINAL SECONDS
LARGER THAN LIFE
SO CLEARLY
DREAM BIG
HDMI
HDTV

26.

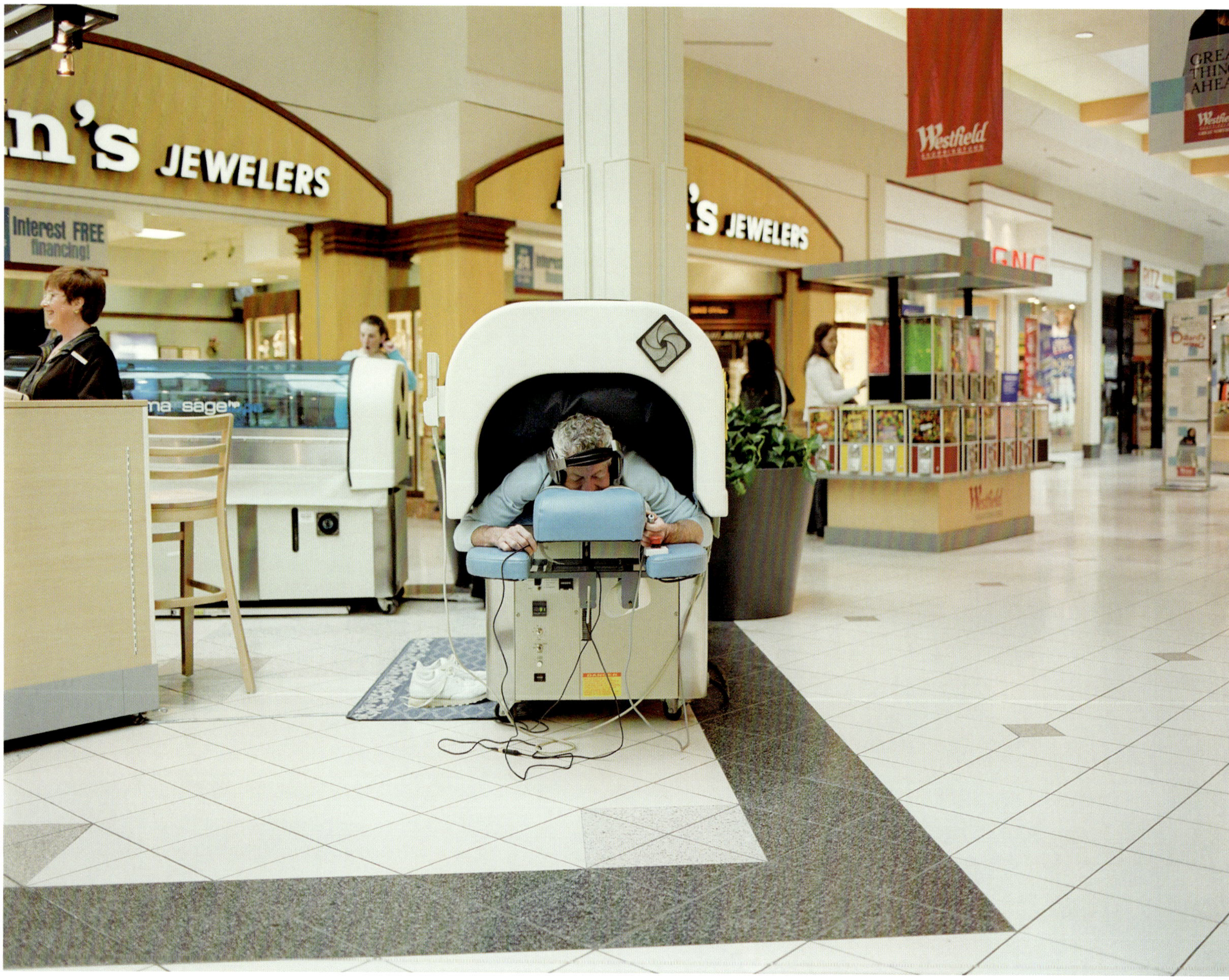
n's JEWELERS
Interest FREE financing!
's JEWELERS
Westfield
Westfield

27.

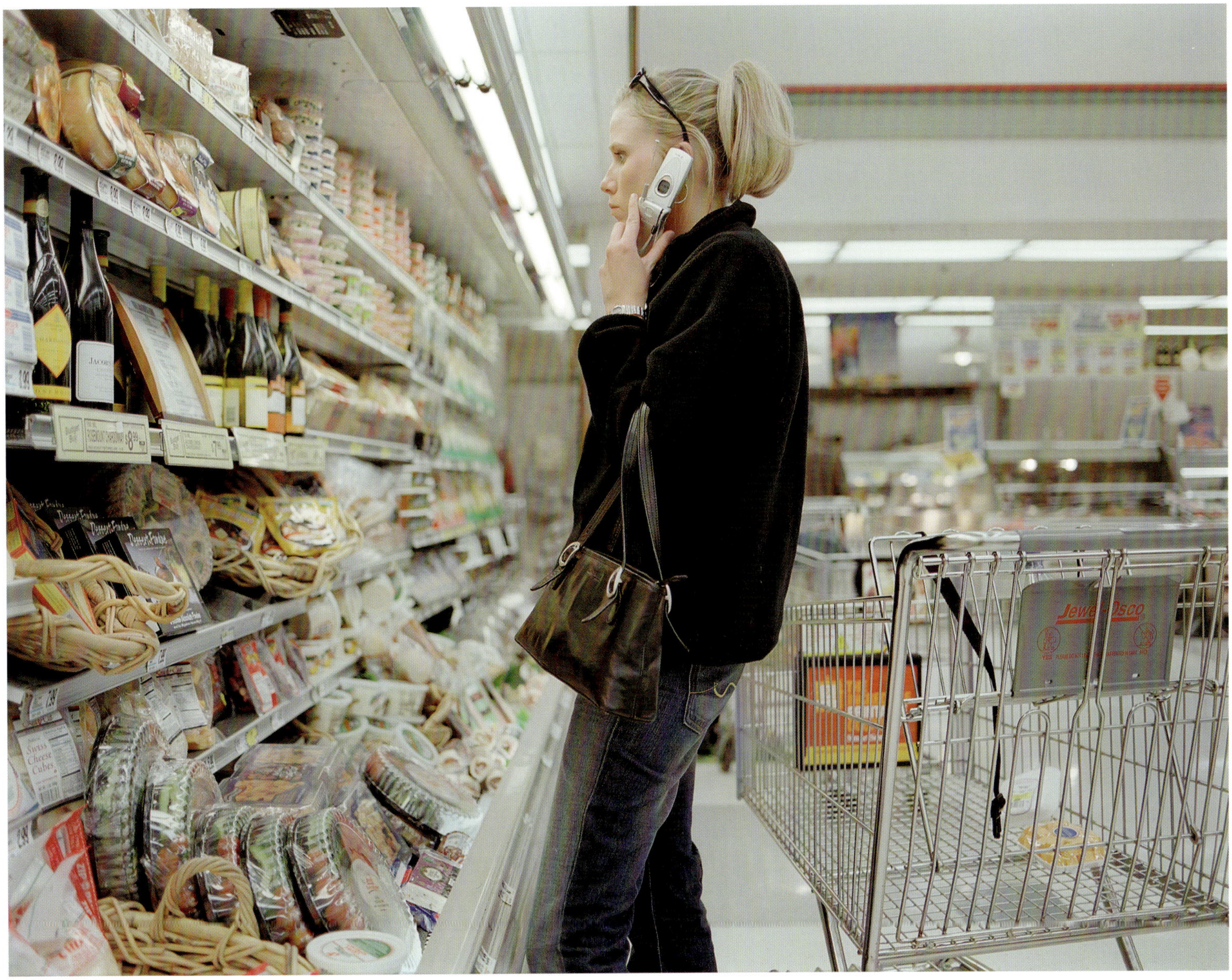

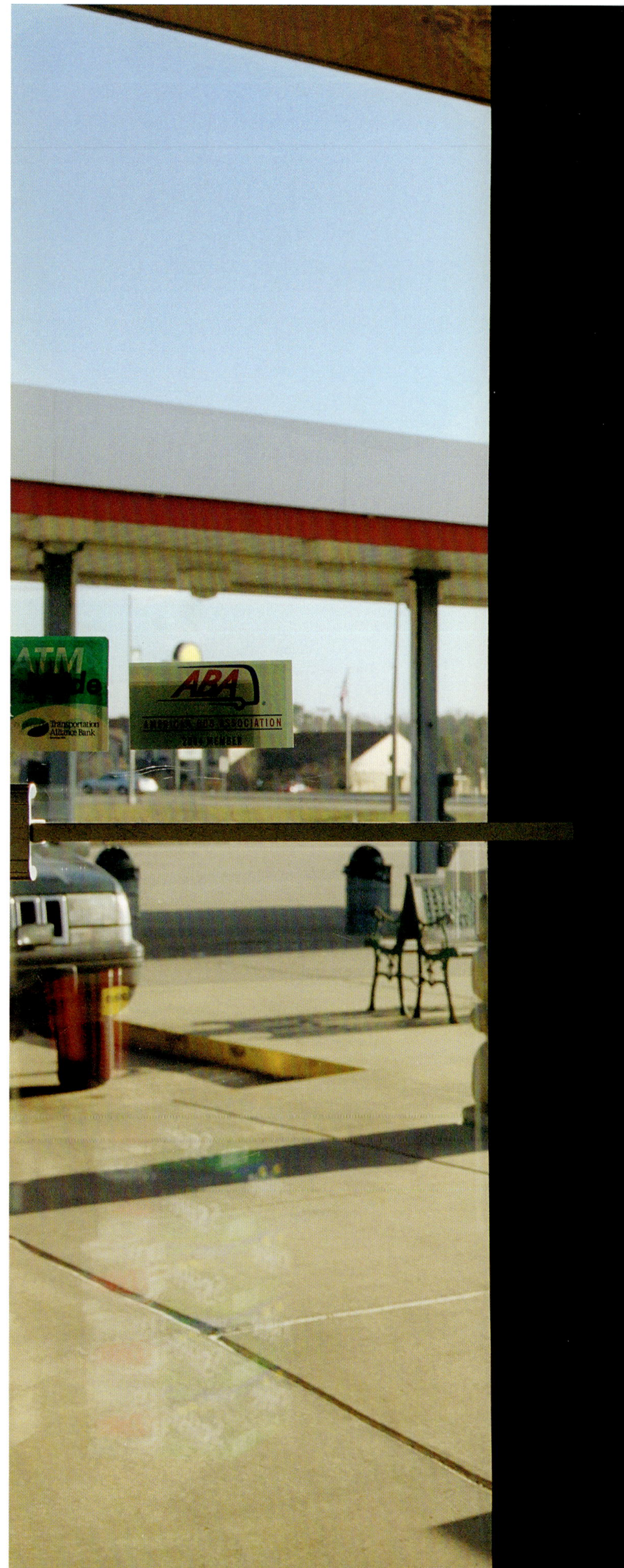
ATM
ABA
Transportation Alliance Bank

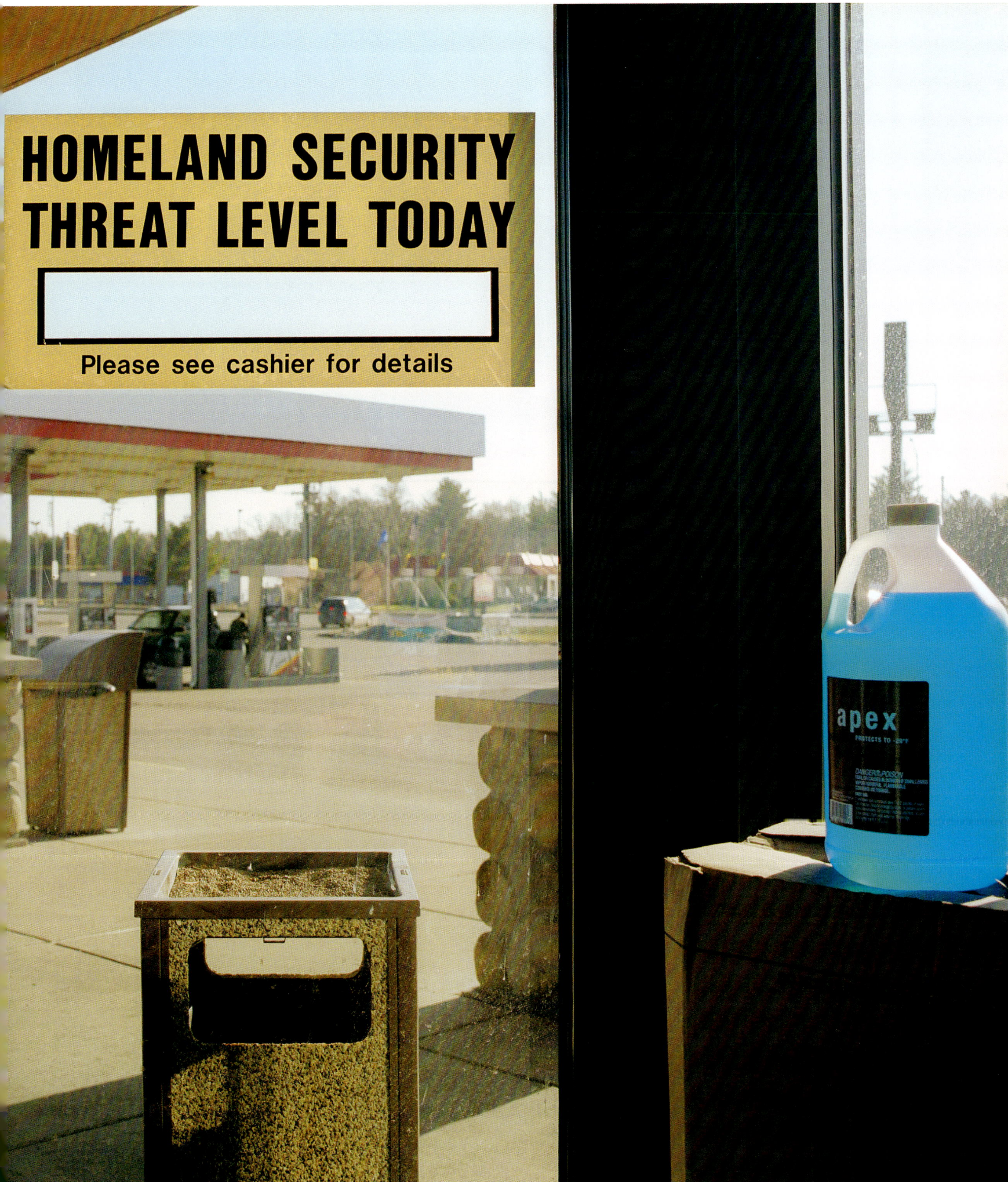
HOMELAND SECURITY
THREAT LEVEL TODAY
Please see cashier for details
apex

29.

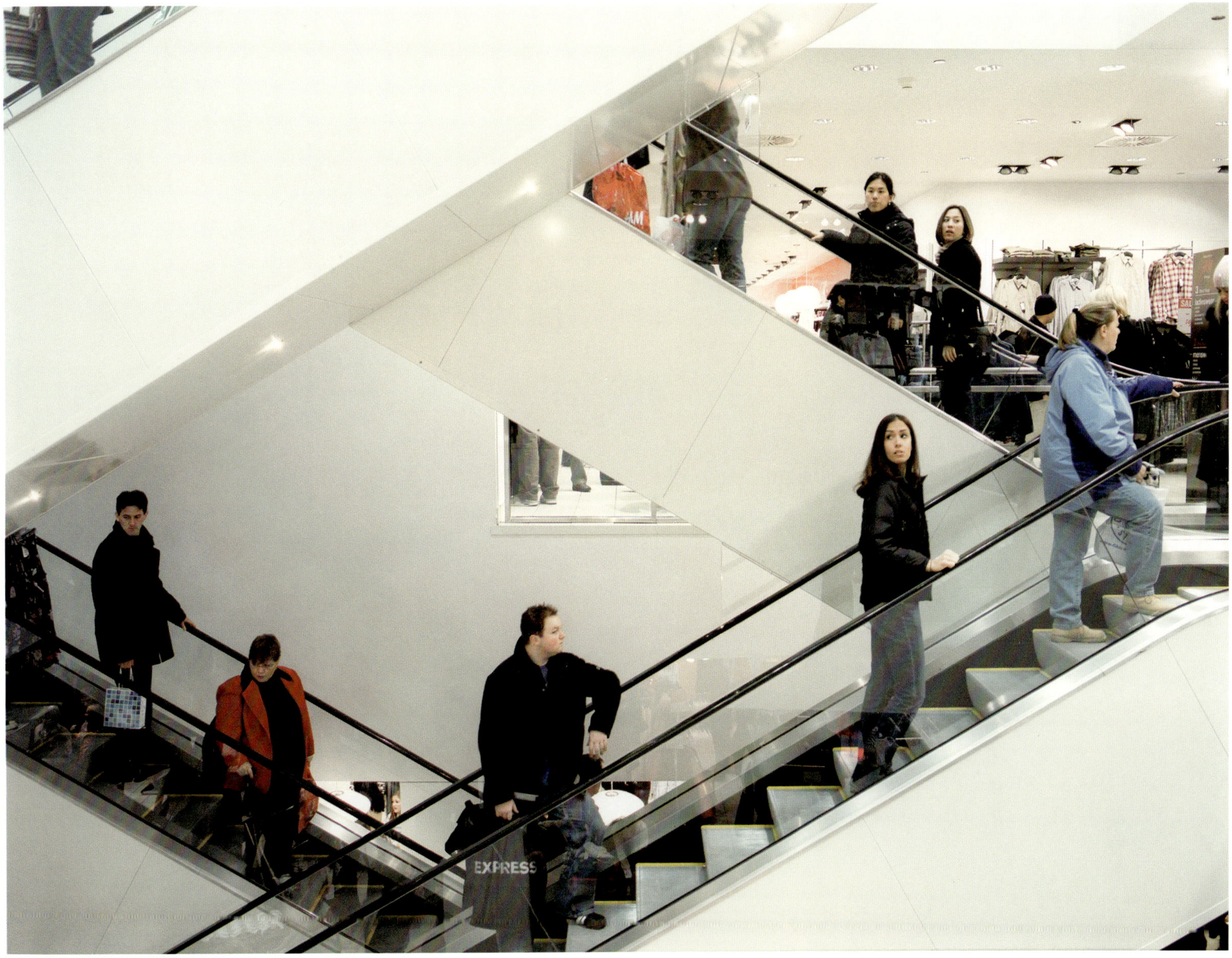

30.

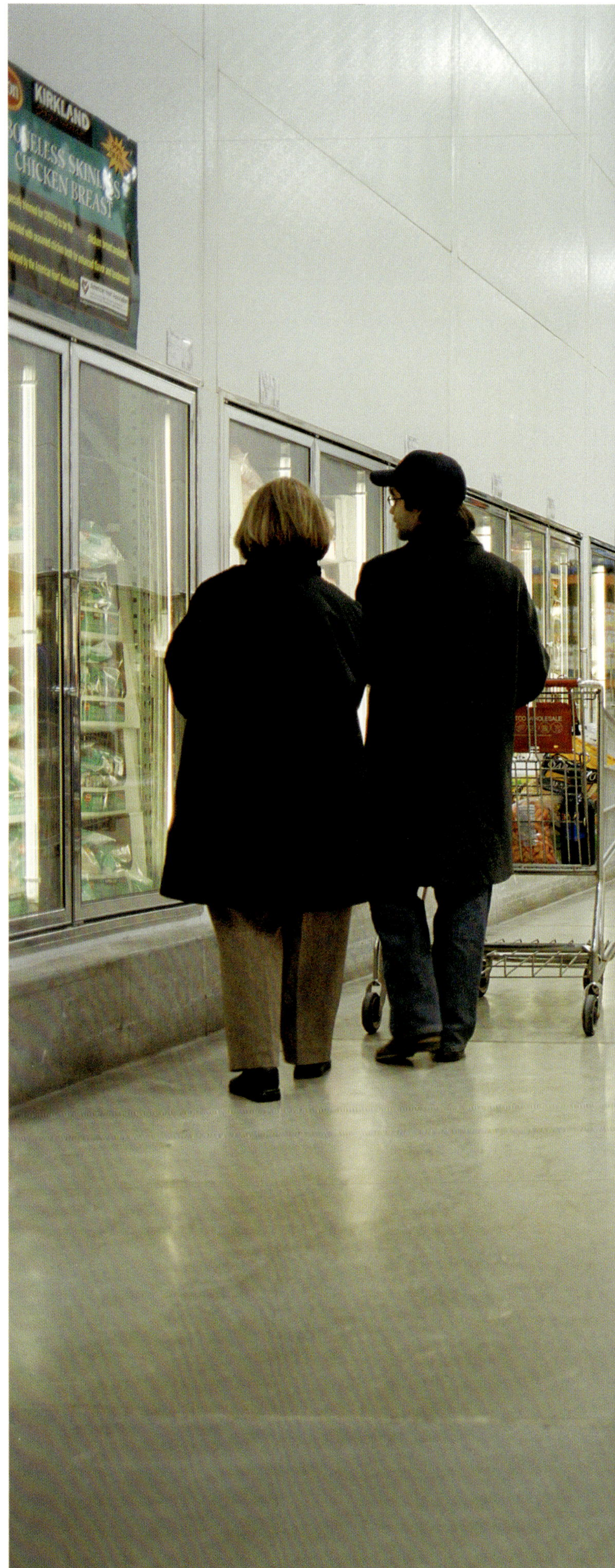

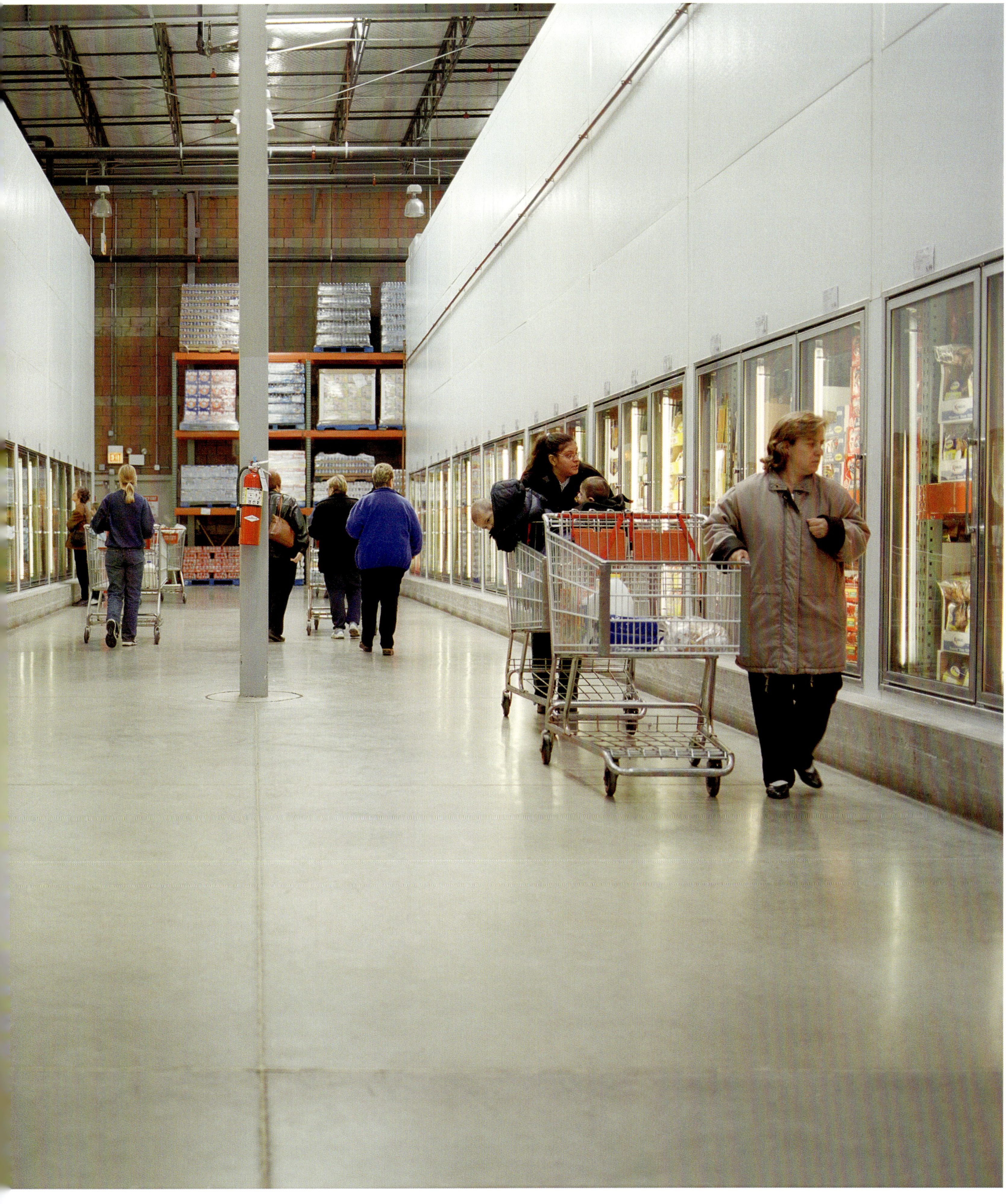

31.

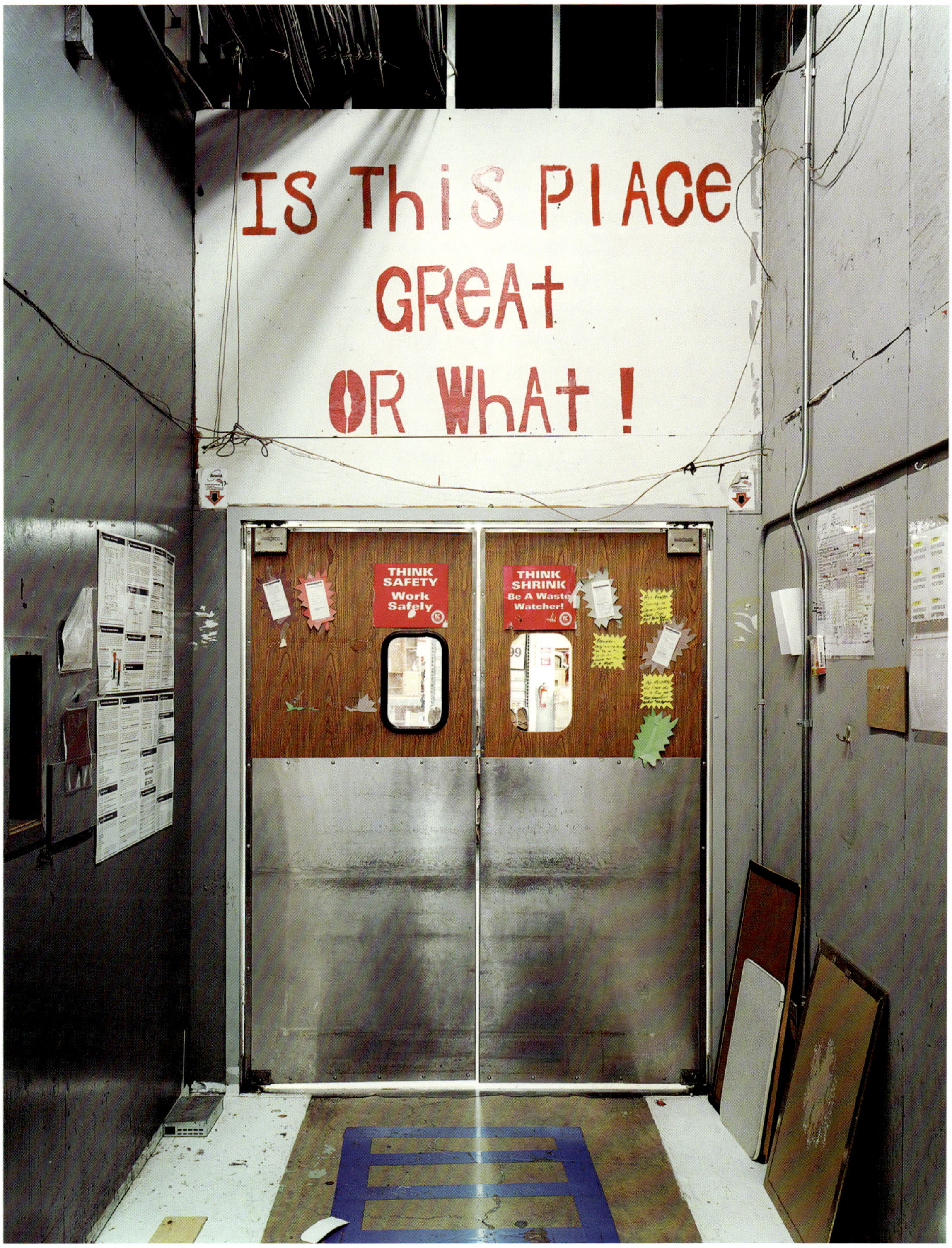
IS ThiS PlACE
GREAt
OR WhAt !
THINK SAFETY Work Safely
THINK SHRINK Be A Waste Watcher!

THRIFT

32.

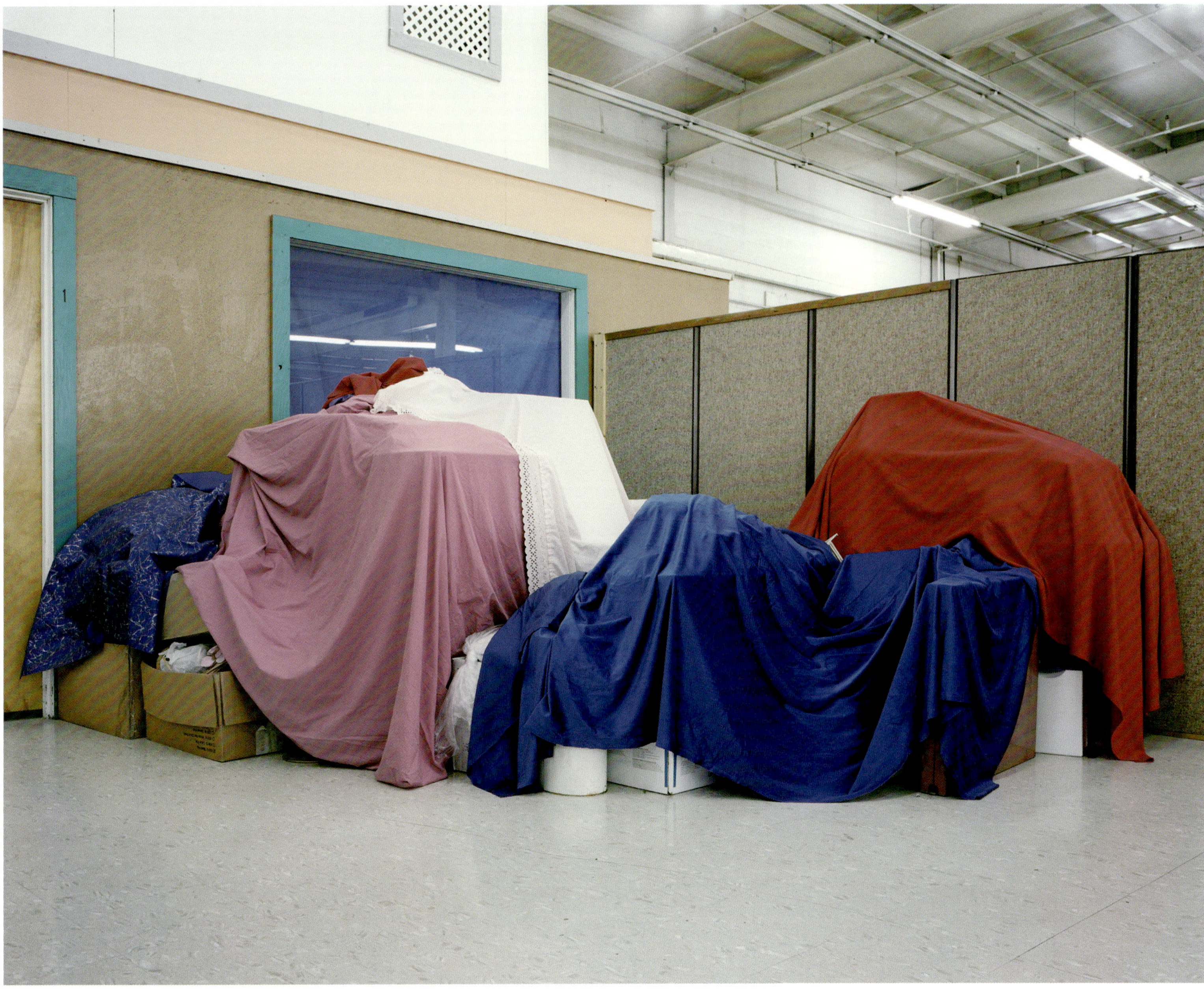

33.

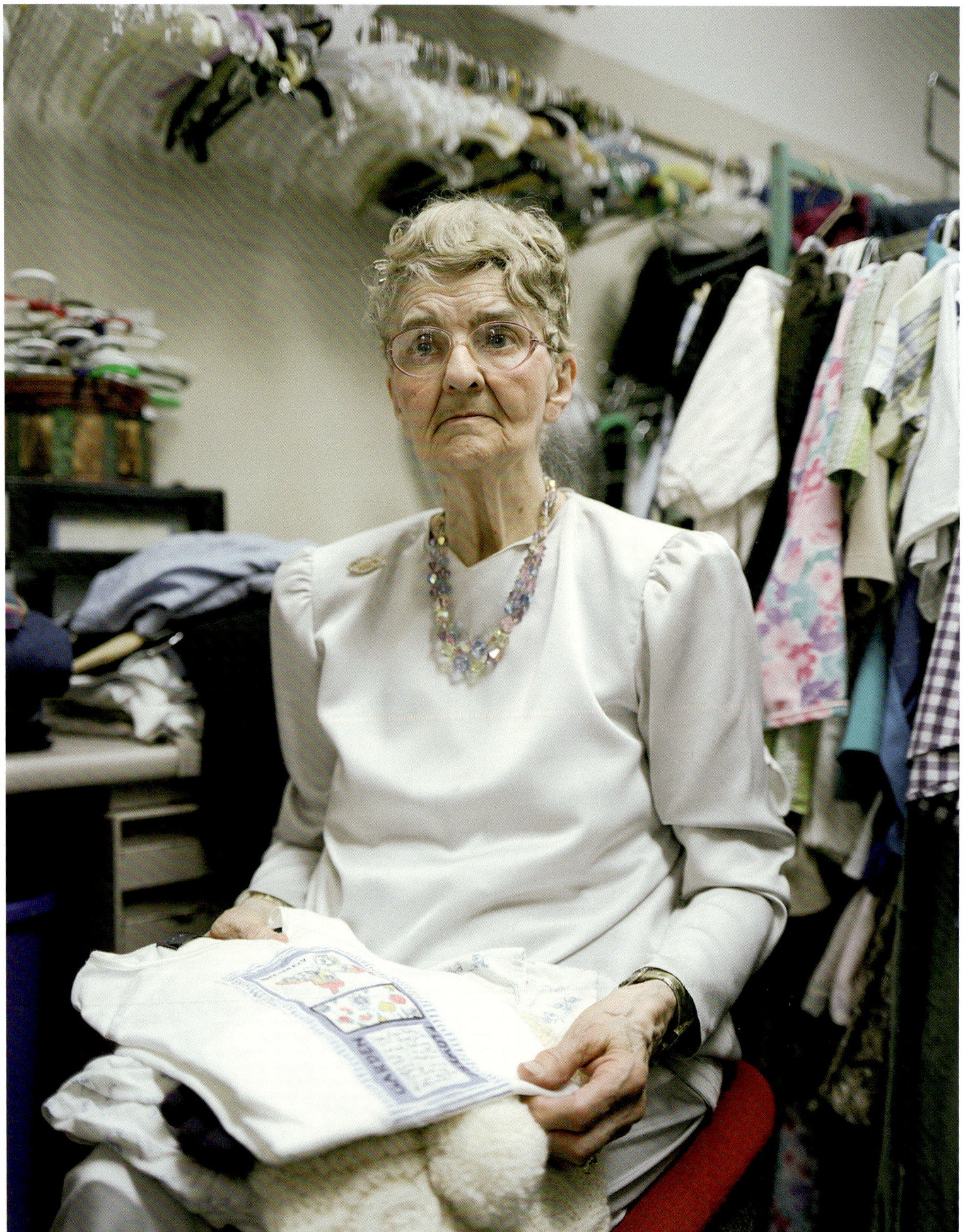

34.

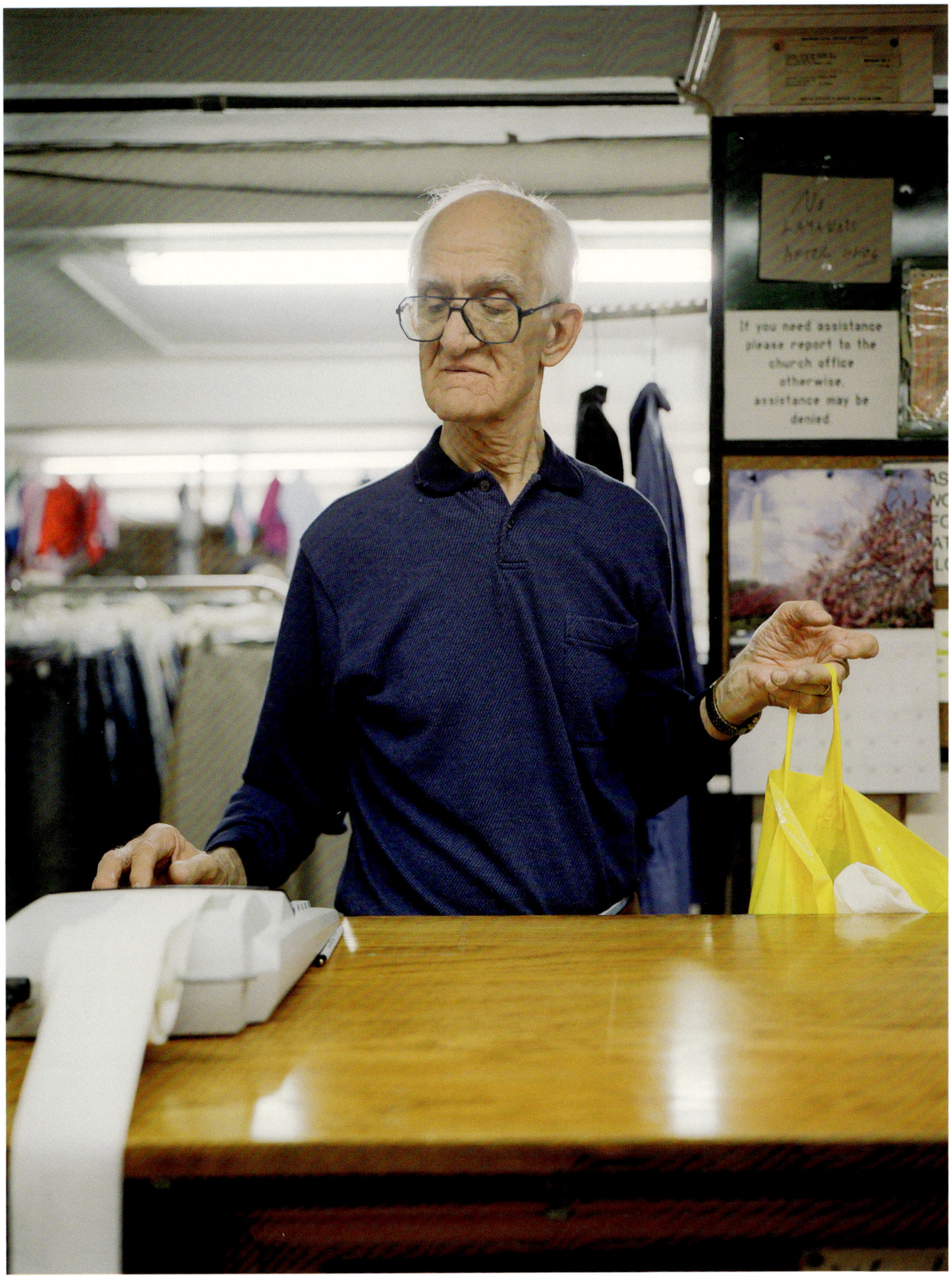
If you need assistance
please report to the
church office
otherwise,
assistance may be
denied.

35.

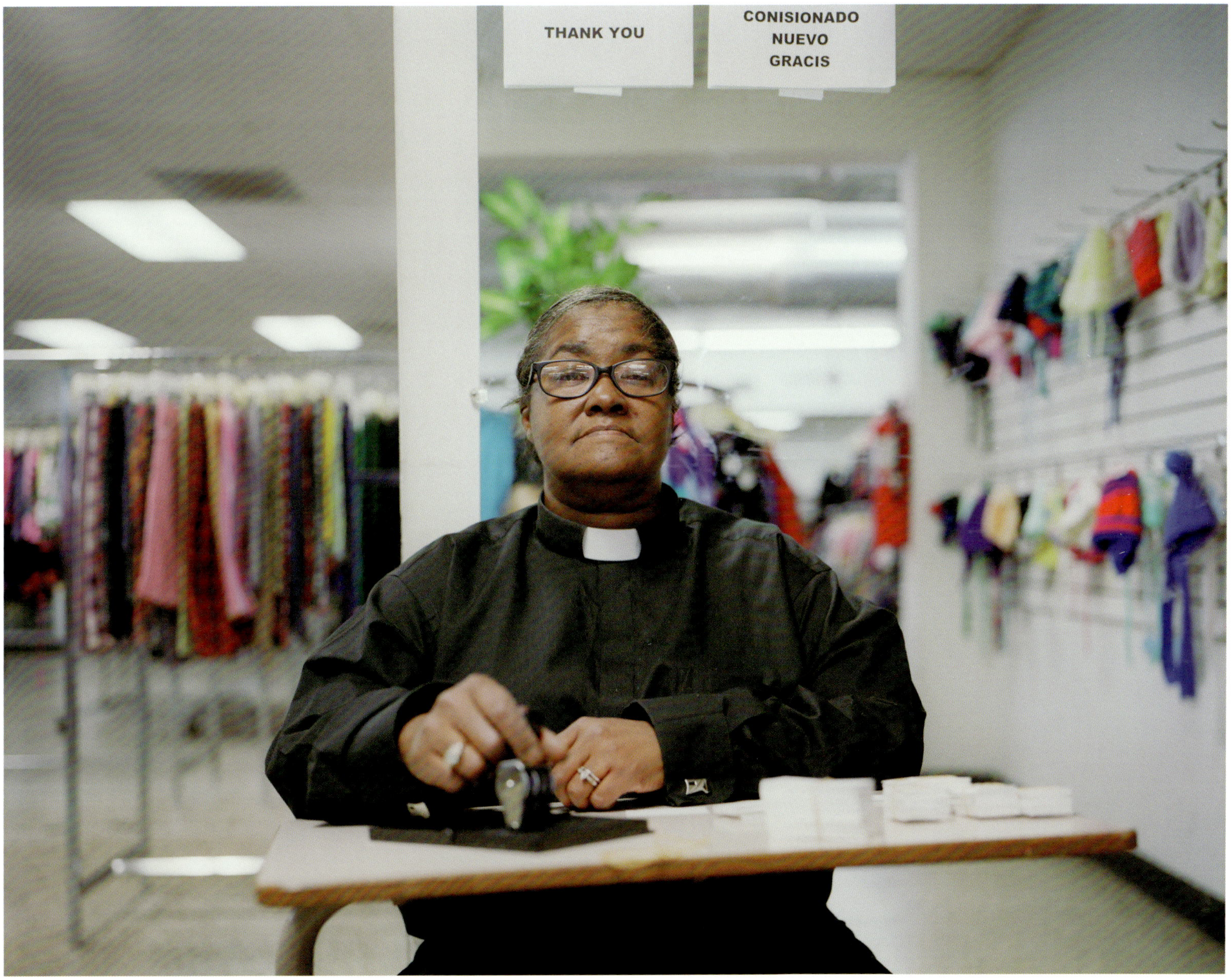

36.

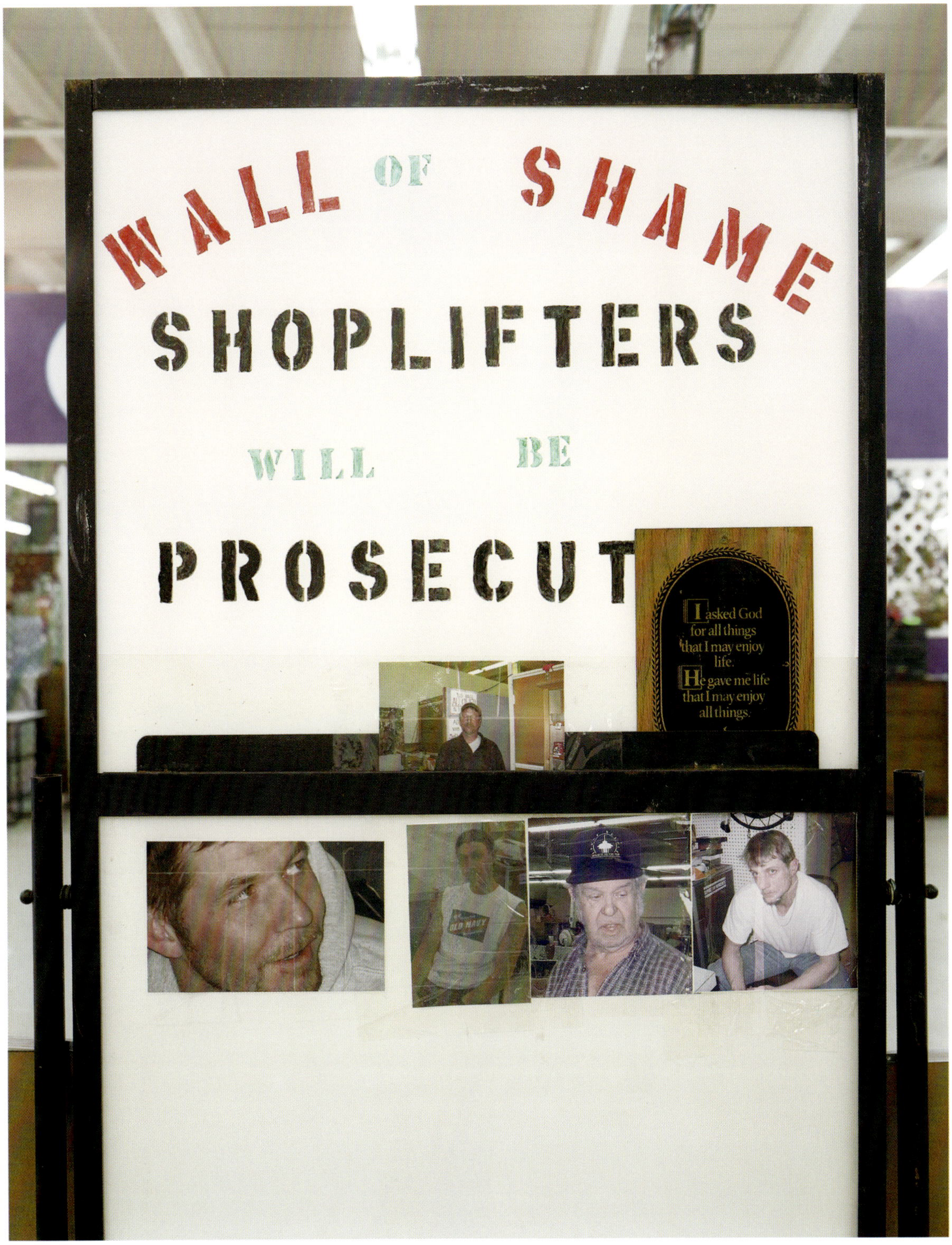
WALL OF SHAME
SHOPLIFTERS
WILL BE
PROSECUT
I asked God for all things that I may enjoy life.
He gave me life that I may enjoy all things.

37.

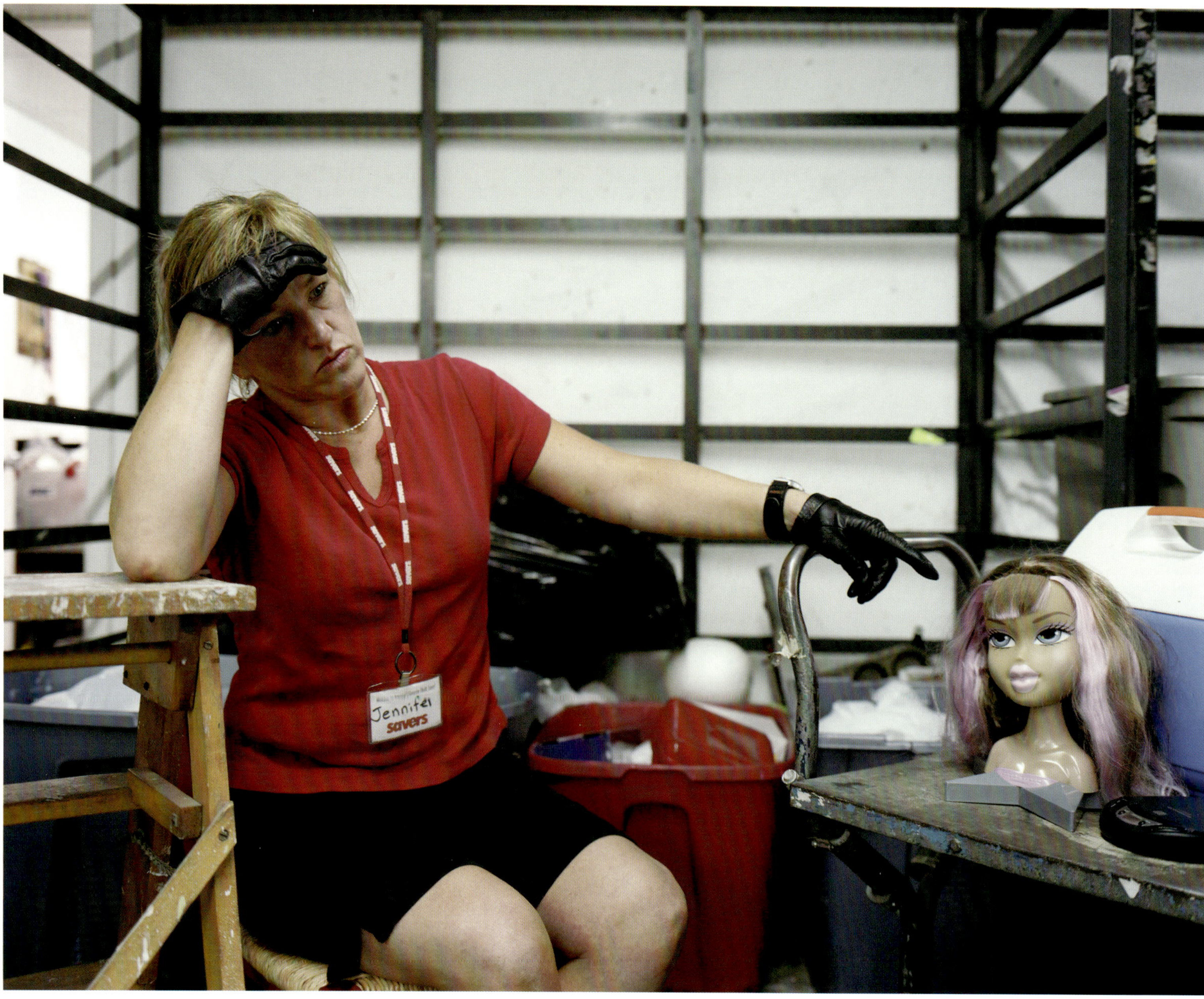

38.

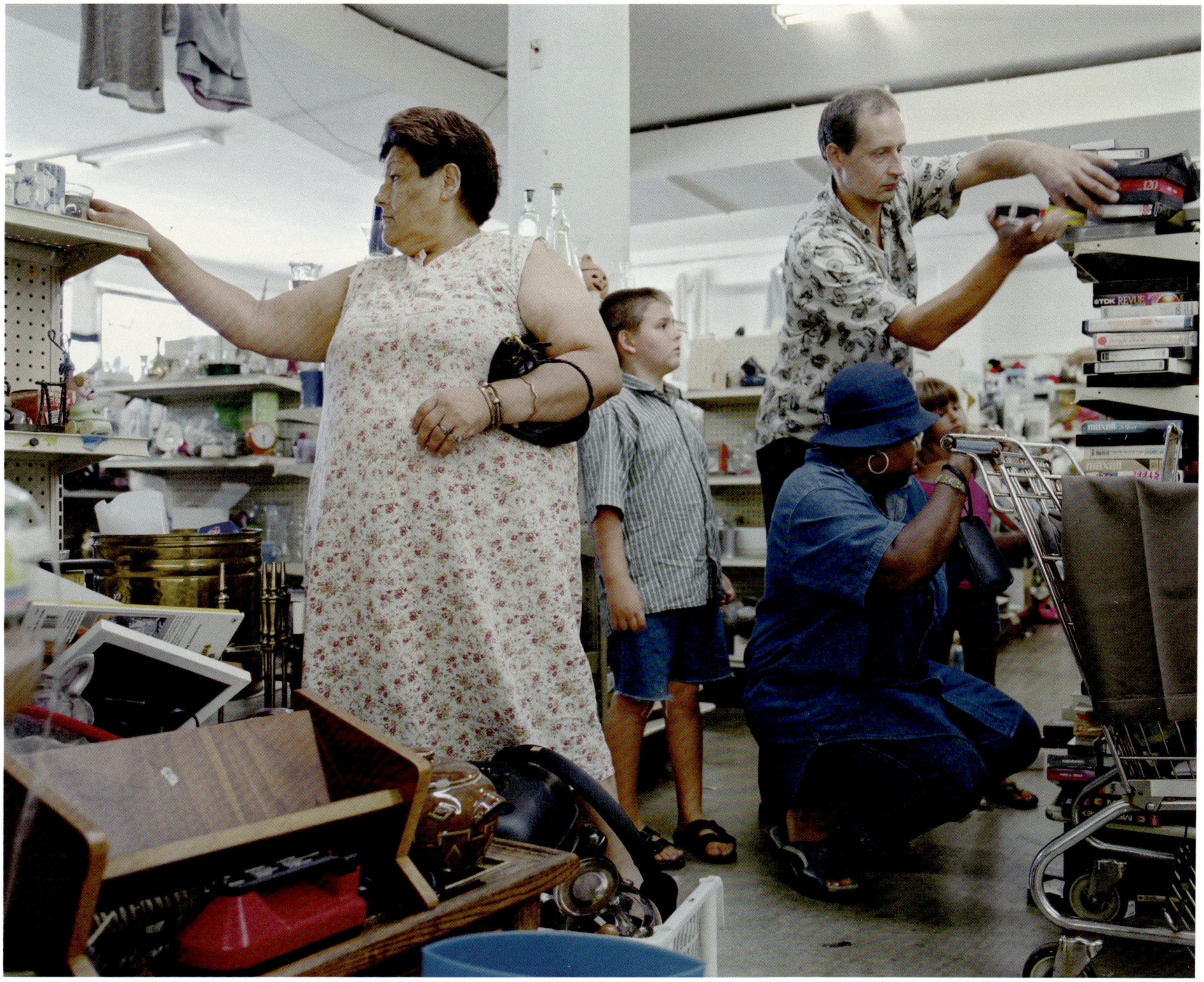

39.

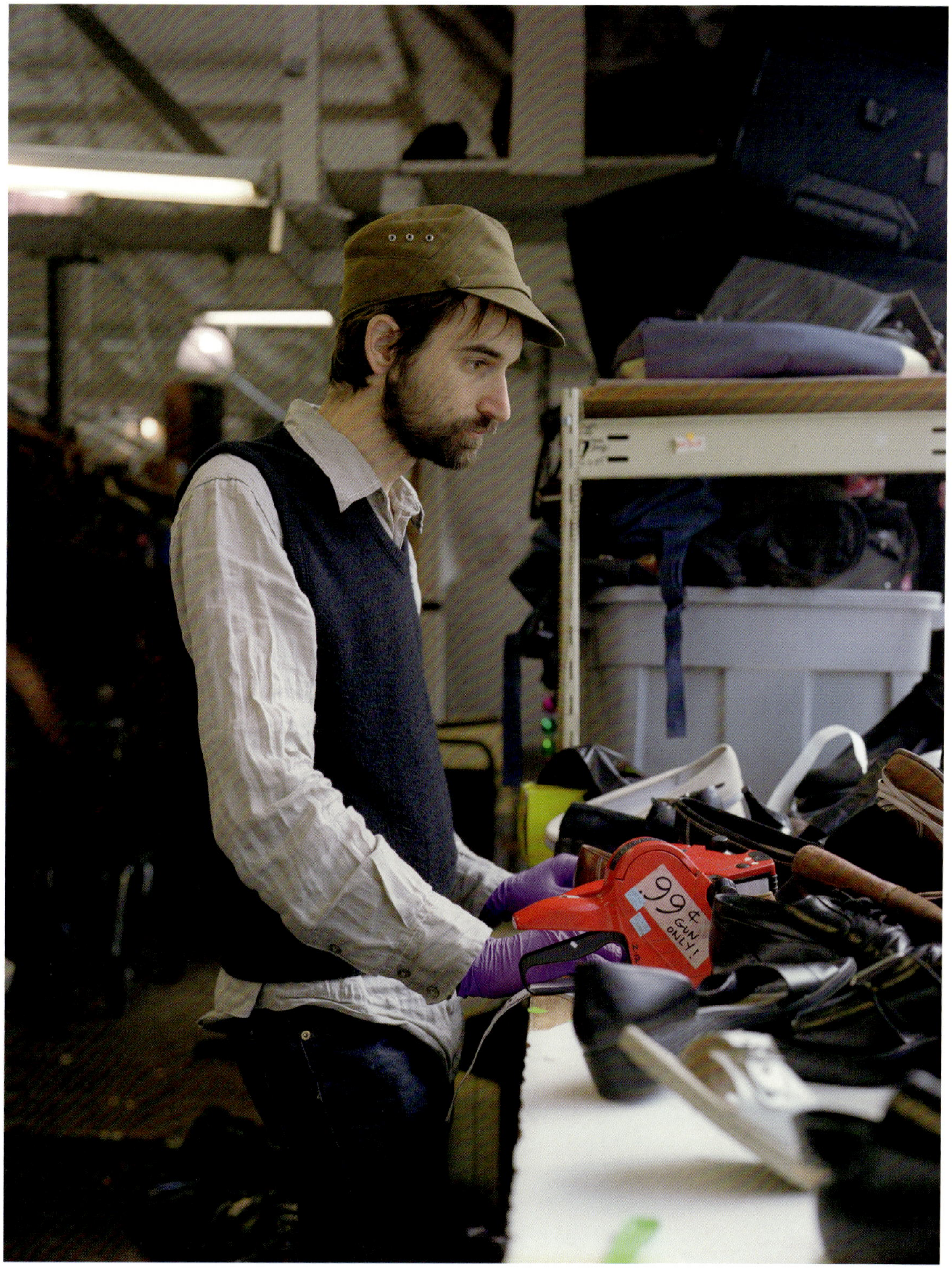

40.

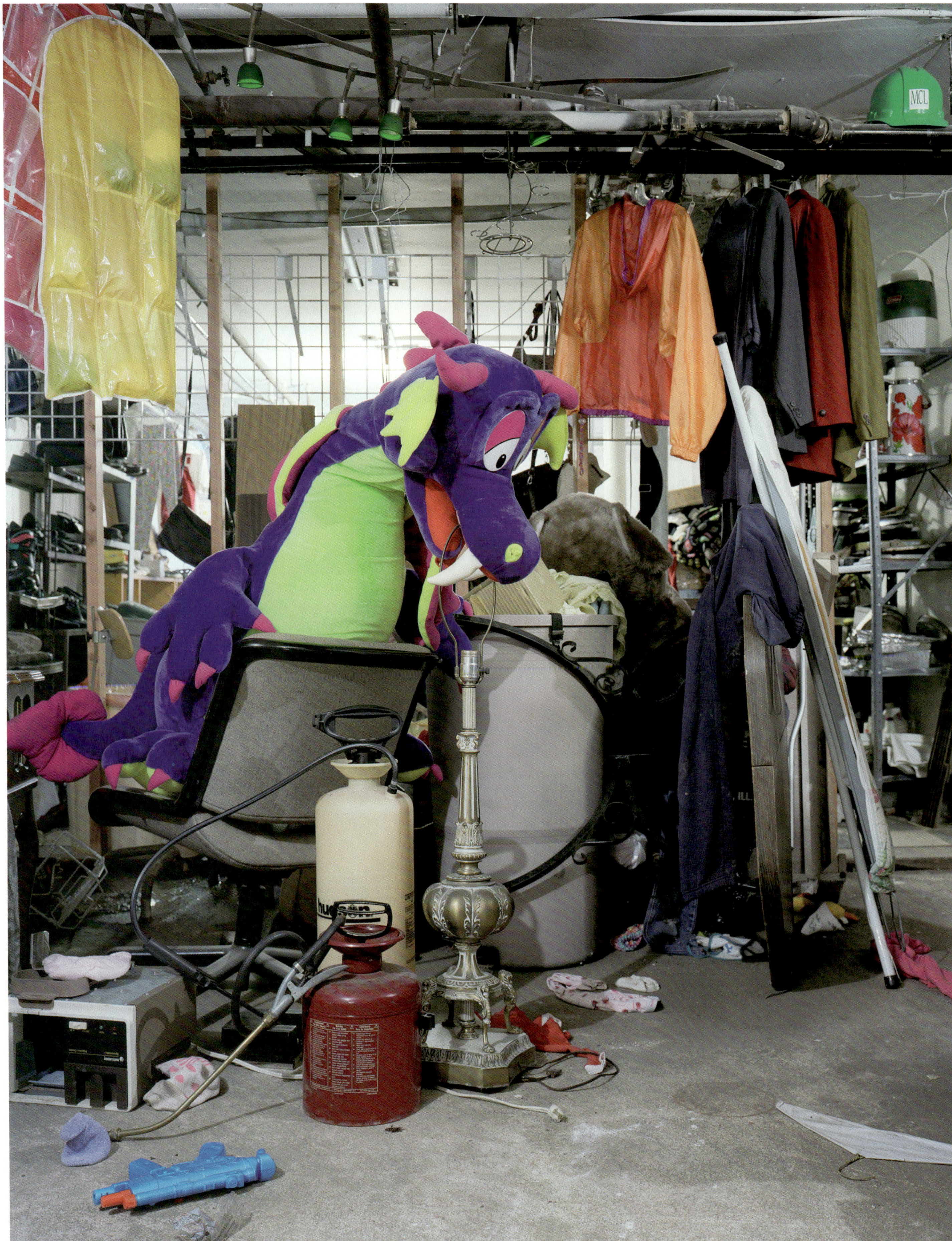

41.

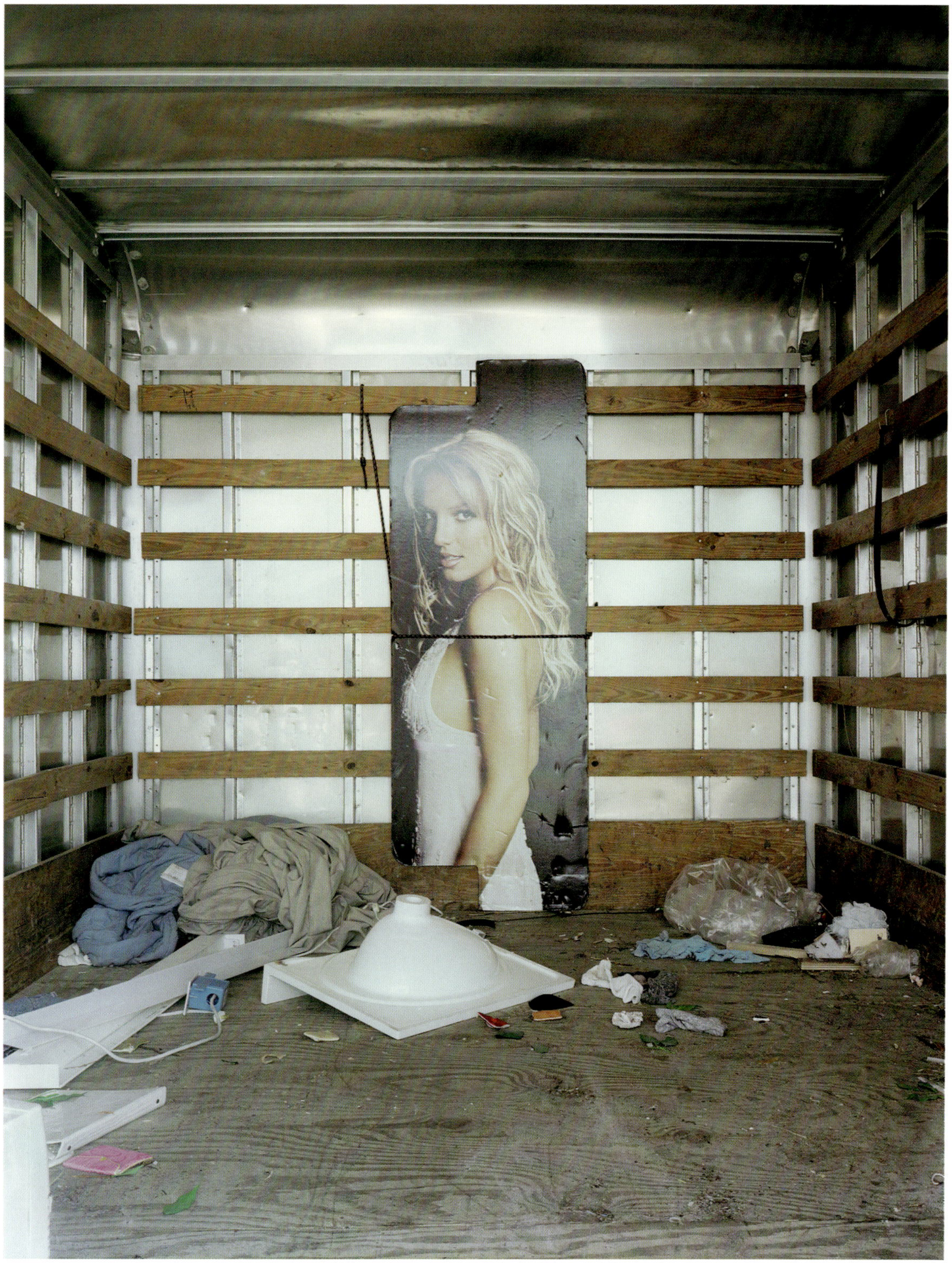

42.

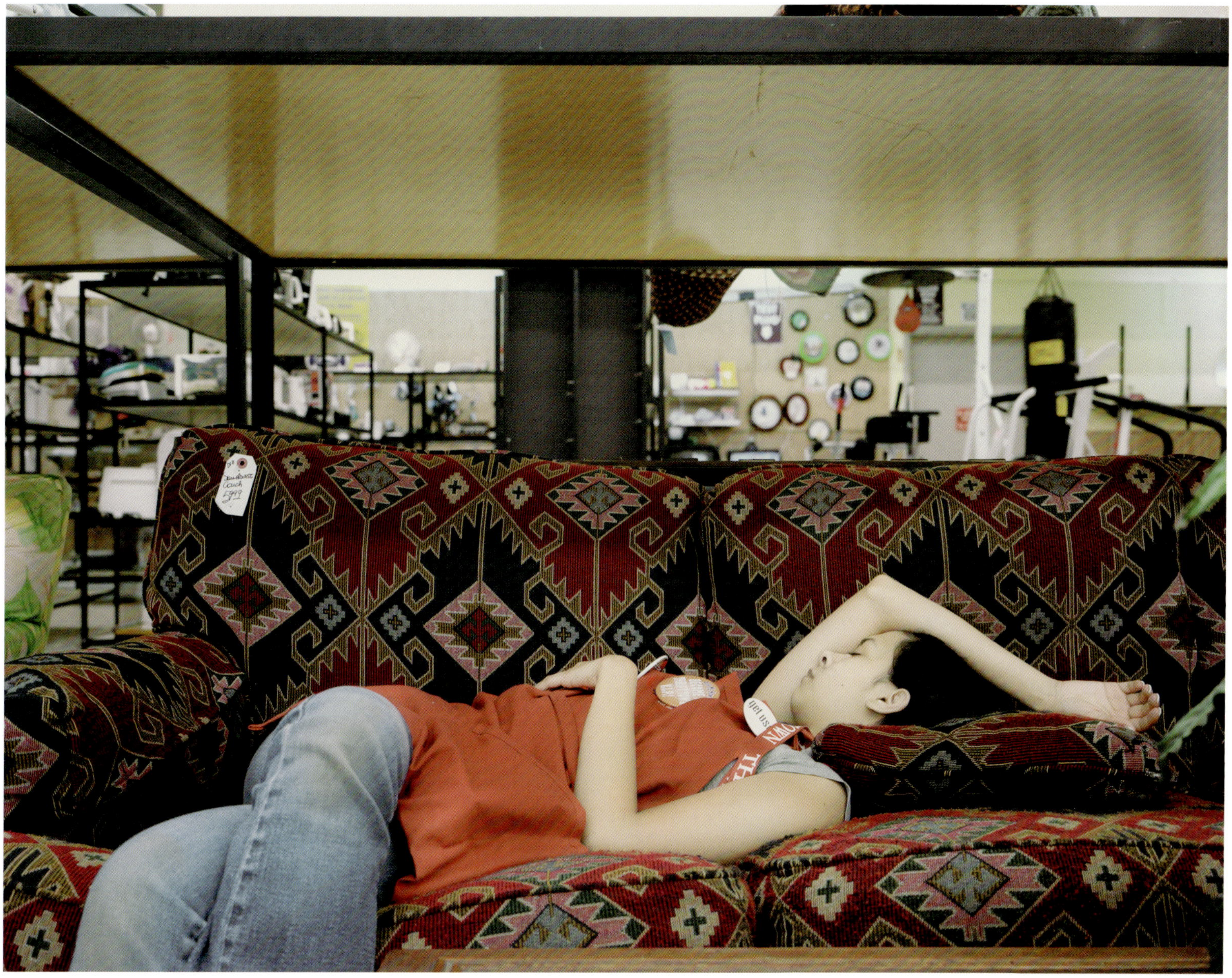

43.

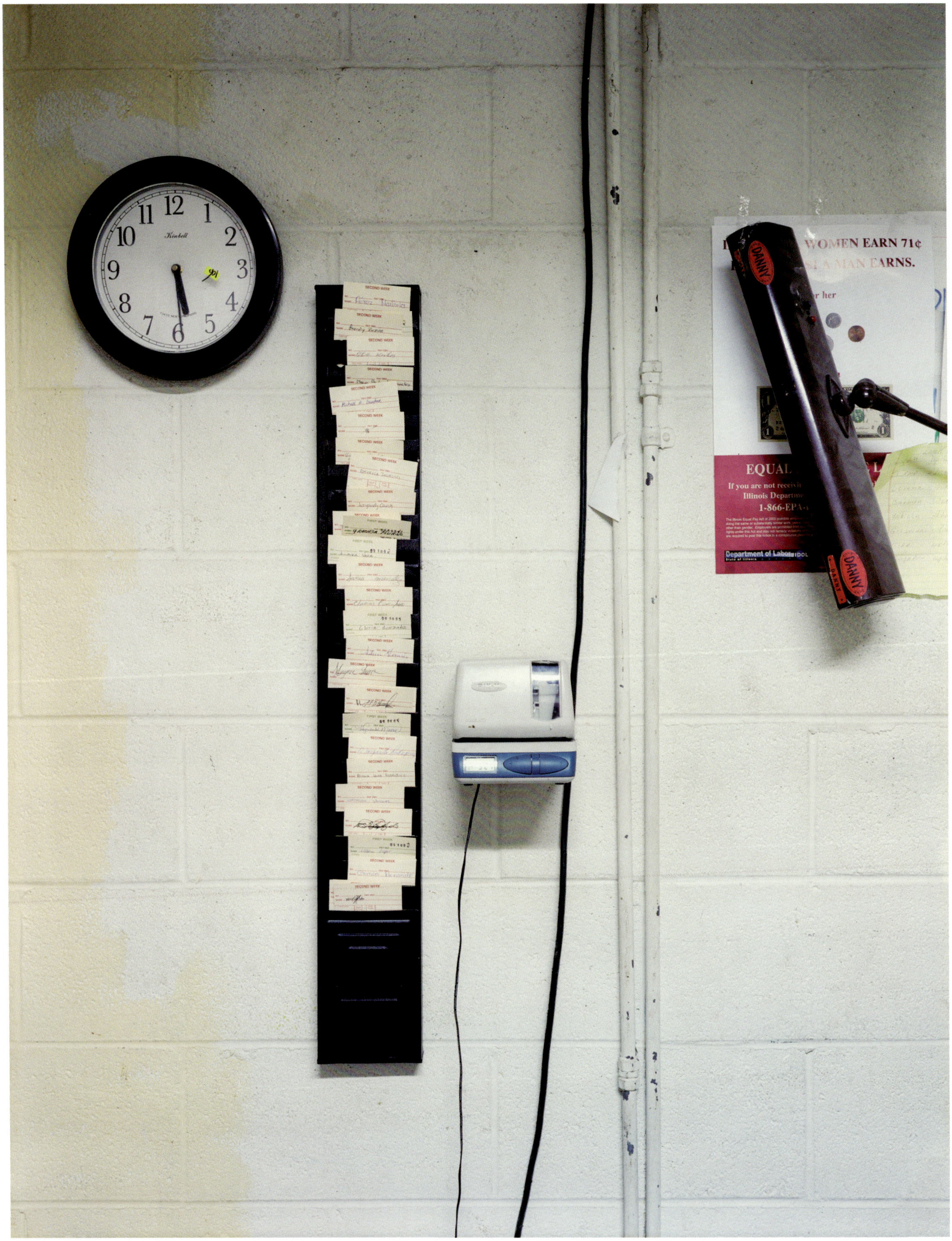
WOMEN EARN 71¢
DANNY
EQUAL
Illinois Departme
1-866-EPA-
Department of Labor
DANNY

44.

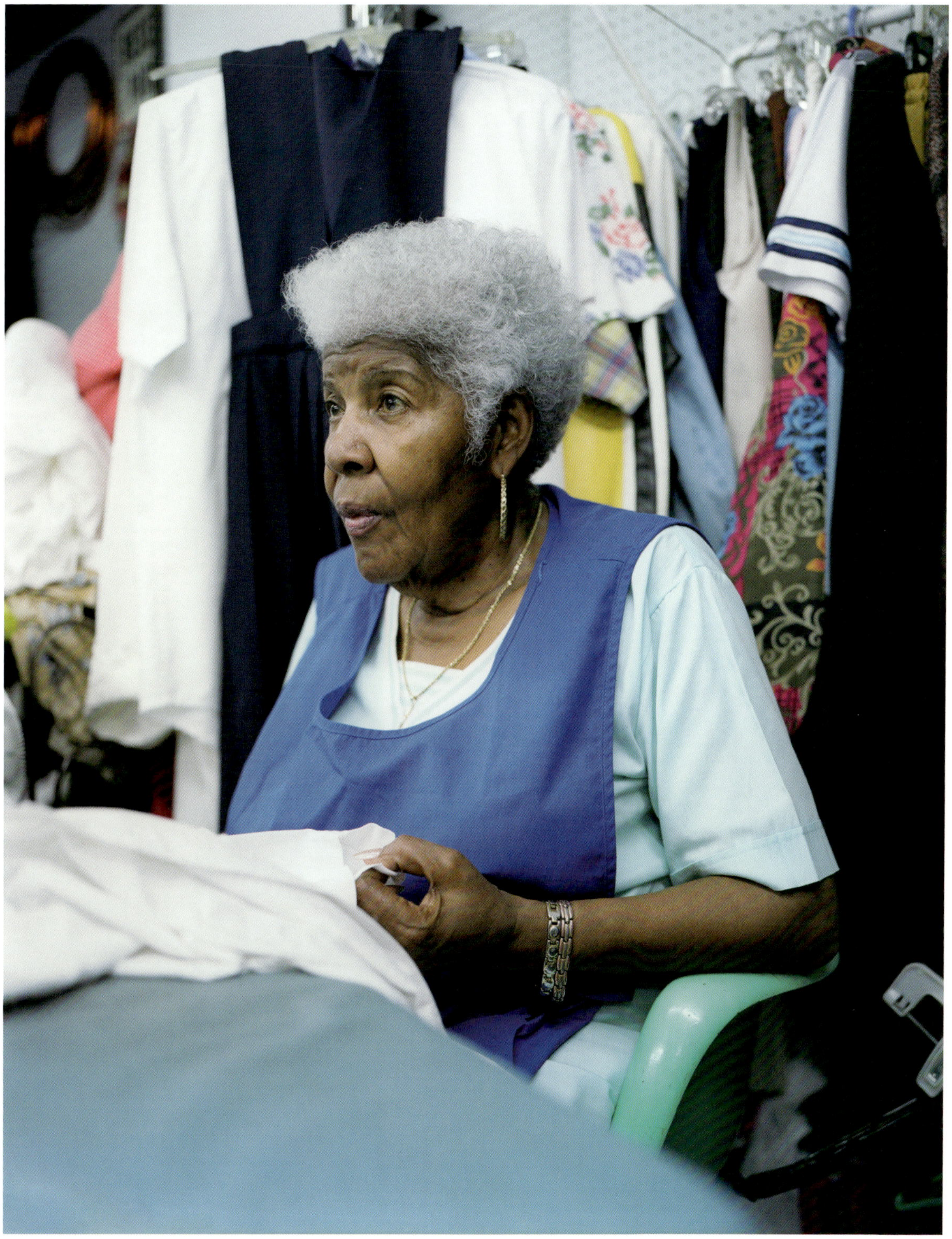

45.

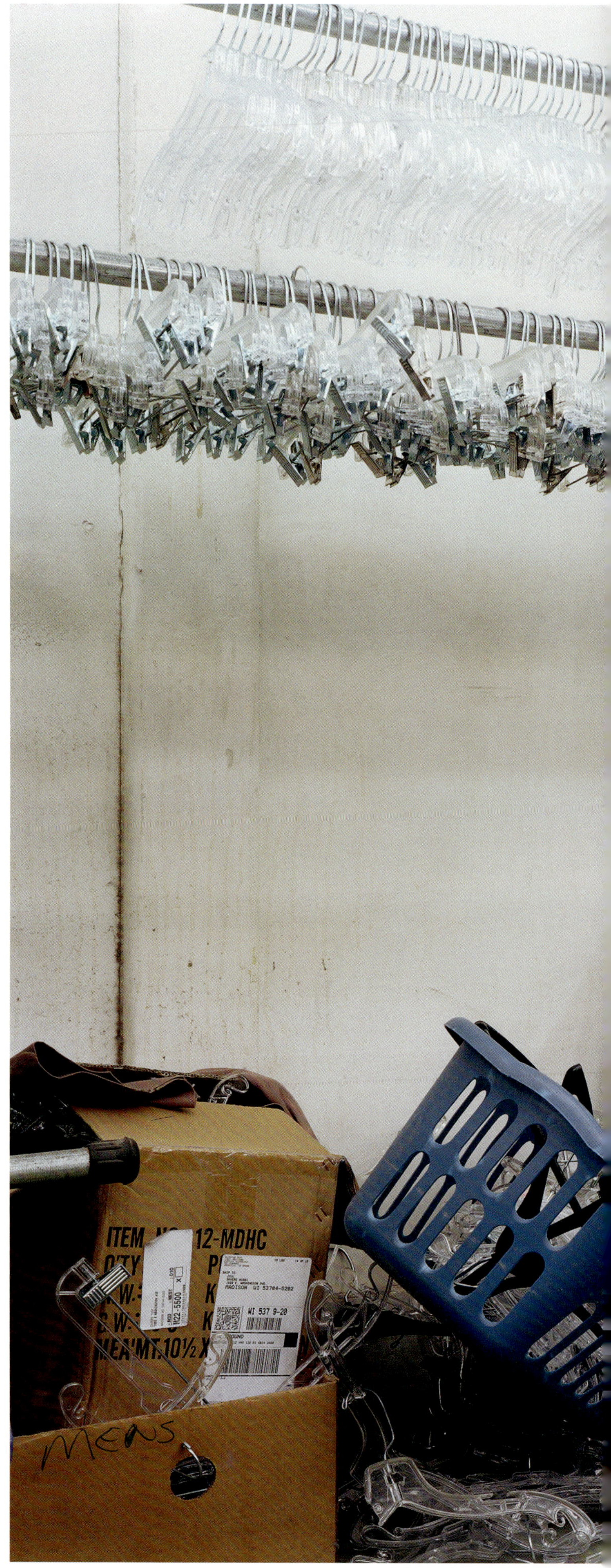

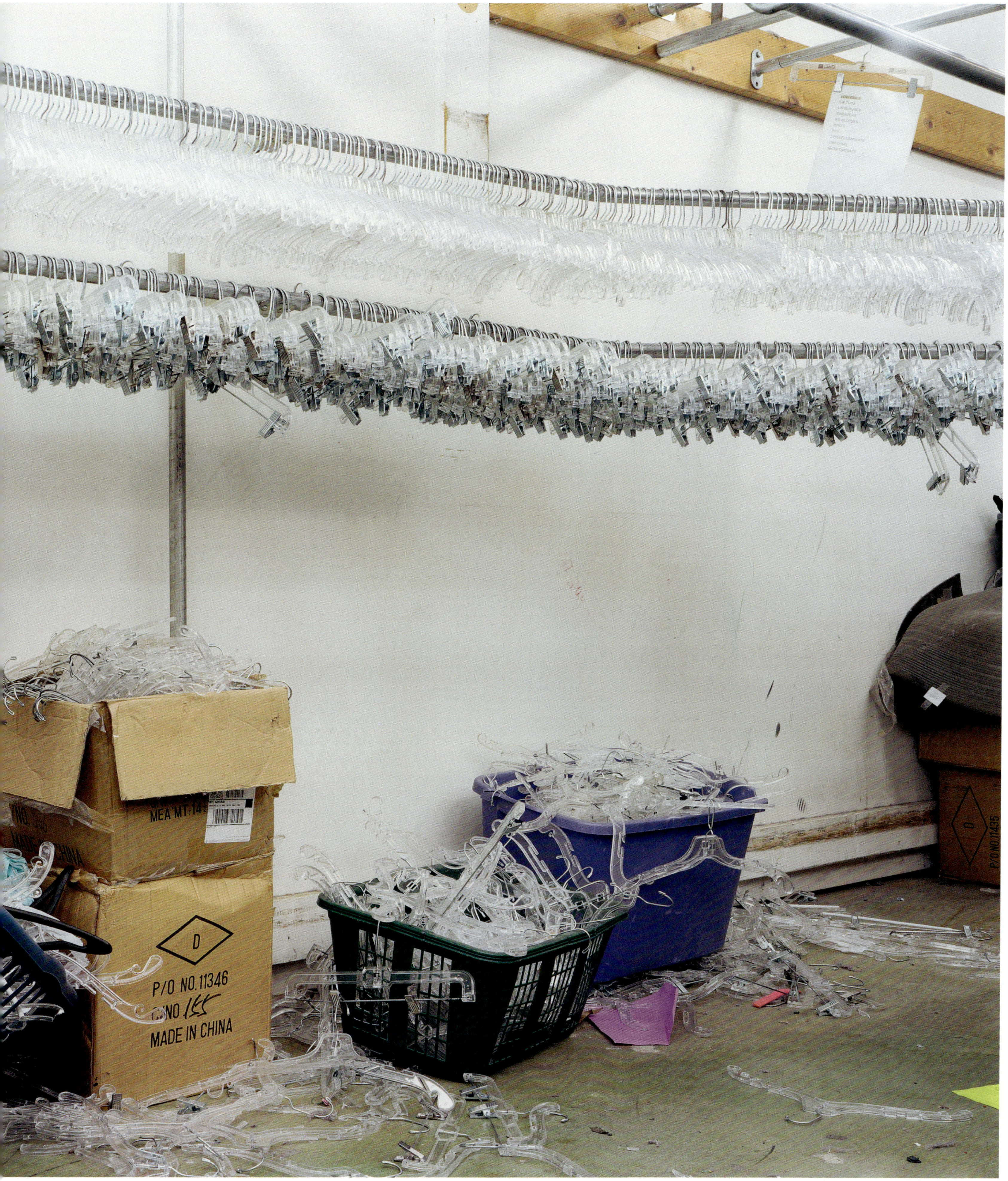
D
P/O NO.11346
MADE IN CHINA
D
P/O NO.11435

46.

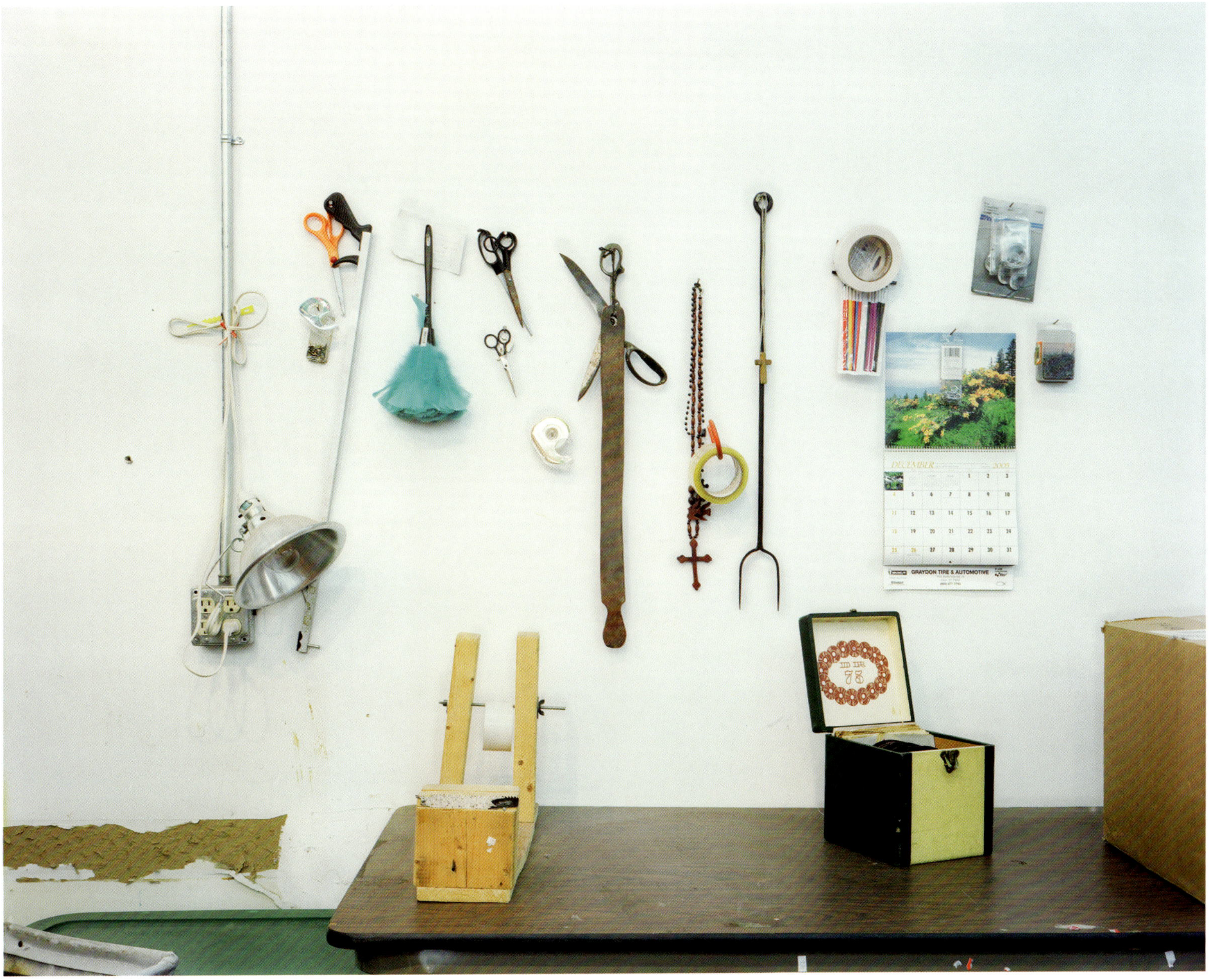

47.

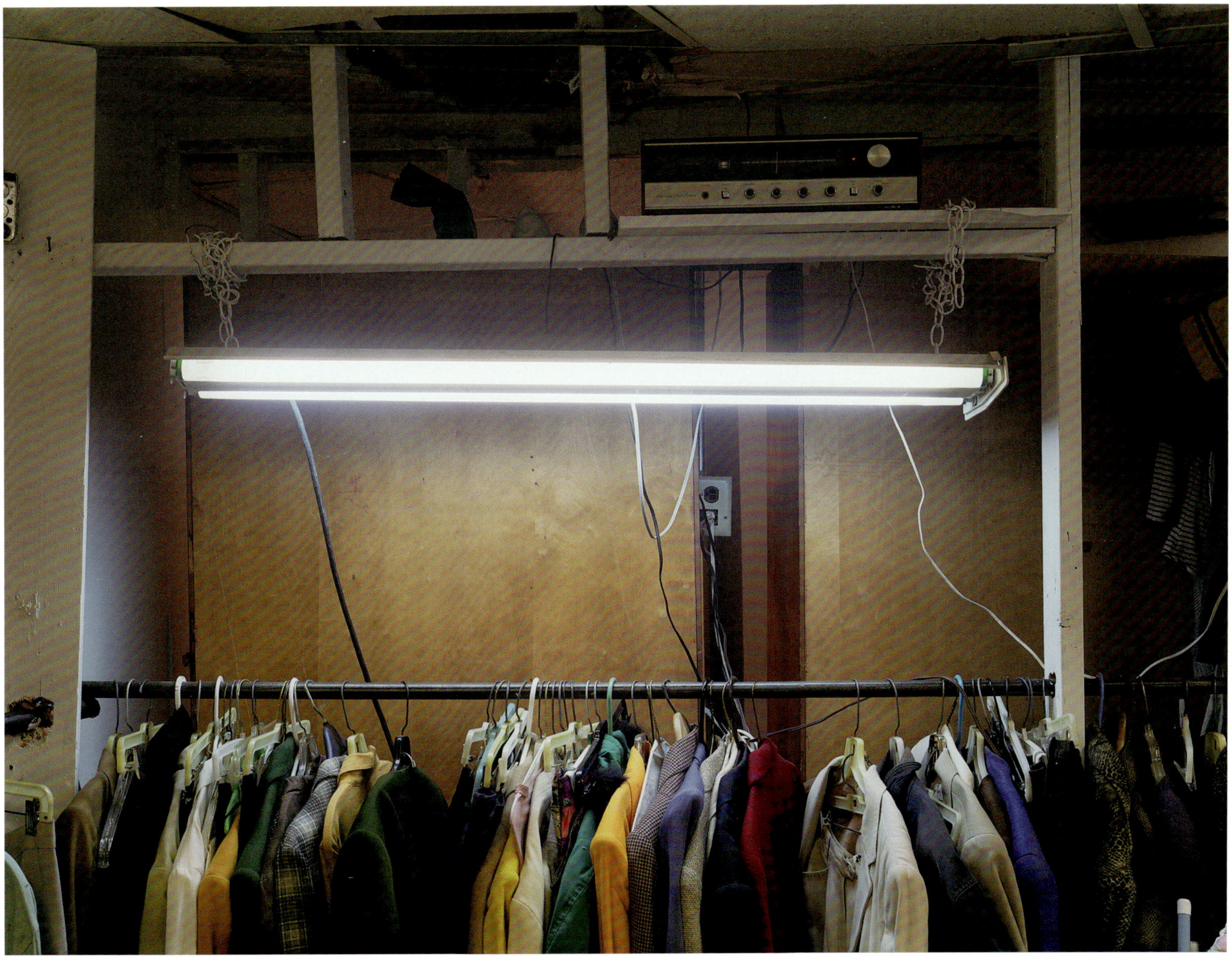

48.

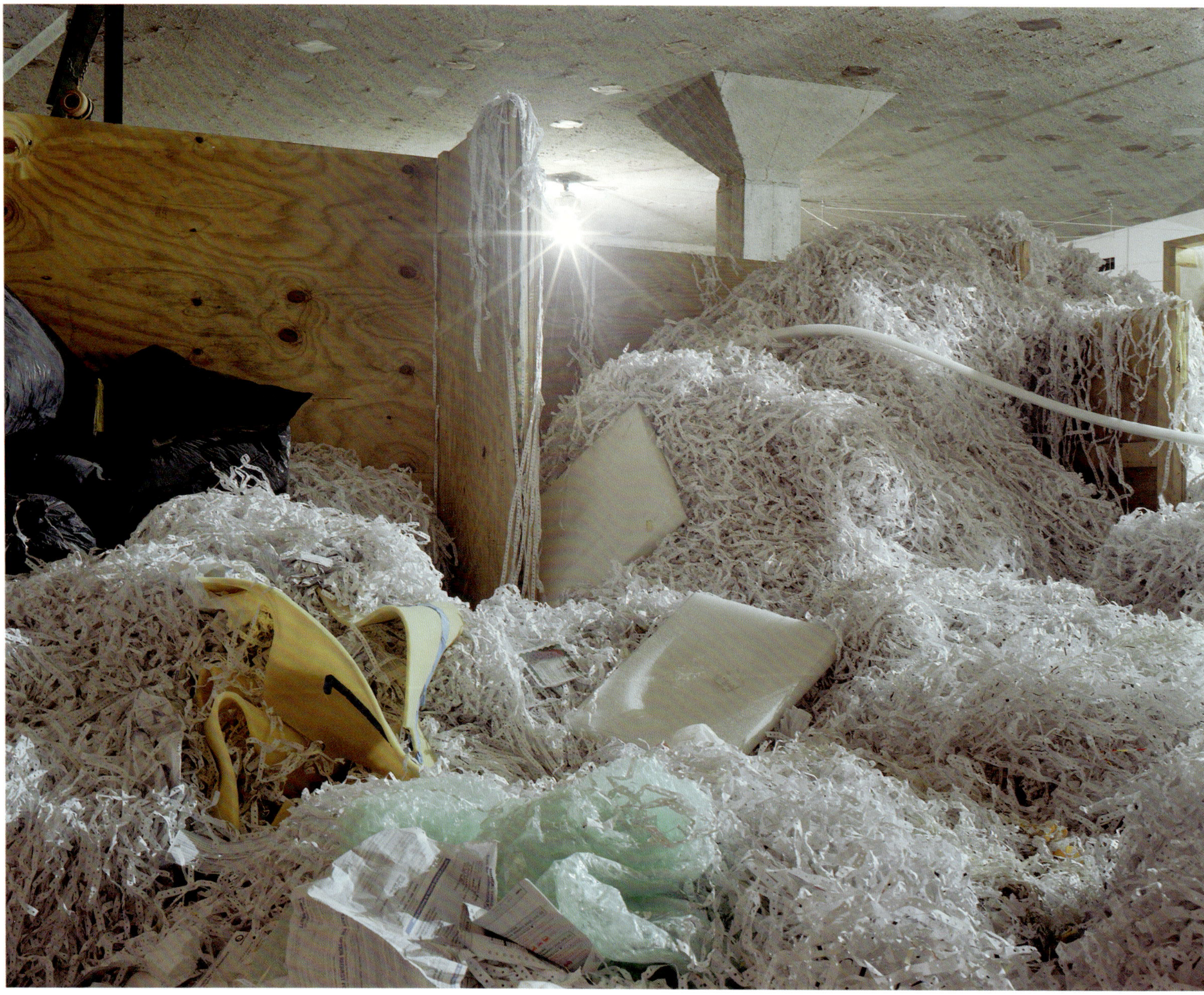

49.

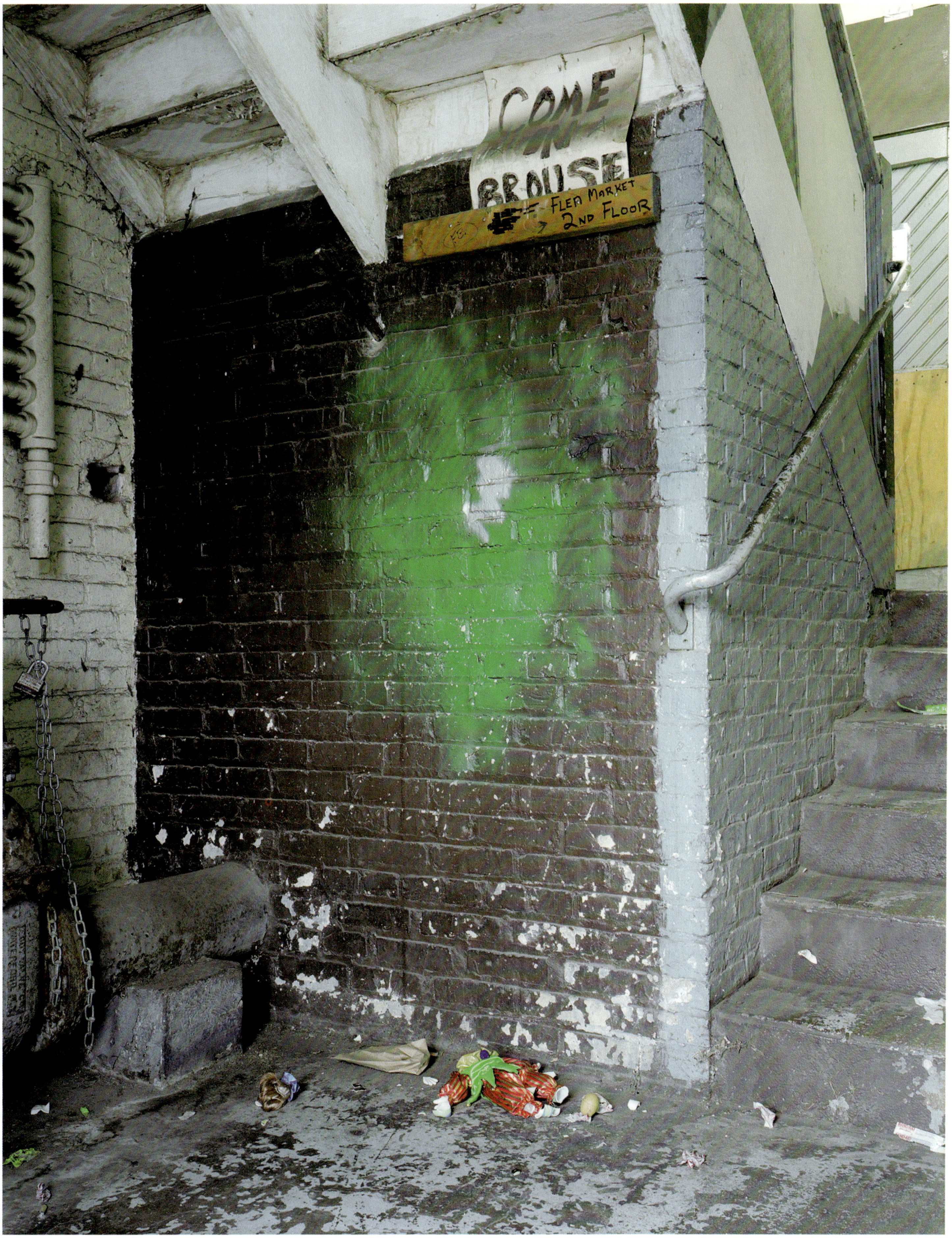

50.

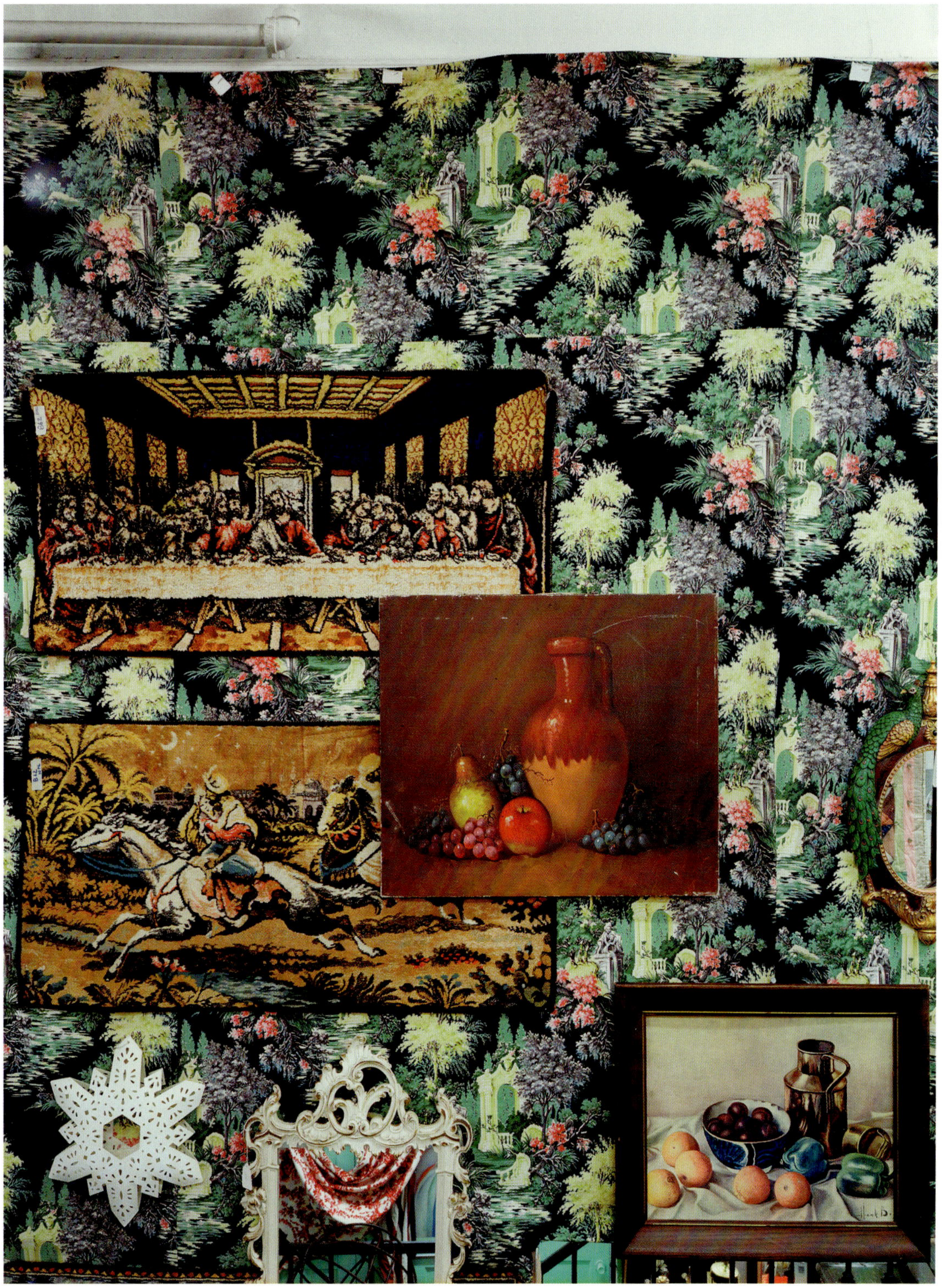

51.

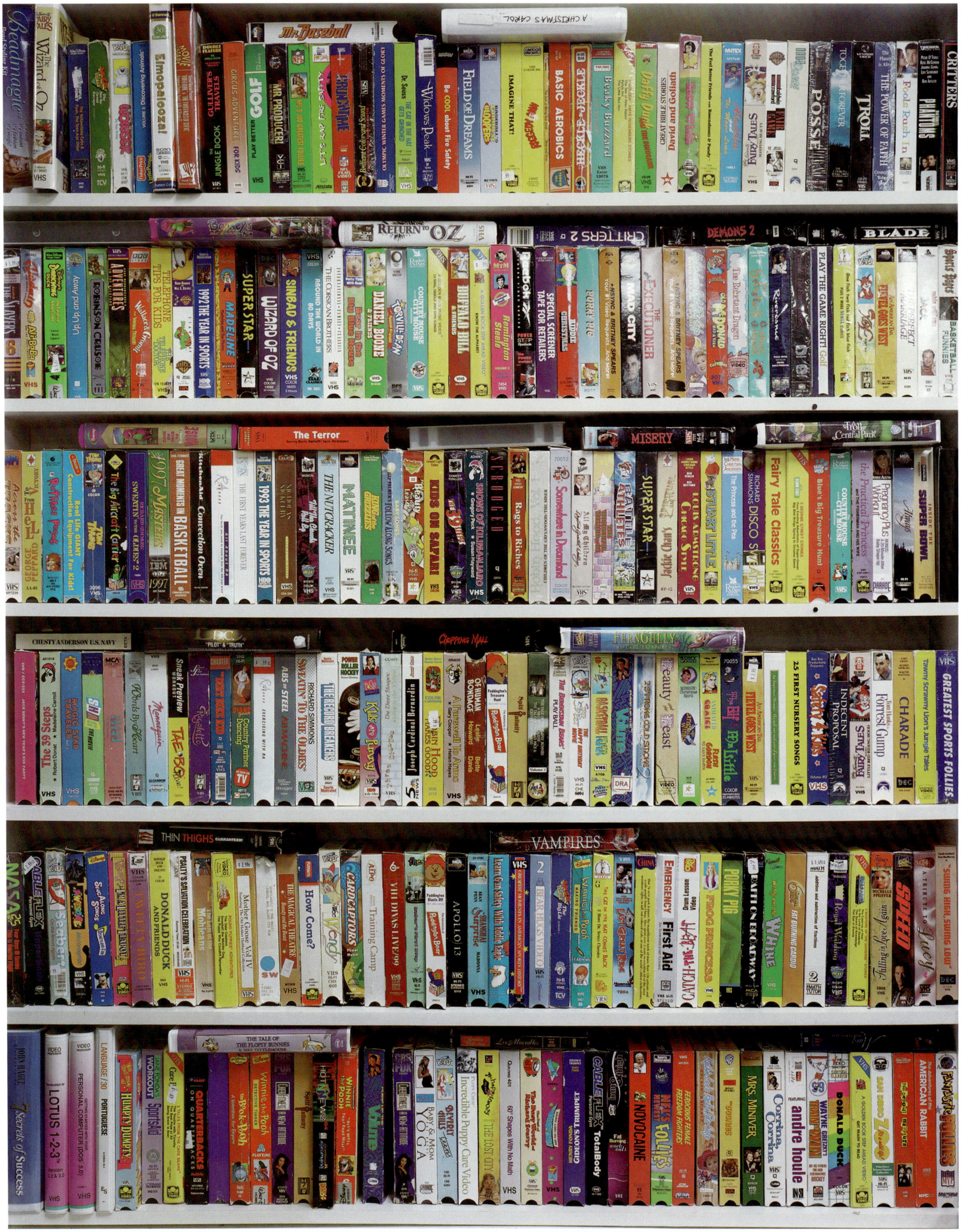

Beadmagic
The Wizard of Oz
Elmopalooza!
Mr. Baseball
A CHRISTMAS CAROL
JUNGLE BOOK
CIRCUS ADVENTURES FOR KIDS
GOLF
MR. PRODUCER
Widows Peak
Be COOL about Fire Safety
FIELD OF DREAMS
IMAGINE THAT!
BASIC AEROBICS
Barney's Buzzard
Daffy Duck
Dogs and Gorgons
Fairy Tales
POSSE
FOREVER
TROLL
THE POWER OF FAITH
Fools Rush In
CRITTERS
RETURN TO OZ
CRITTERS 2
DEMONS 2
BLADE
Aladdin
ROBINSON CRUSOE
ADVENTURES
TELEPHONE TIPS FOR KIDS
1992 THE YEAR IN SPORTS
MADELINE
SUPER STAR
WIZARD OF OZ
SINBAD & FRIENDS
AROUND THE WORLD IN 80 DAYS
THE CORSICAN BROTHERS
DANIEL BOONE
BUFFALO BILL
Remington Steele
SPECIAL SCREENER TAPE FOR RETAILERS
MAD CITY
THE EXECUTIONER
The Reluctant Dragon
PLAY THE GAME RIGHT! Golf
BASKETBALL FUNNIES
The Terror
MISERY
Troll in Central Park
Construction Equipment For Kids!
The Big Aircraft Carrier
1997 Mysteries
GREAT MOMENTS IN BASKETBALL
Convection Oven
THE FIRST YEARS LAST FOREVER
1993 THE YEAR IN SPORTS
THE NUTCRACKER
MATINEE
KIDS ON SAFARI
SNOWS OF KILIMANJARO
SCROOGED
Rags to Riches
Somewhere in Dreamland
SUPER STAR
STUART LITTLE
The Princess and the Pea
RICHARD SIMMONS DISCO SWEAT
Fairy Tale Classics
Blue's Big Treasure Hunt
COUNTRY MOUSE CITY MOUSE
the Practical Princess
SUPER BOWL
CHESTY ANDERSON U.S. NAVY
Chopping Mall
FERNGULLY
The 39 Steps
Sneak Preview
ABS of STEEL
SWEATIN' TO THE OLDIES
RICHARD SIMMONS
Kids
Joseph Cardinal Bernardin
A Farewell To Arms
OF HUMAN BONDAGE
Robin Hood
Paddington Bear
The Elf
25 FIRST NURSERY SONGS
INDECENT PROPOSAL
Forrest Gump
CHARADE
GREATEST SPORTS FOLLIES
THIN THIGHS
VAMPIRES
NASA
CABLEFLEX
DONALD DUCK AND FRIENDS
Mother Goose Vol. IV
How Come?
CARDCAPTORS
Training Camp
APOLLO 13
EMERGENCY First Aid
FROG PRINCESS
PORKY PIG
SPEED
THE TALE OF THE FLOPSY BUNNIES
7 Secrets of Success
LOTUS 1-2-3
PERSONAL COMPUTER (DOS 5.0)
PORTUGUESE
HUMPTY DUMPTY
QUARTERBACKS
Winnie the Pooh
YOGA
Incredible Puppy Care Video
THE LOST CITY
60 Shapes With No Math
CABLEFLEX TotalBody
NOVOCAINE
MRS. MINIVER
Corrina, Corrina
andre houle
DONALD DUCK
AMERICAN RABBIT
FANTASTIC FOLLIES

52.

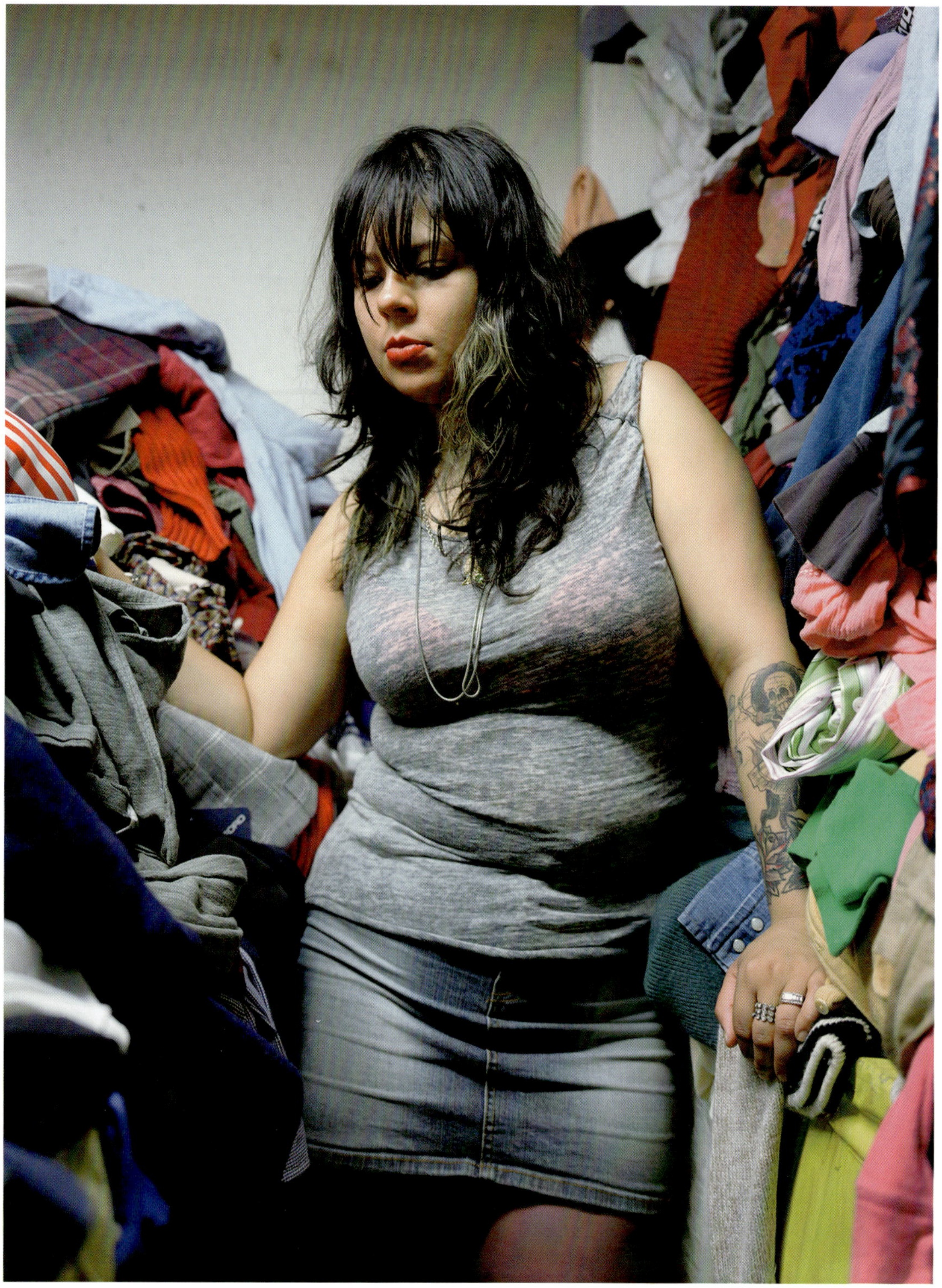

53.

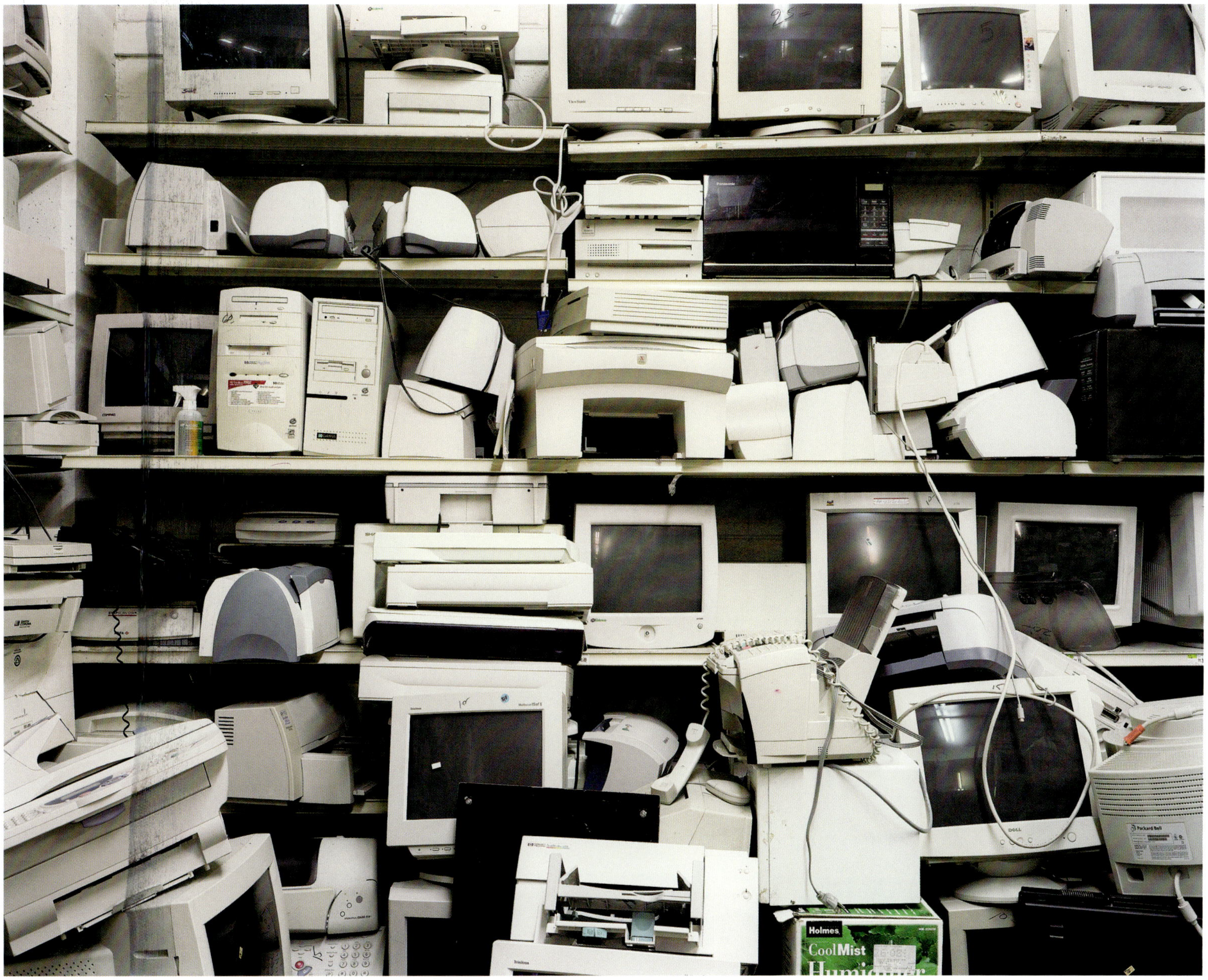

DARK STORES

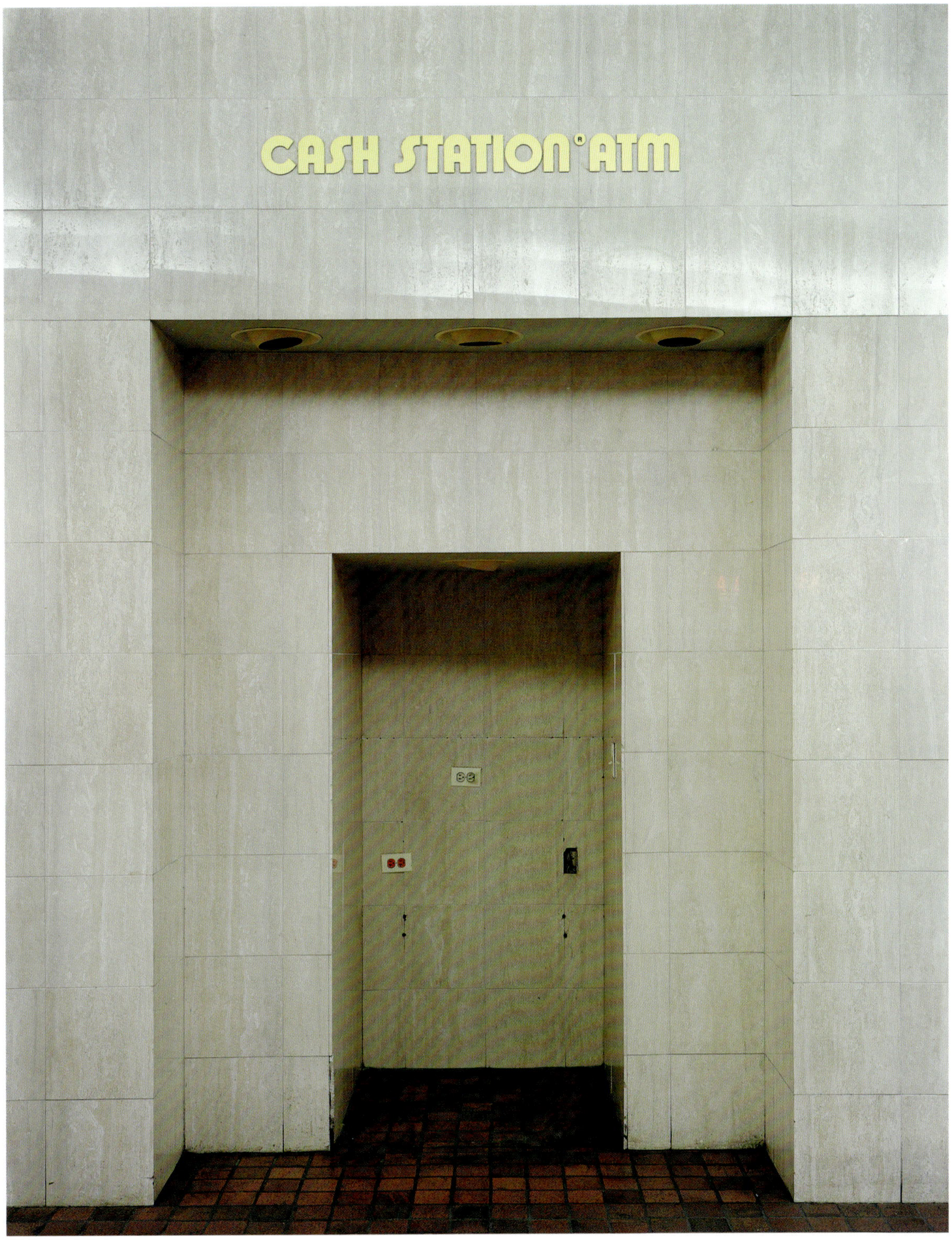

54.

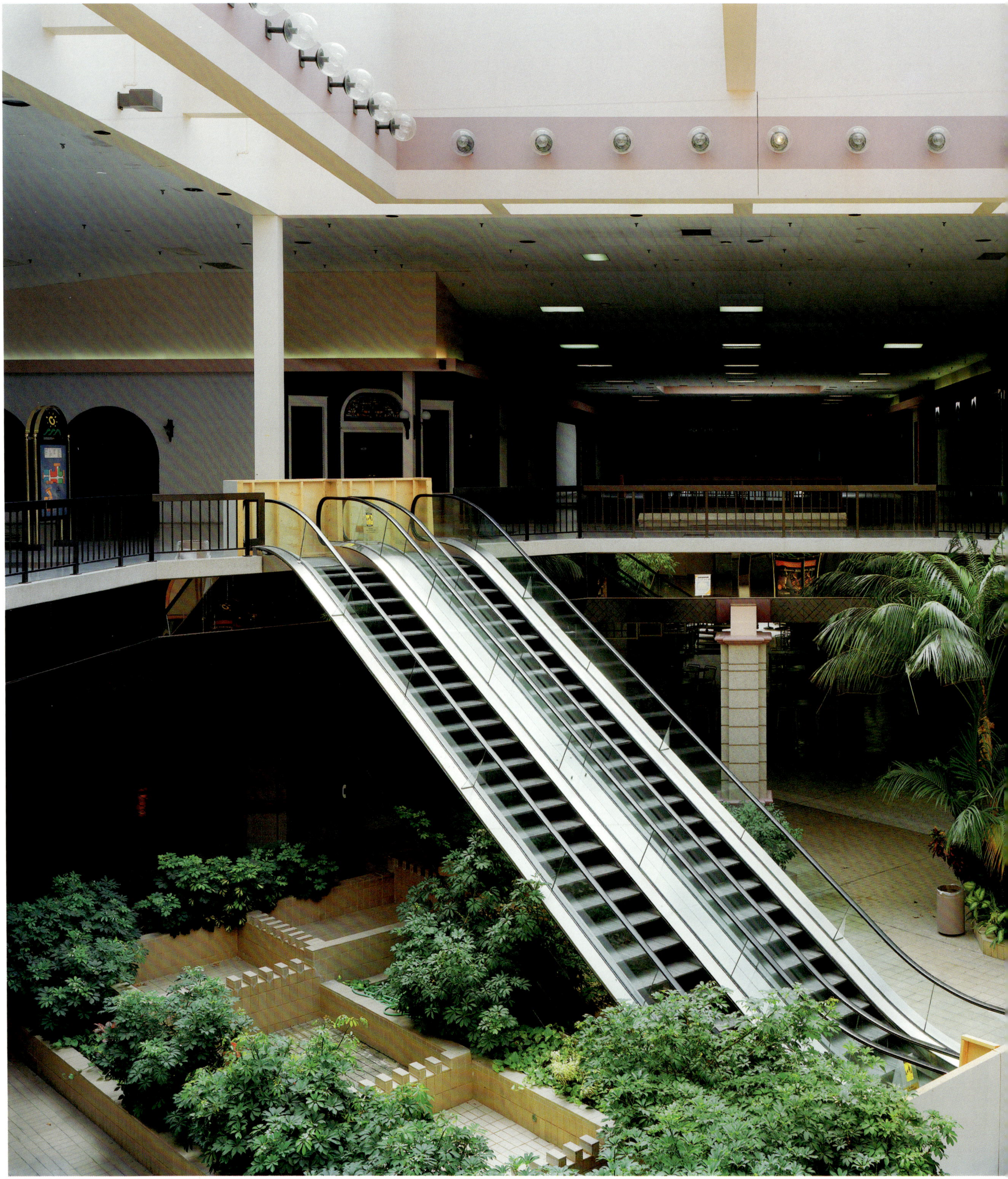

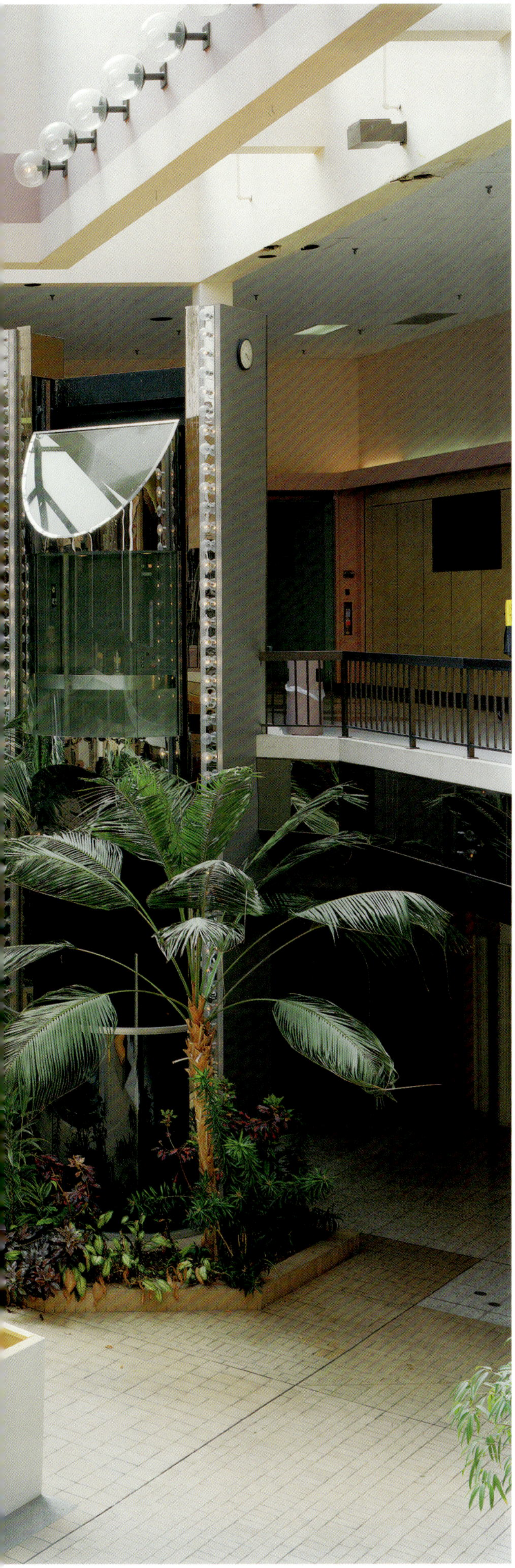

56.

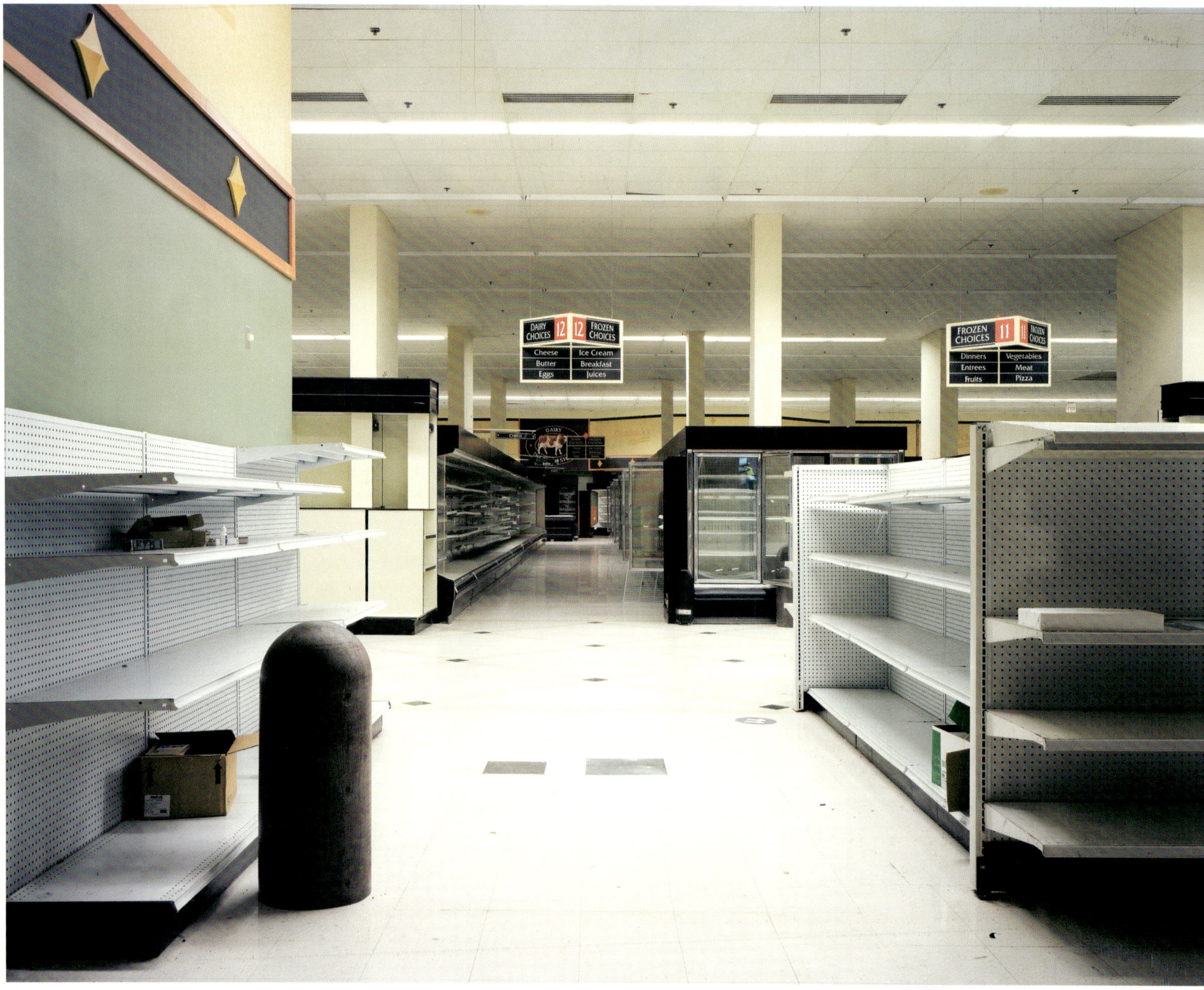
DAIRY CHOICES 12
12 FROZEN CHOICES
Cheese
Butter
Eggs
Ice Cream
Breakfast
Juices
FROZEN CHOICES 11
Dinners
Entrees
Fruits
Vegetables
Meat
Pizza

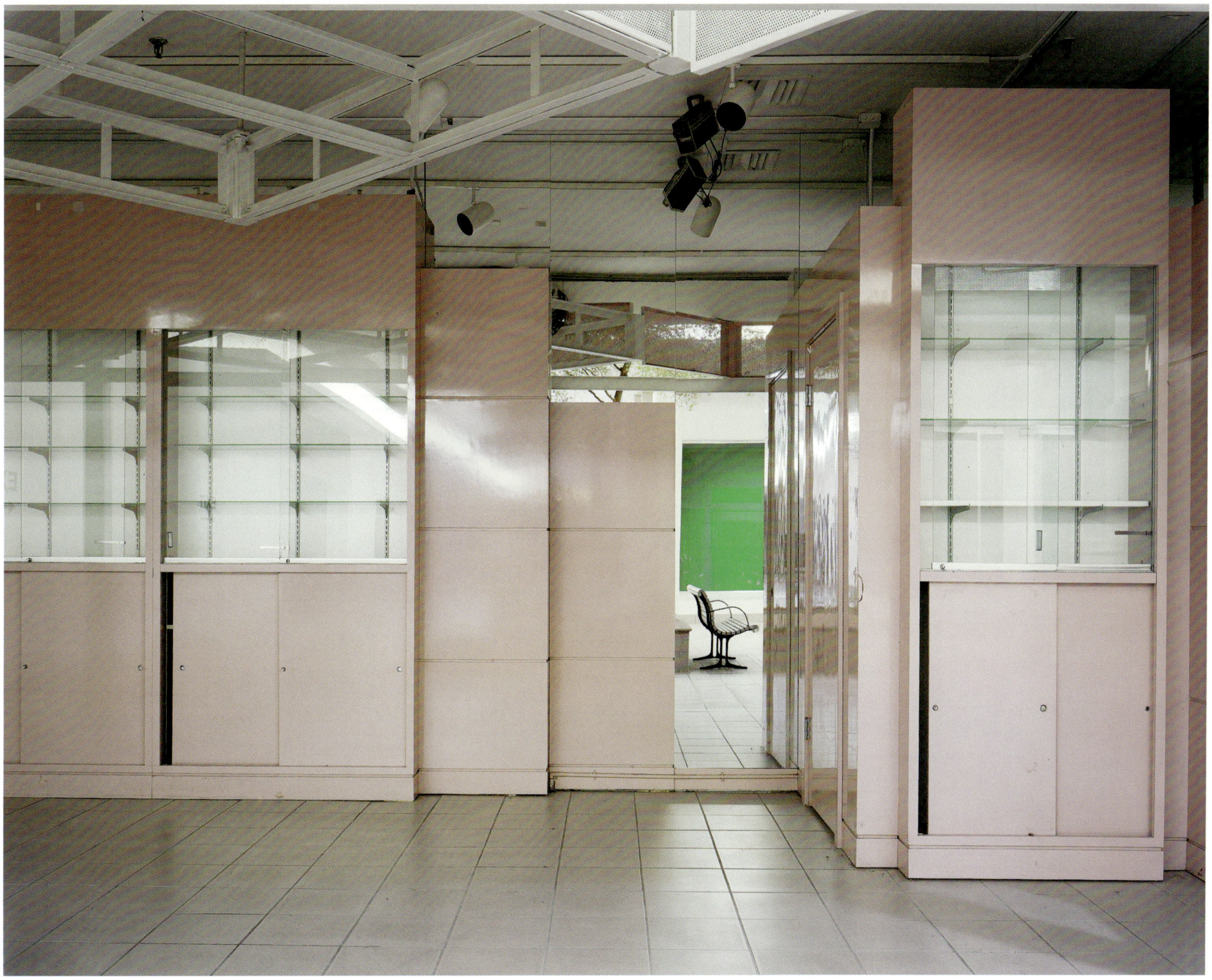

57.

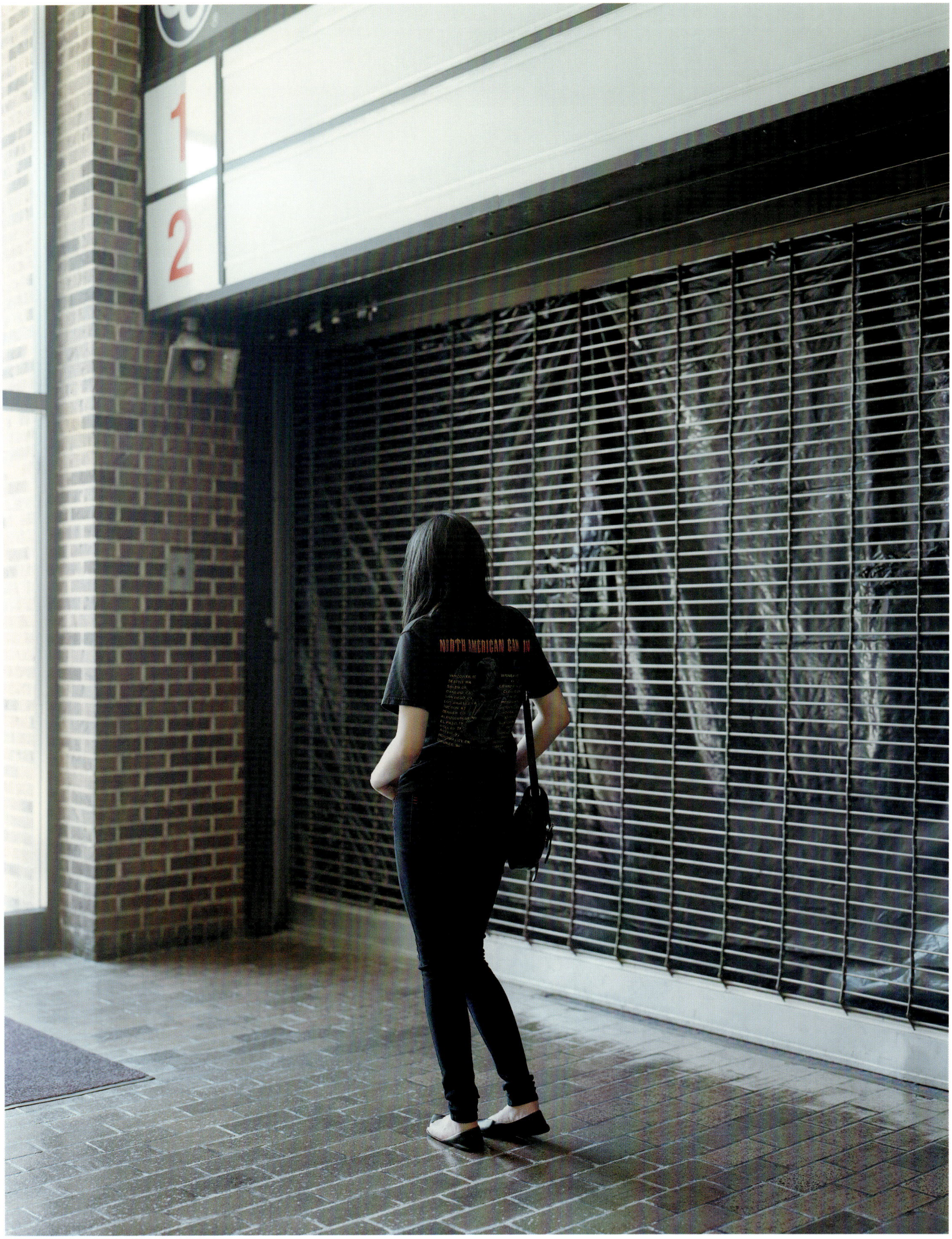
1
2

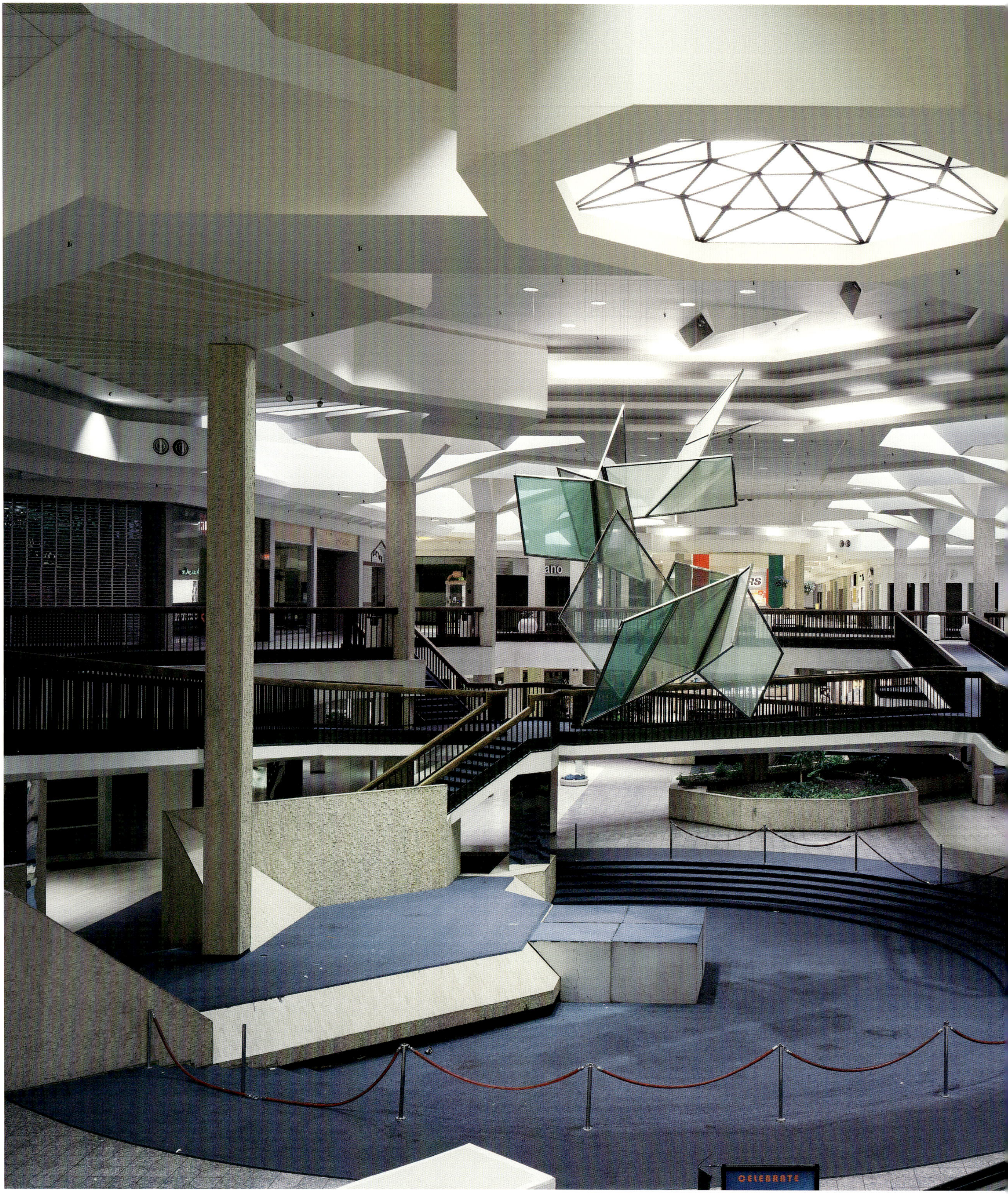
CELEBRATE

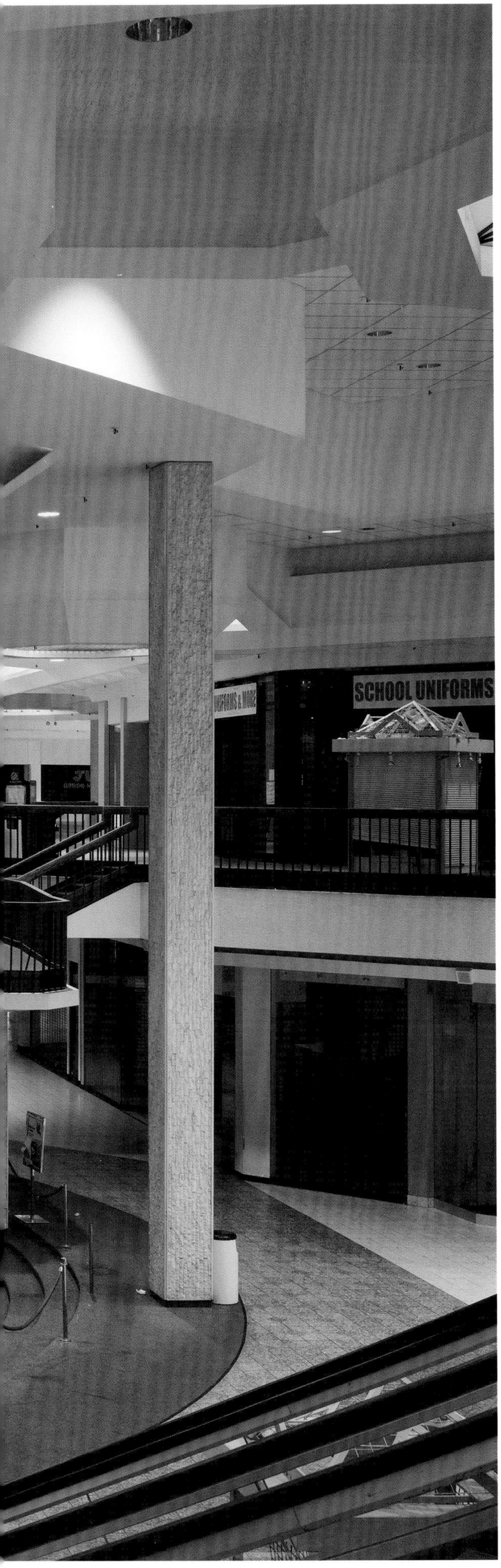
SCHOOL UNIFORMS

60.

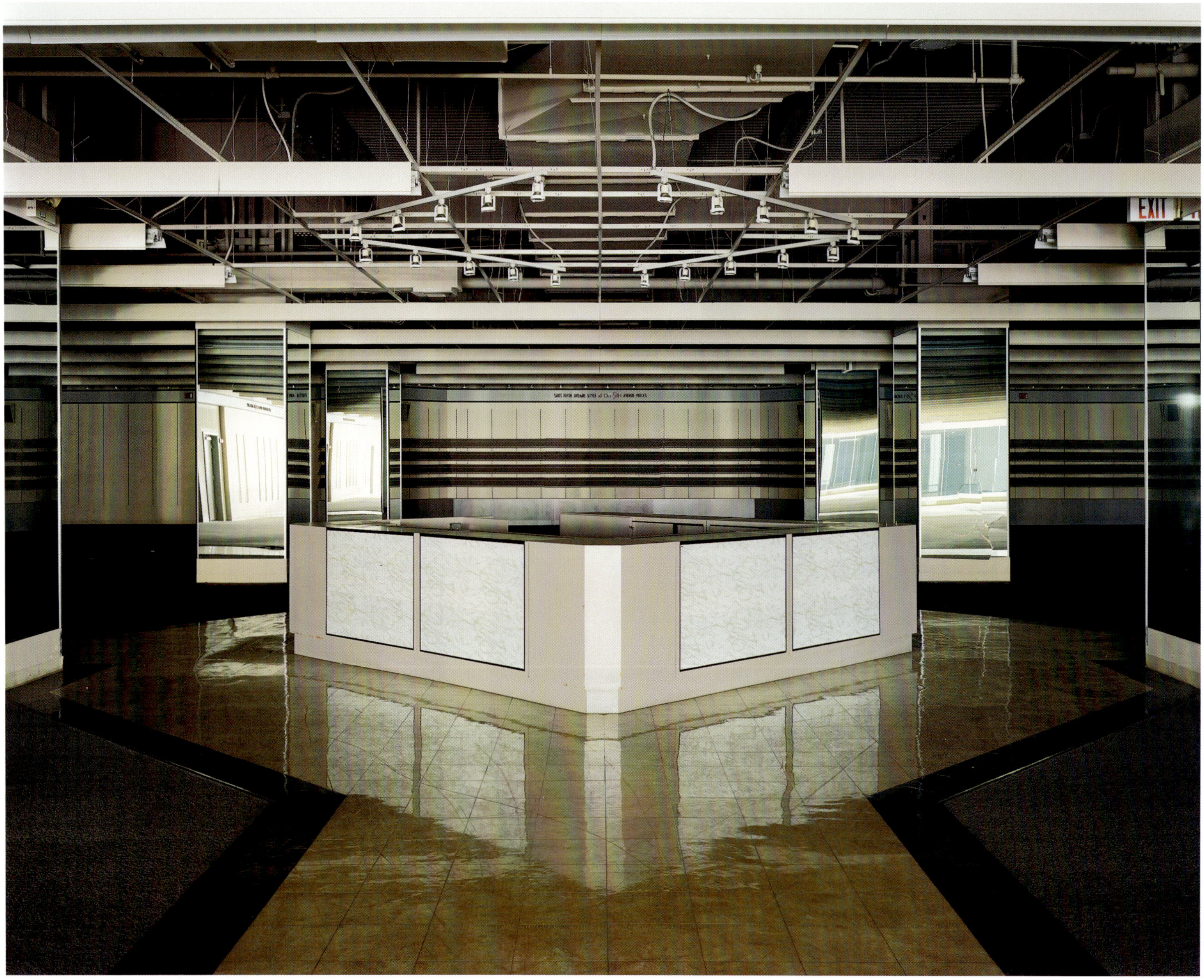

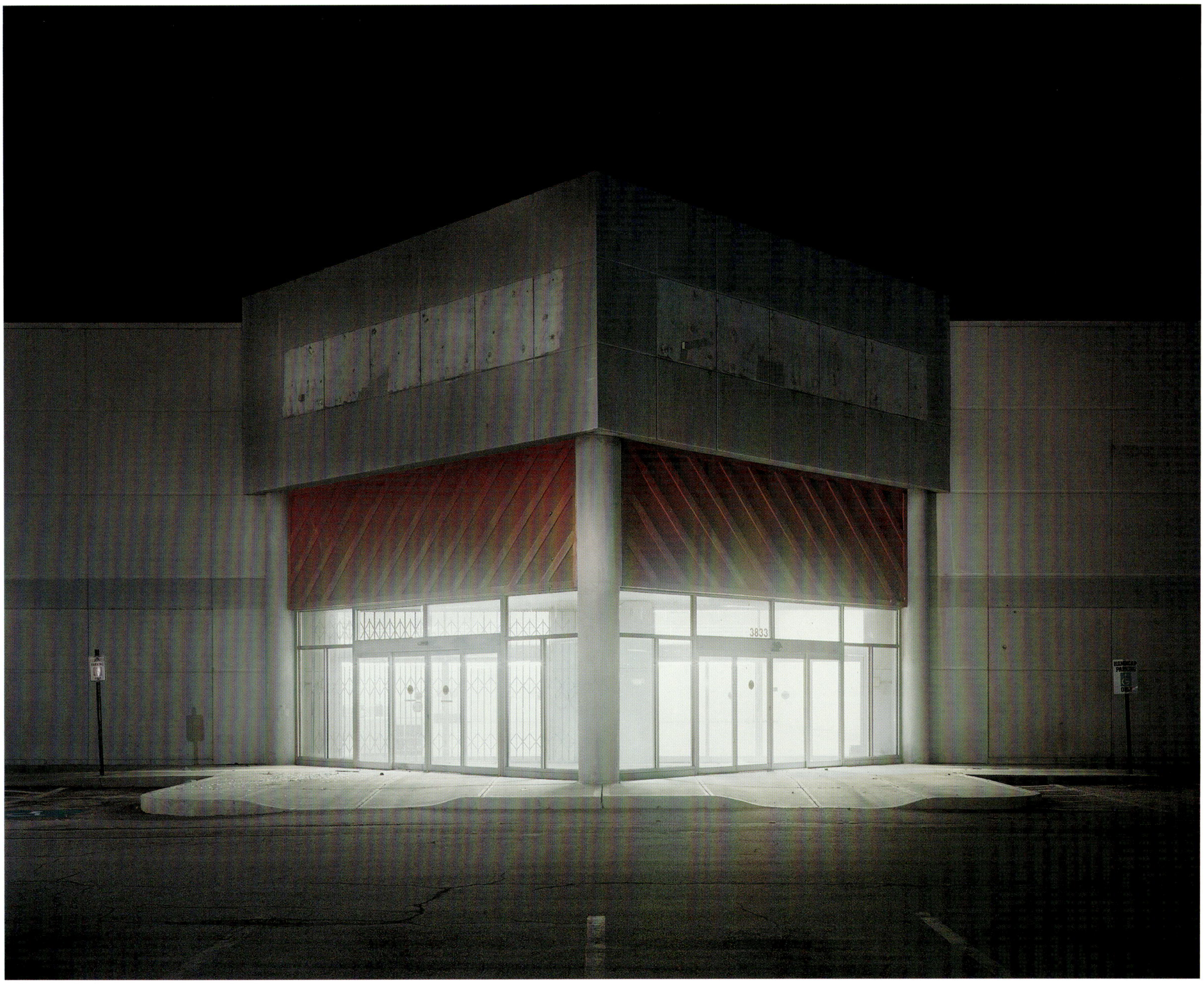

61.

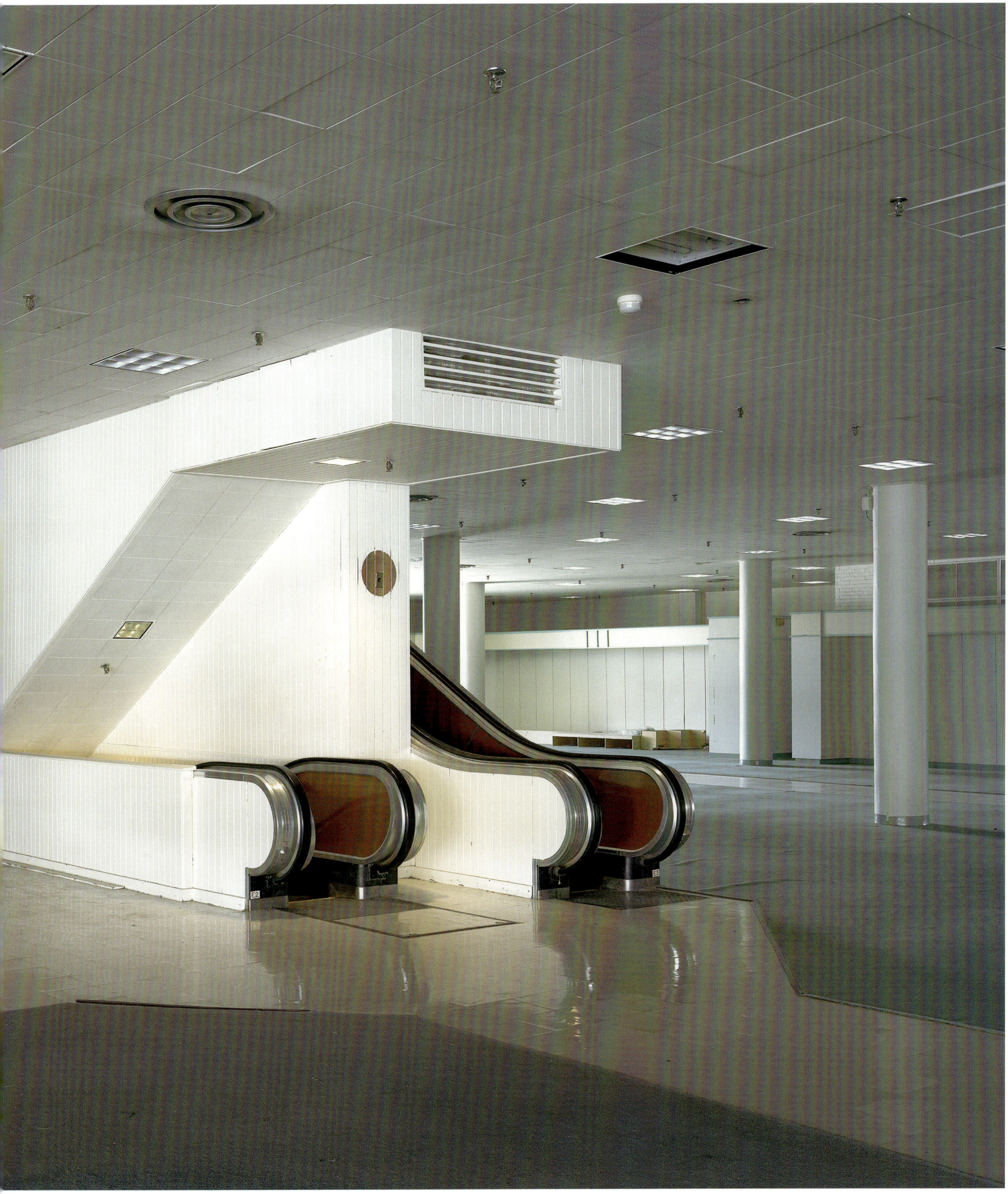

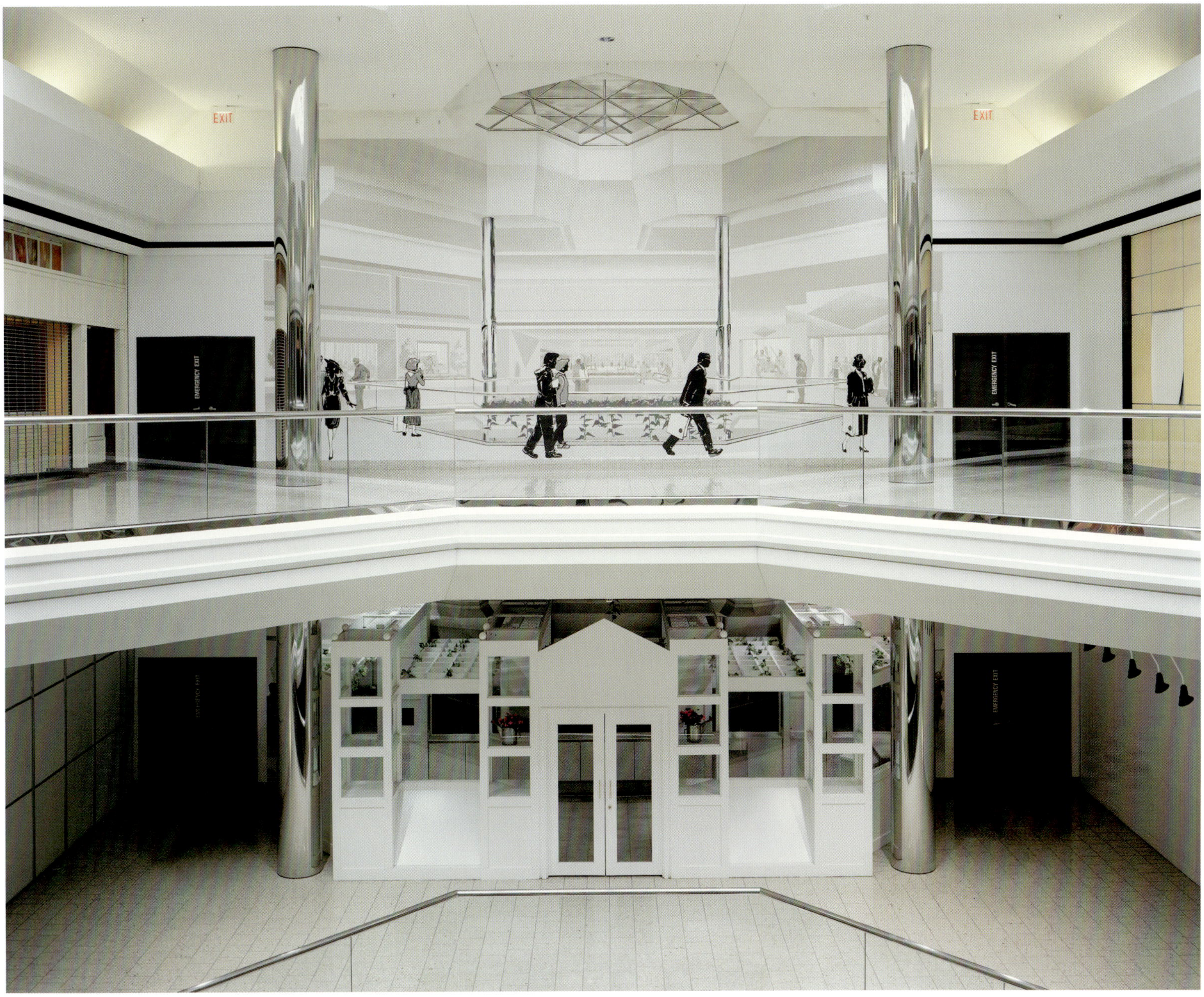

63.

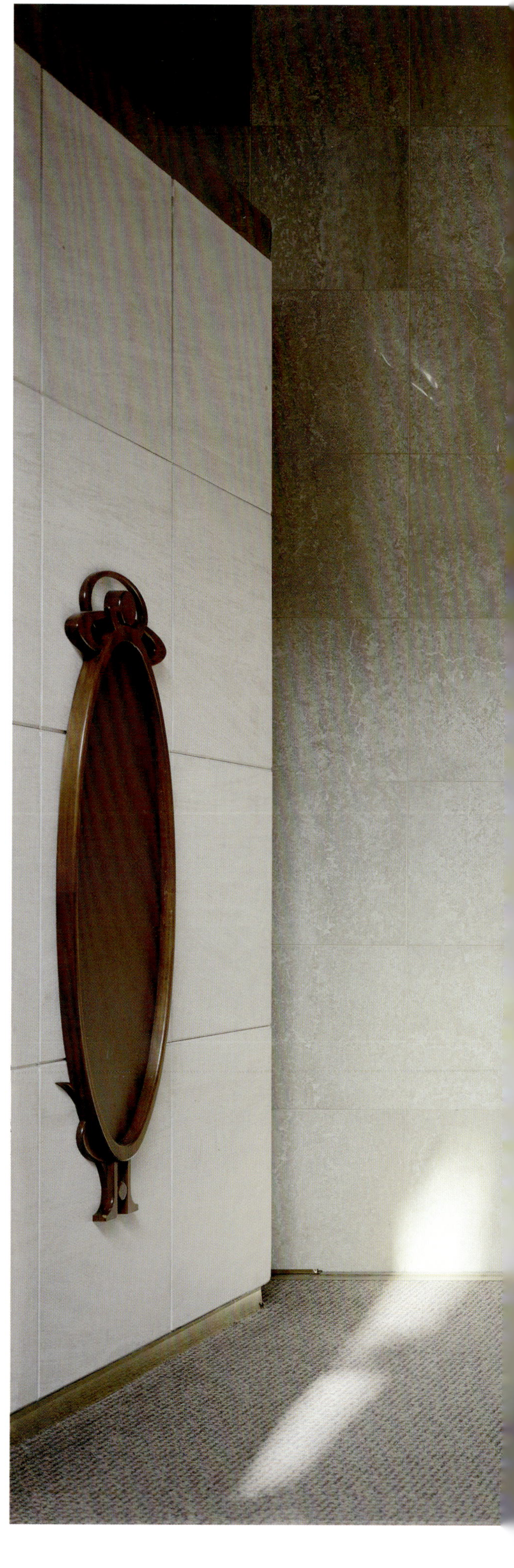

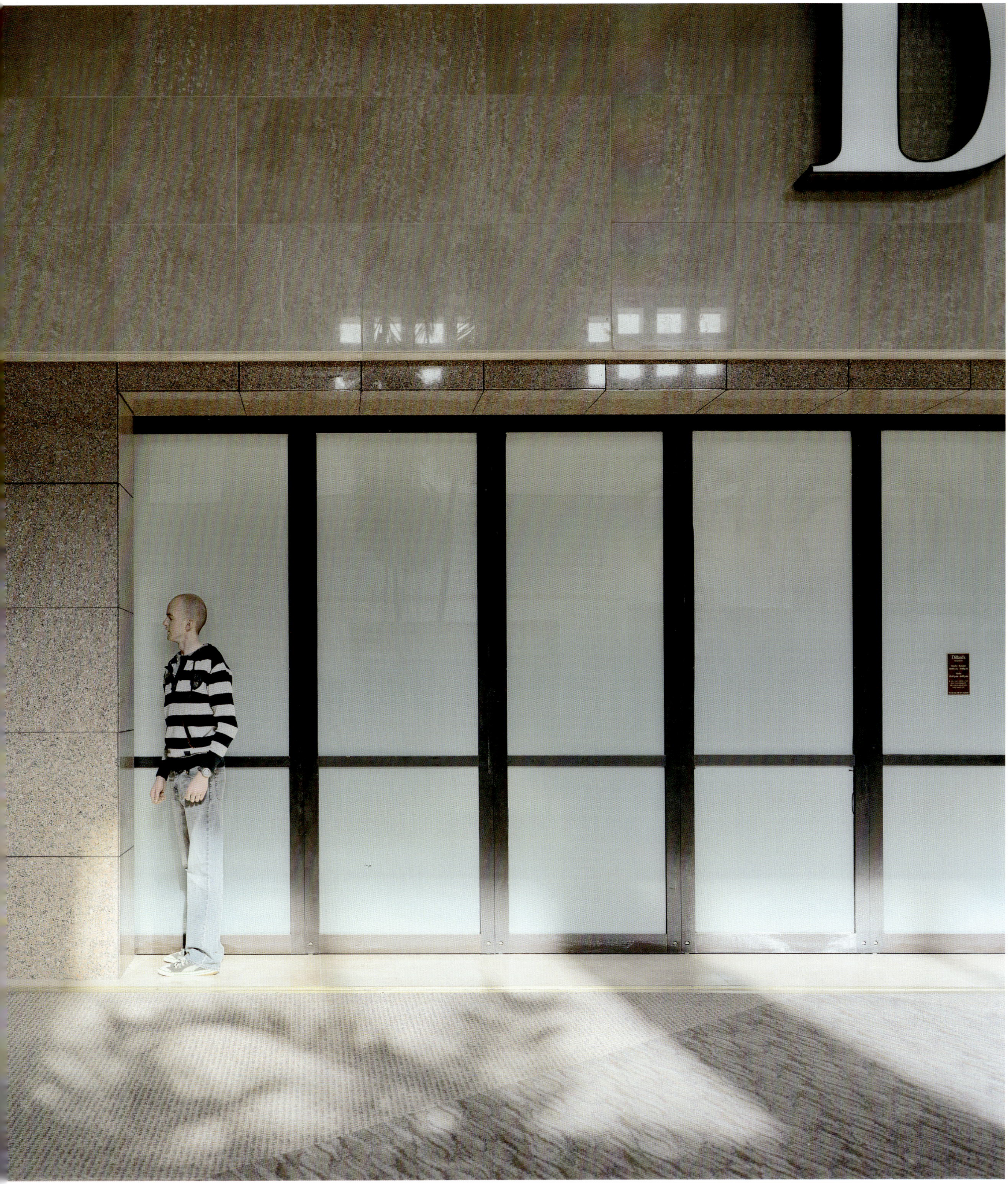

65.

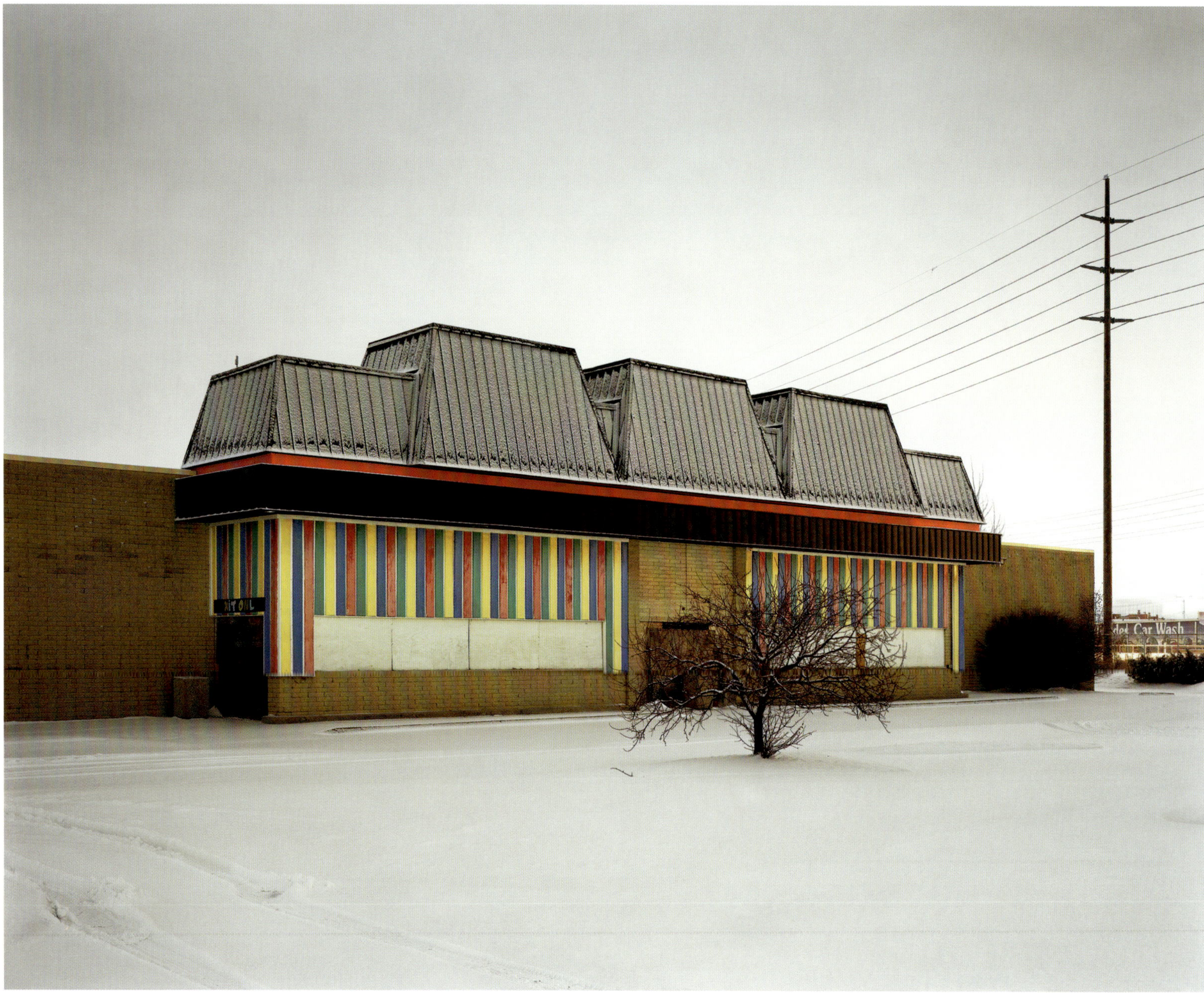

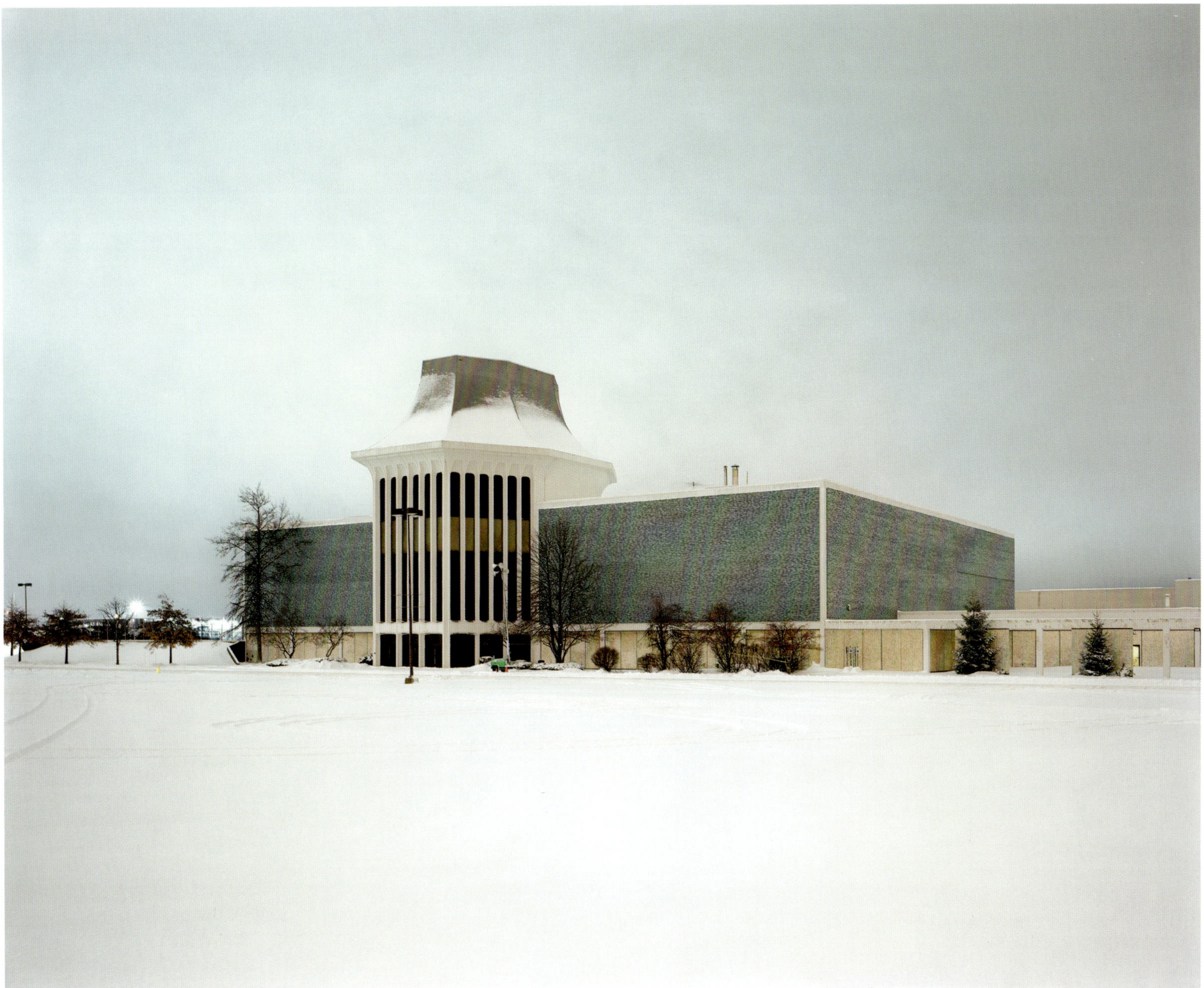

66.

67.

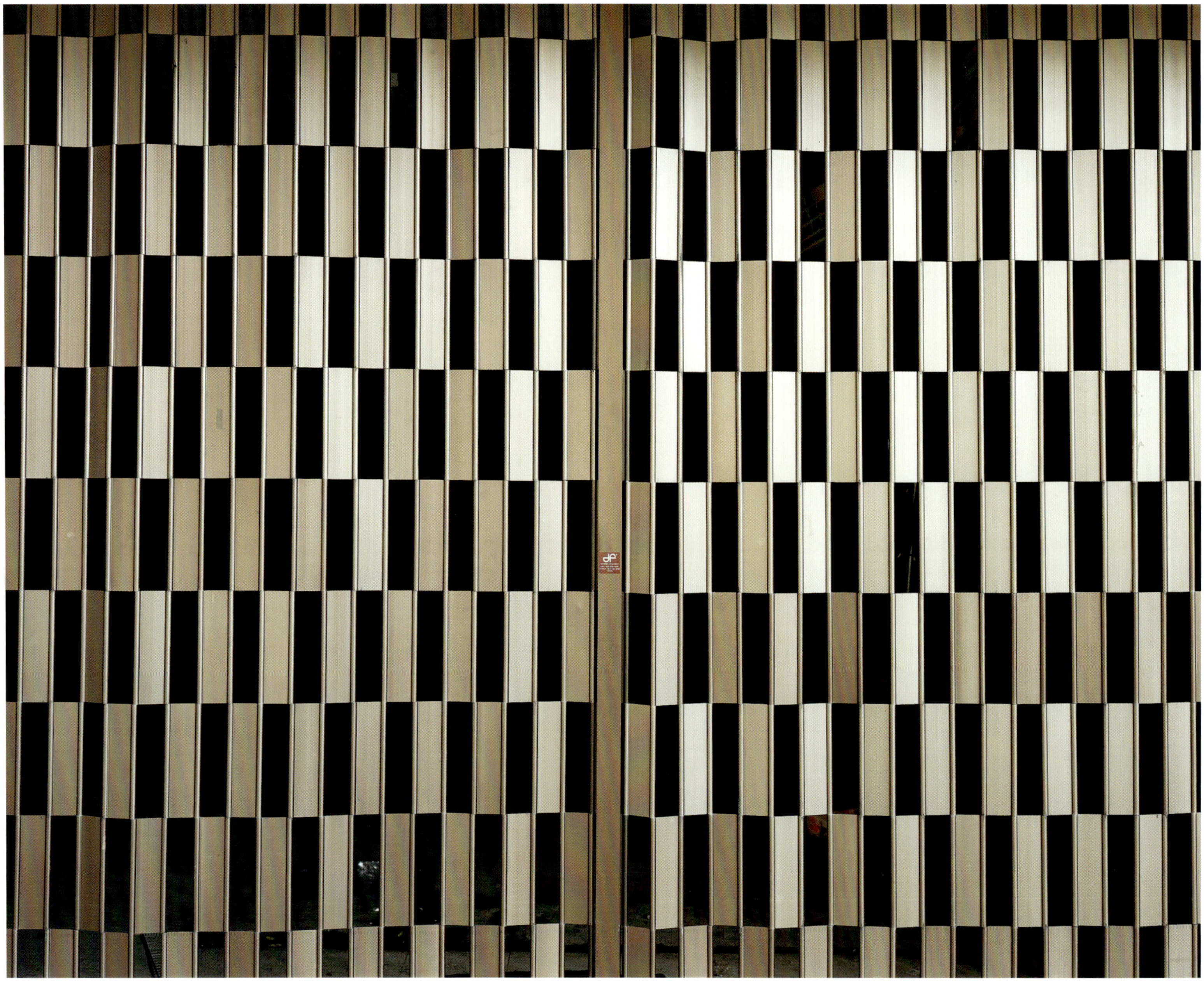

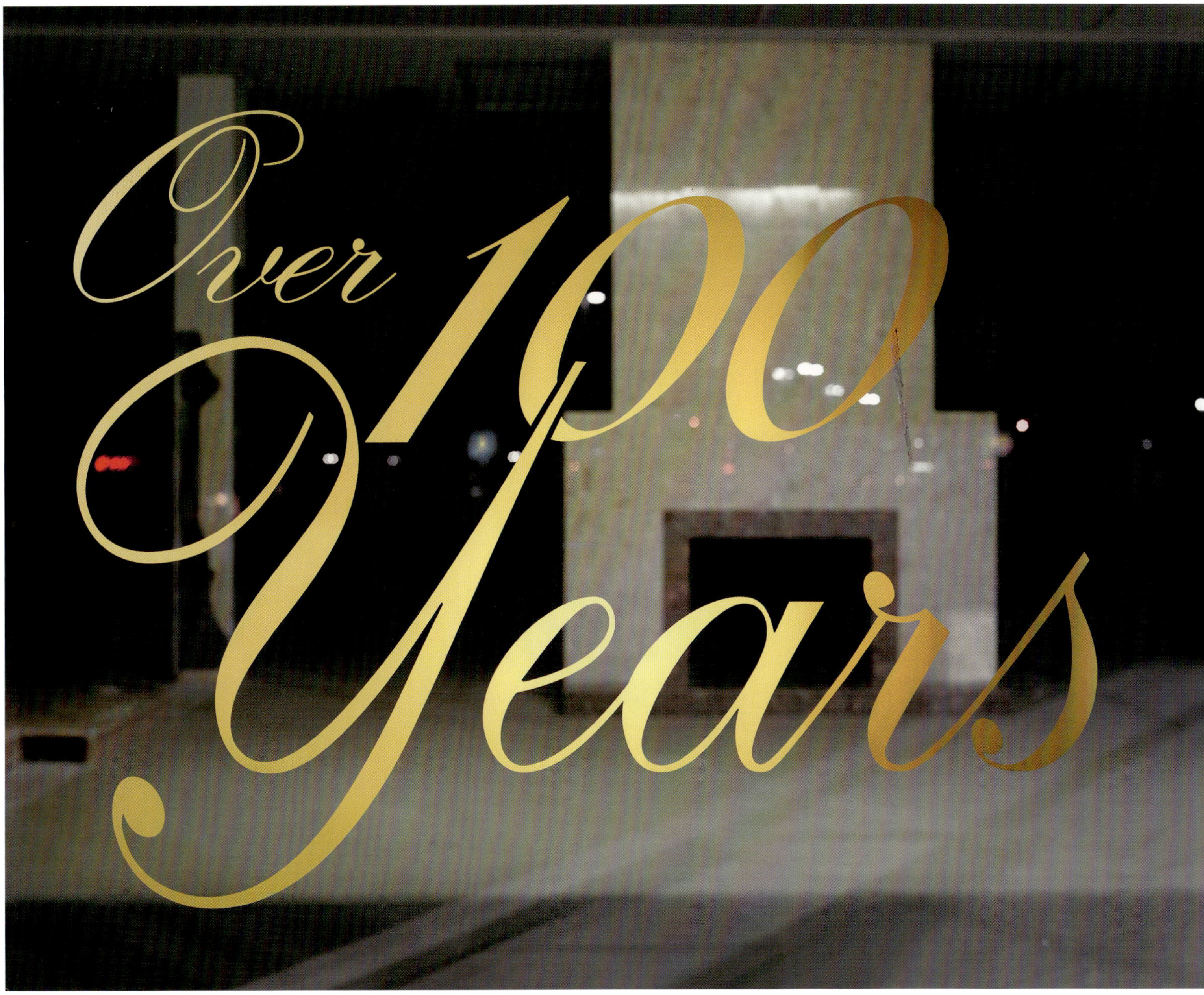
Over 100 Years

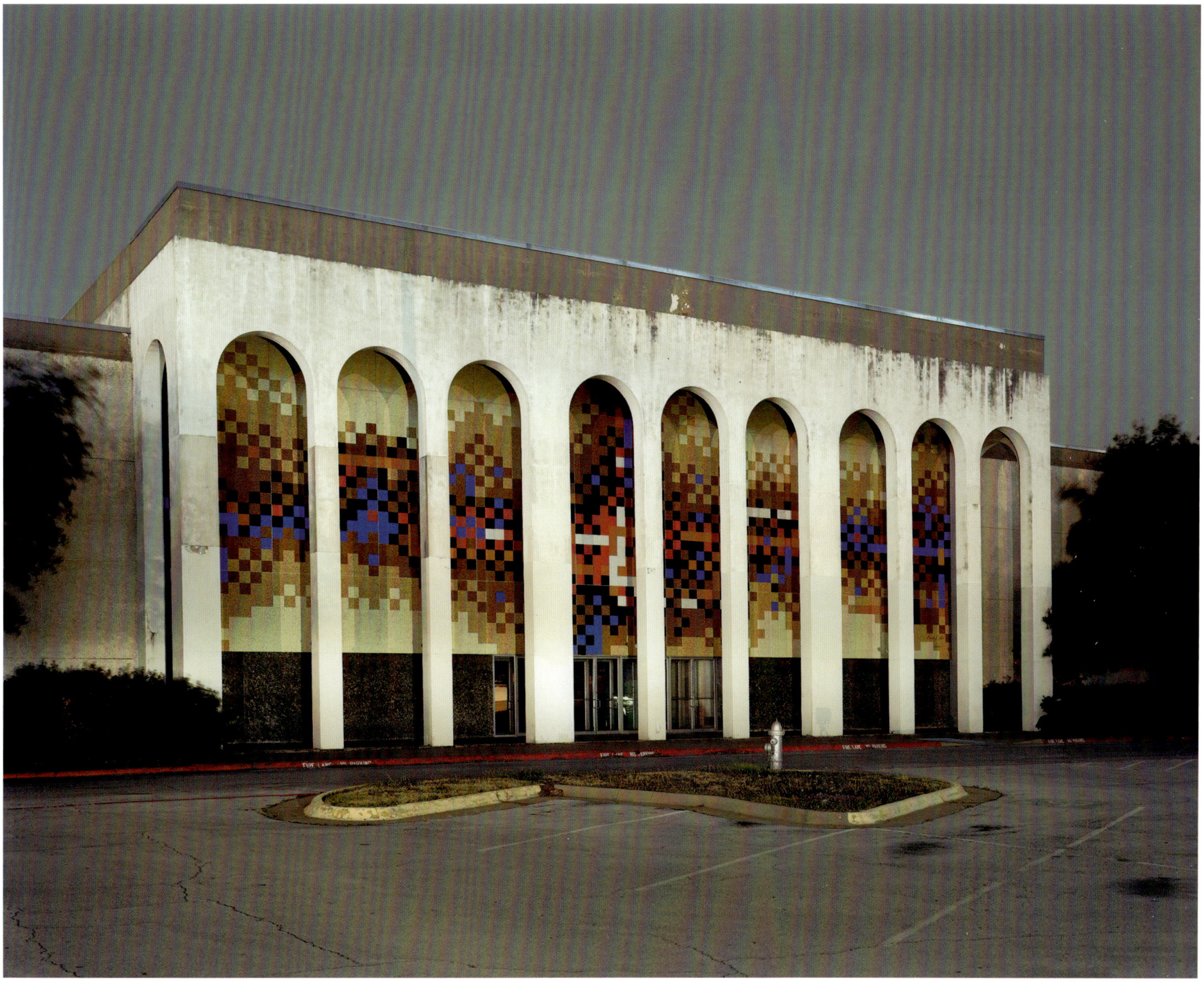

69.

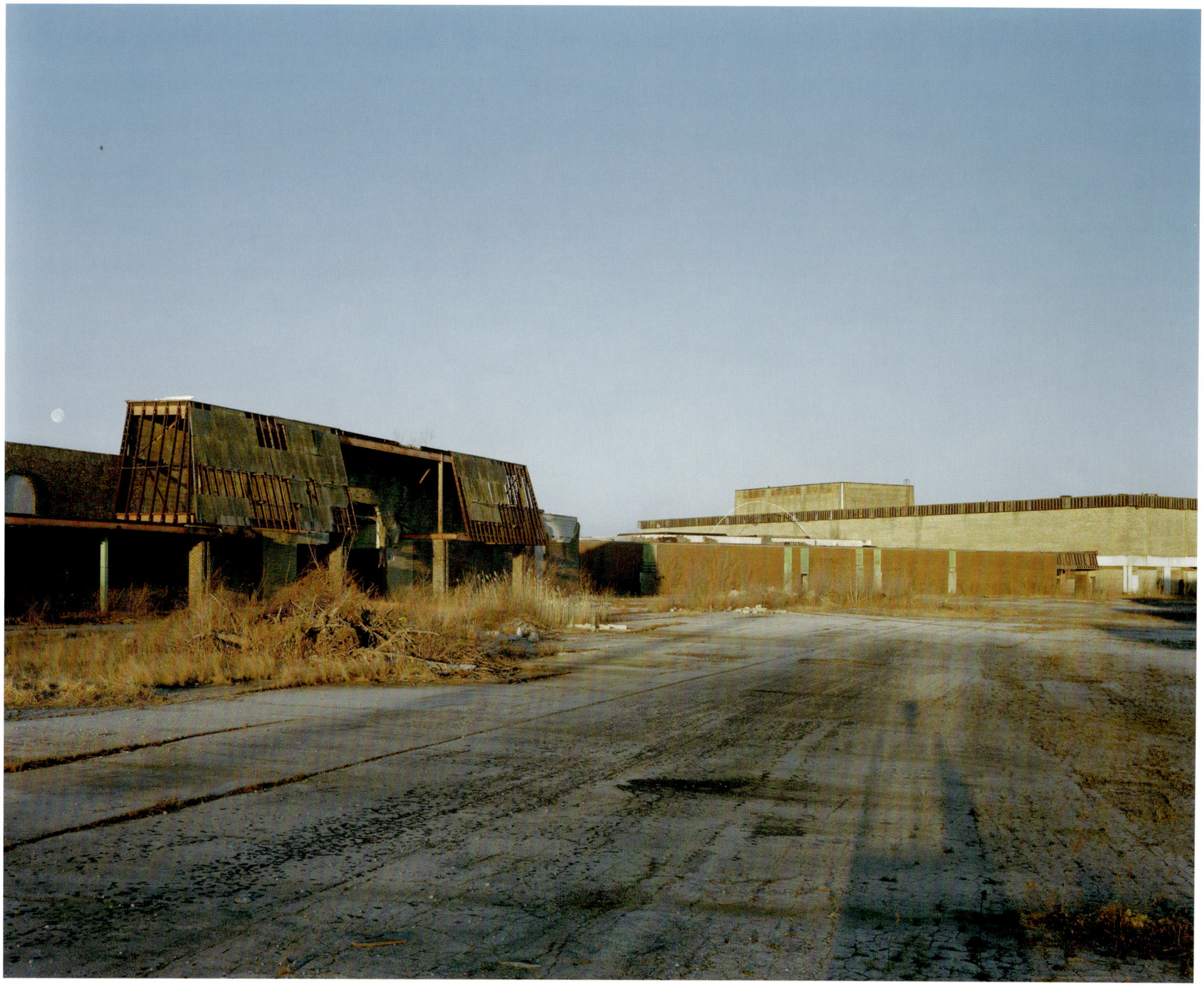

71.

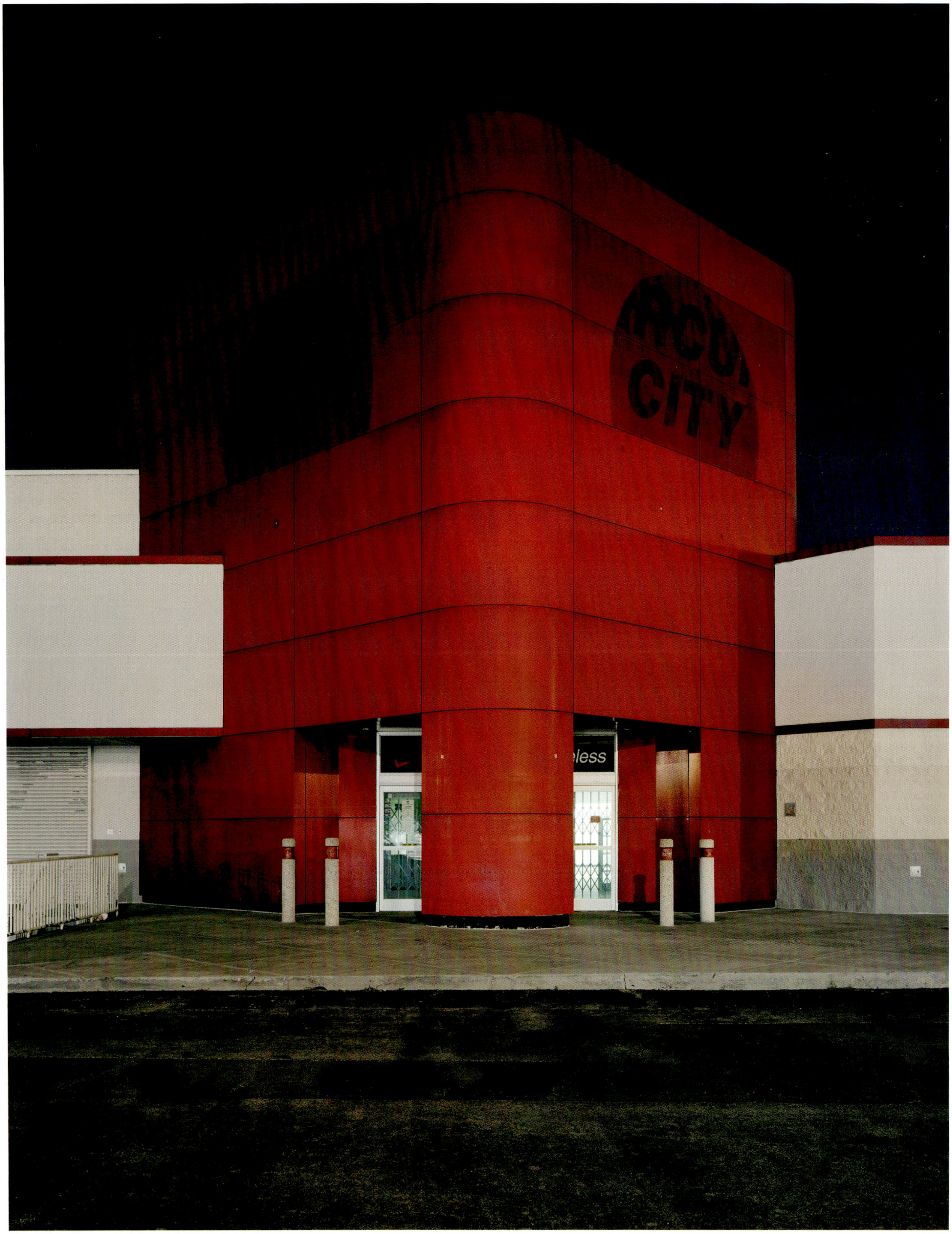
CITY

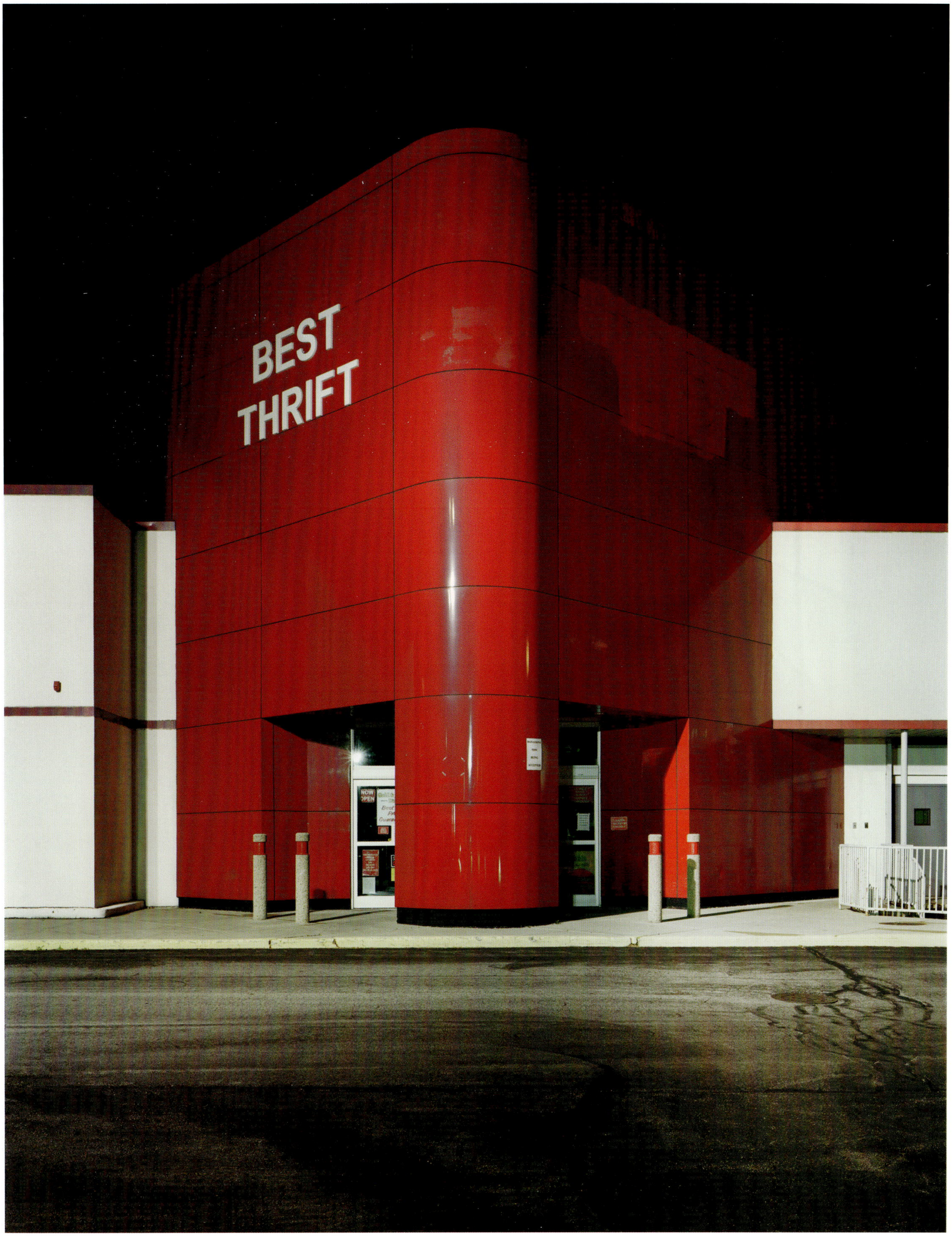

73.

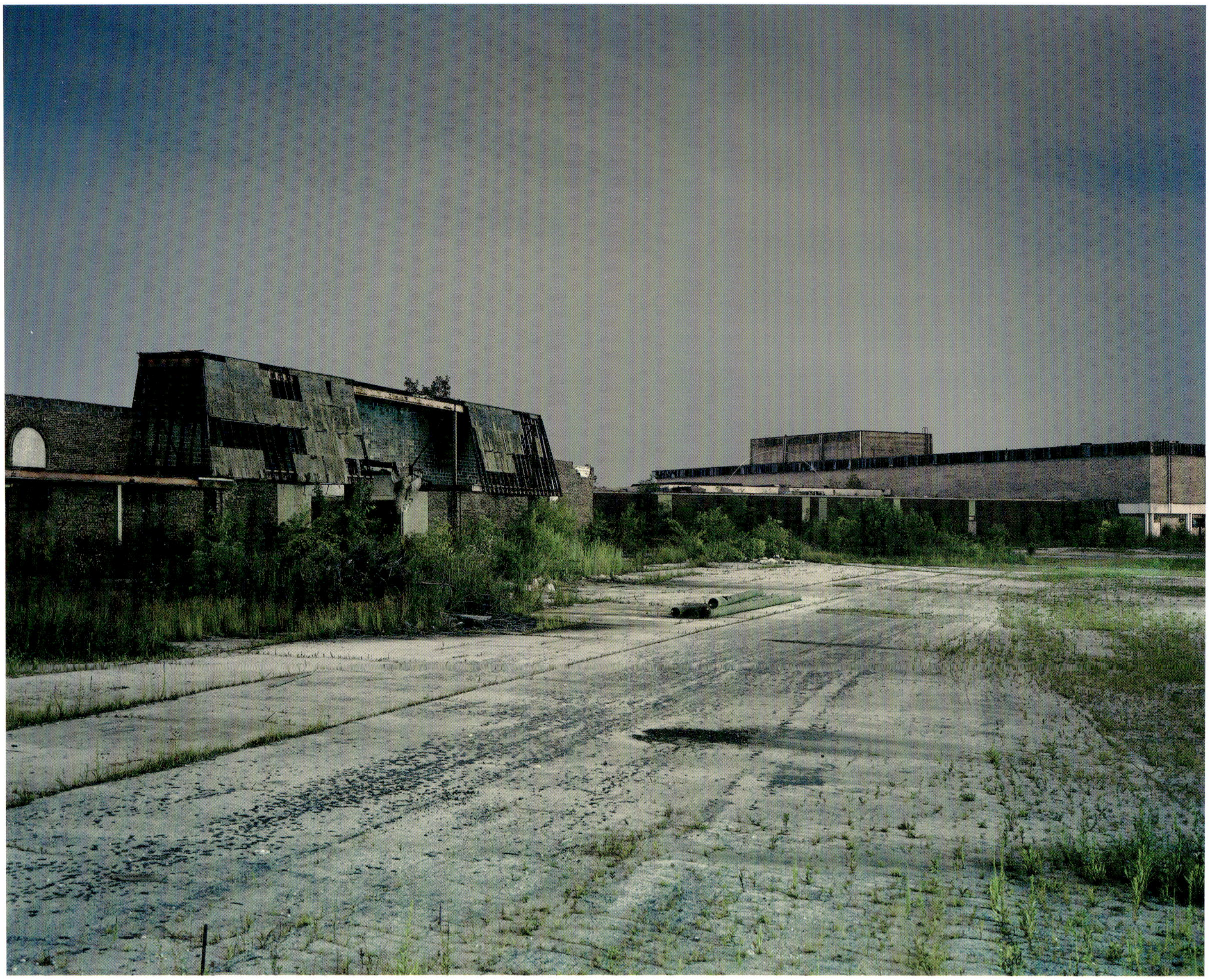

70.

77.

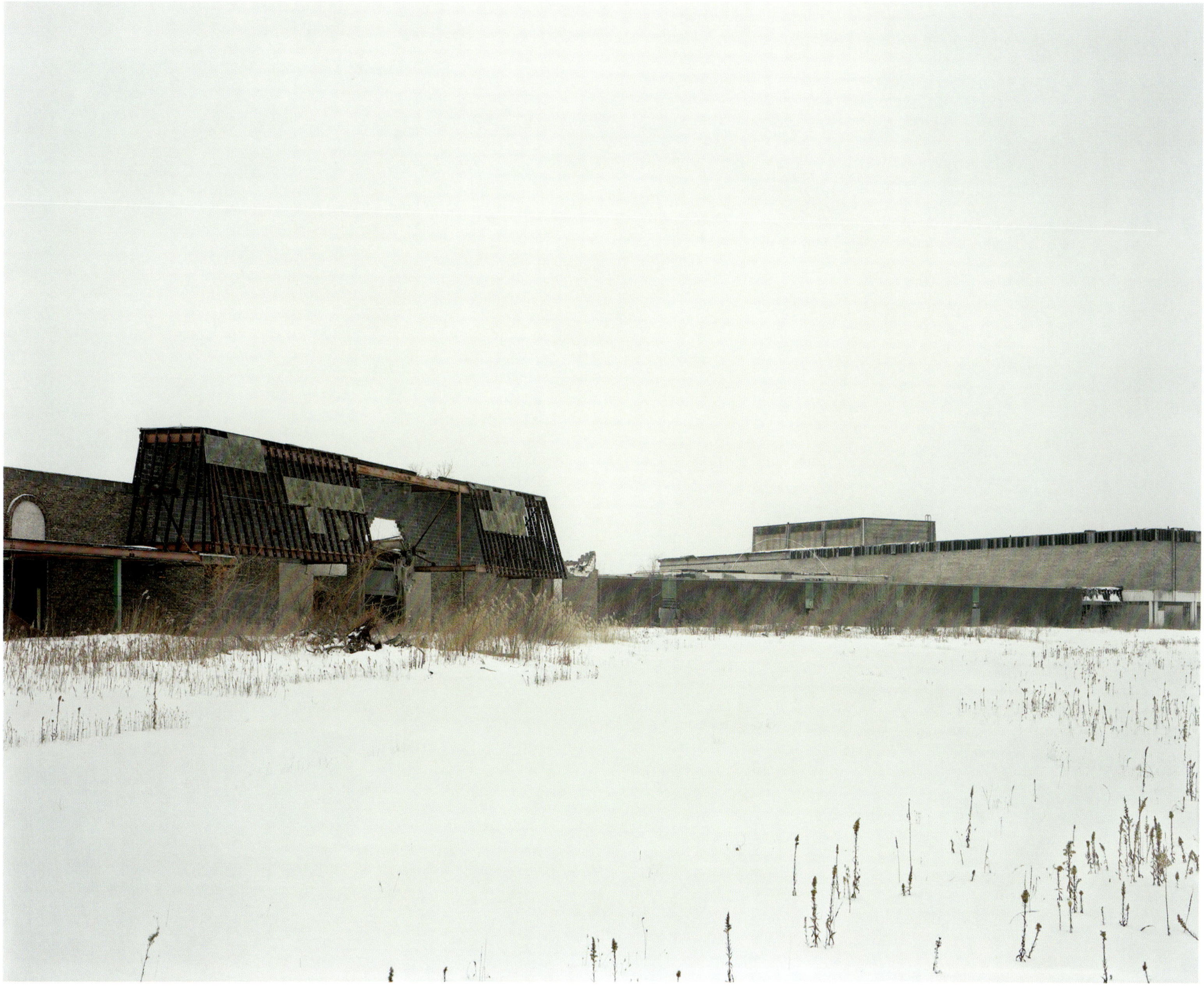

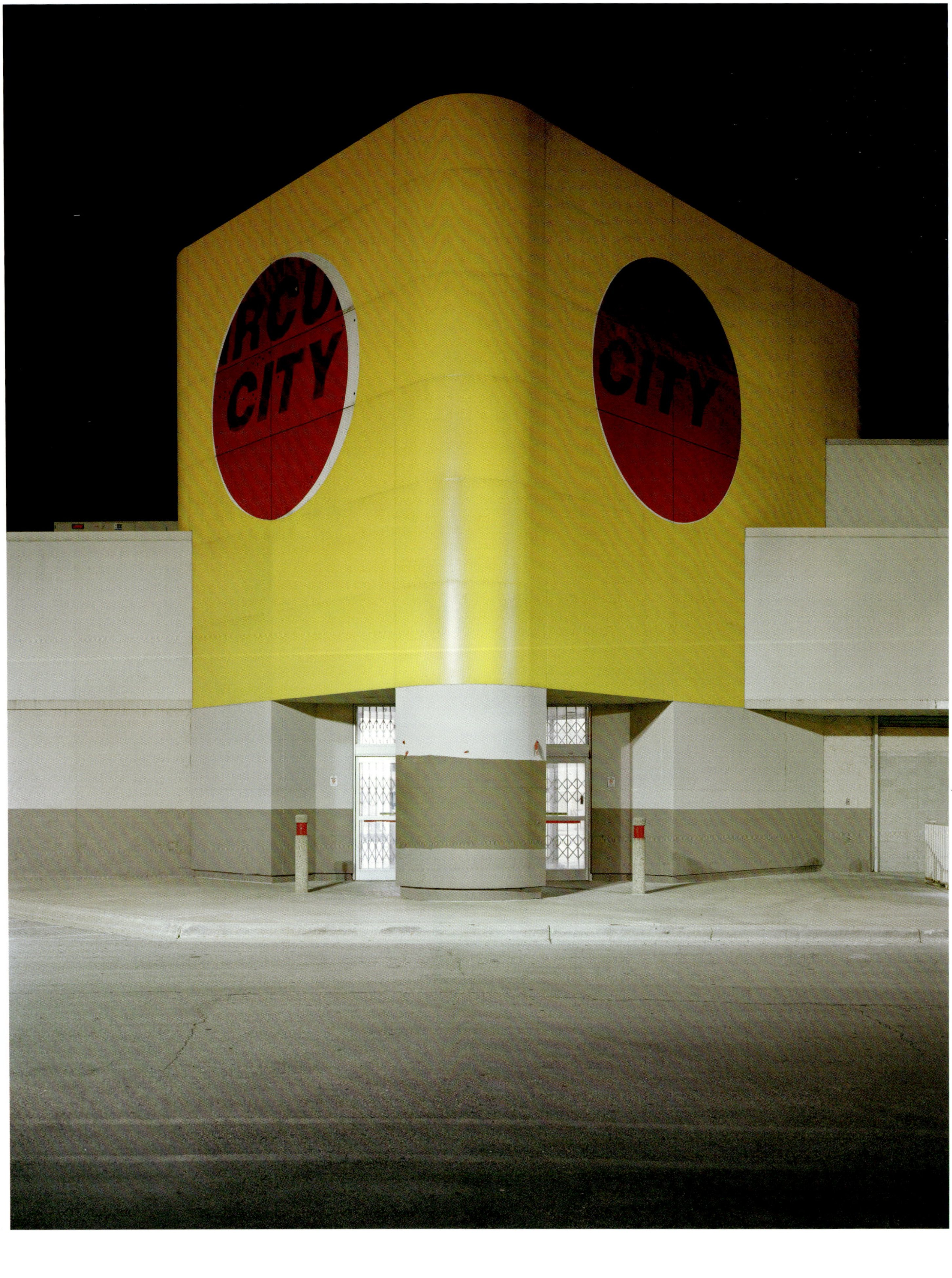
IRCU
CITY
CITY

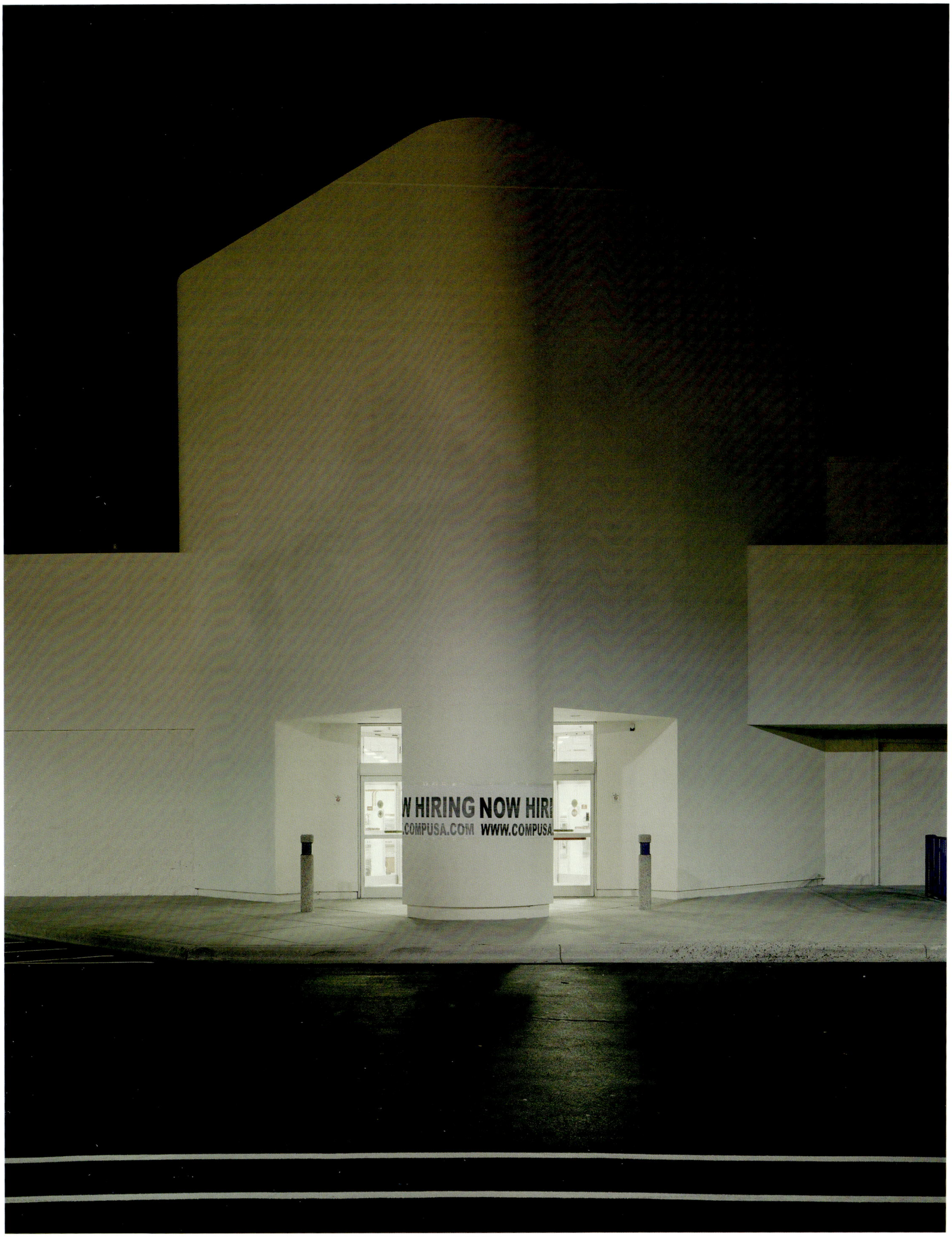

75.

76.

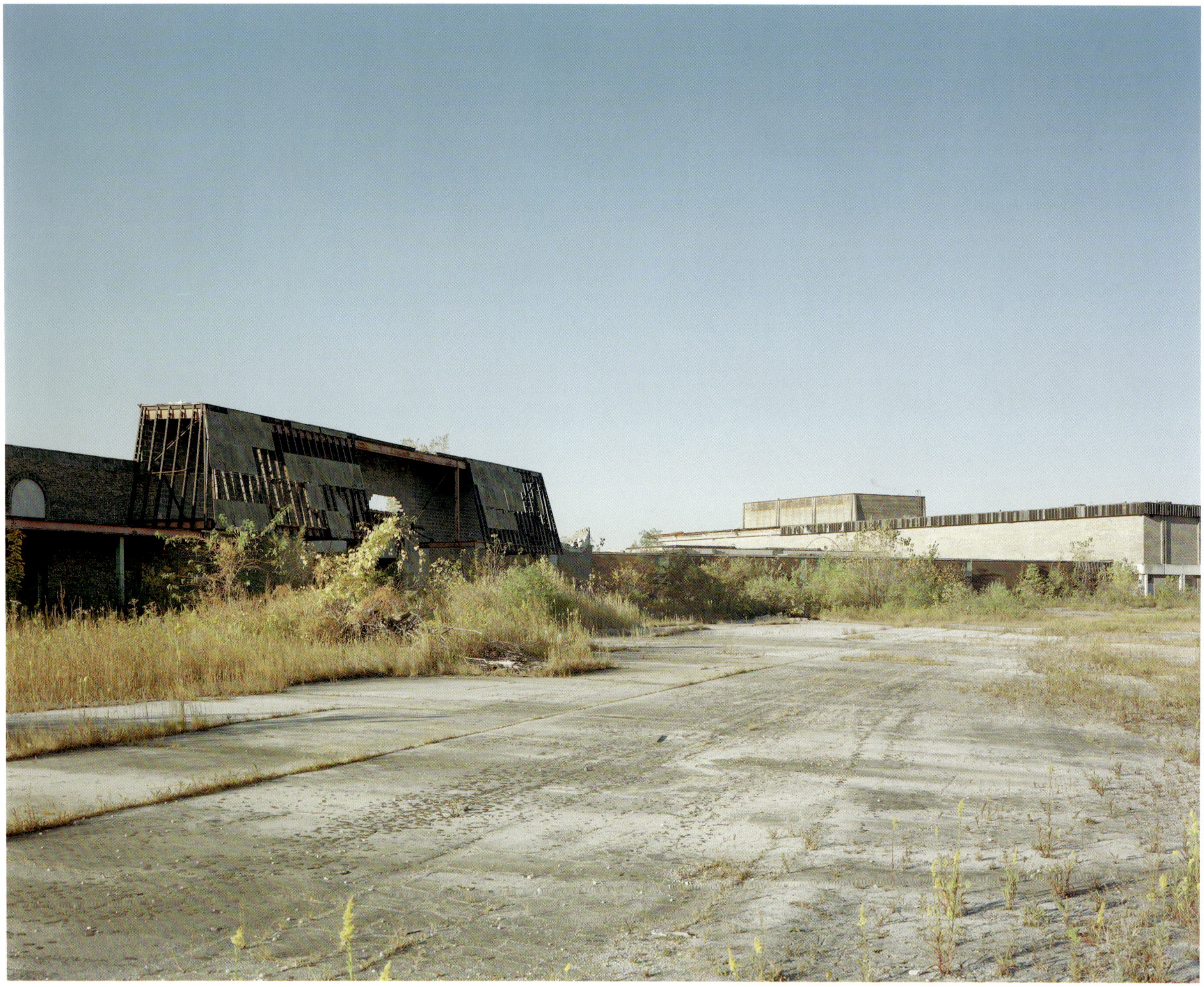

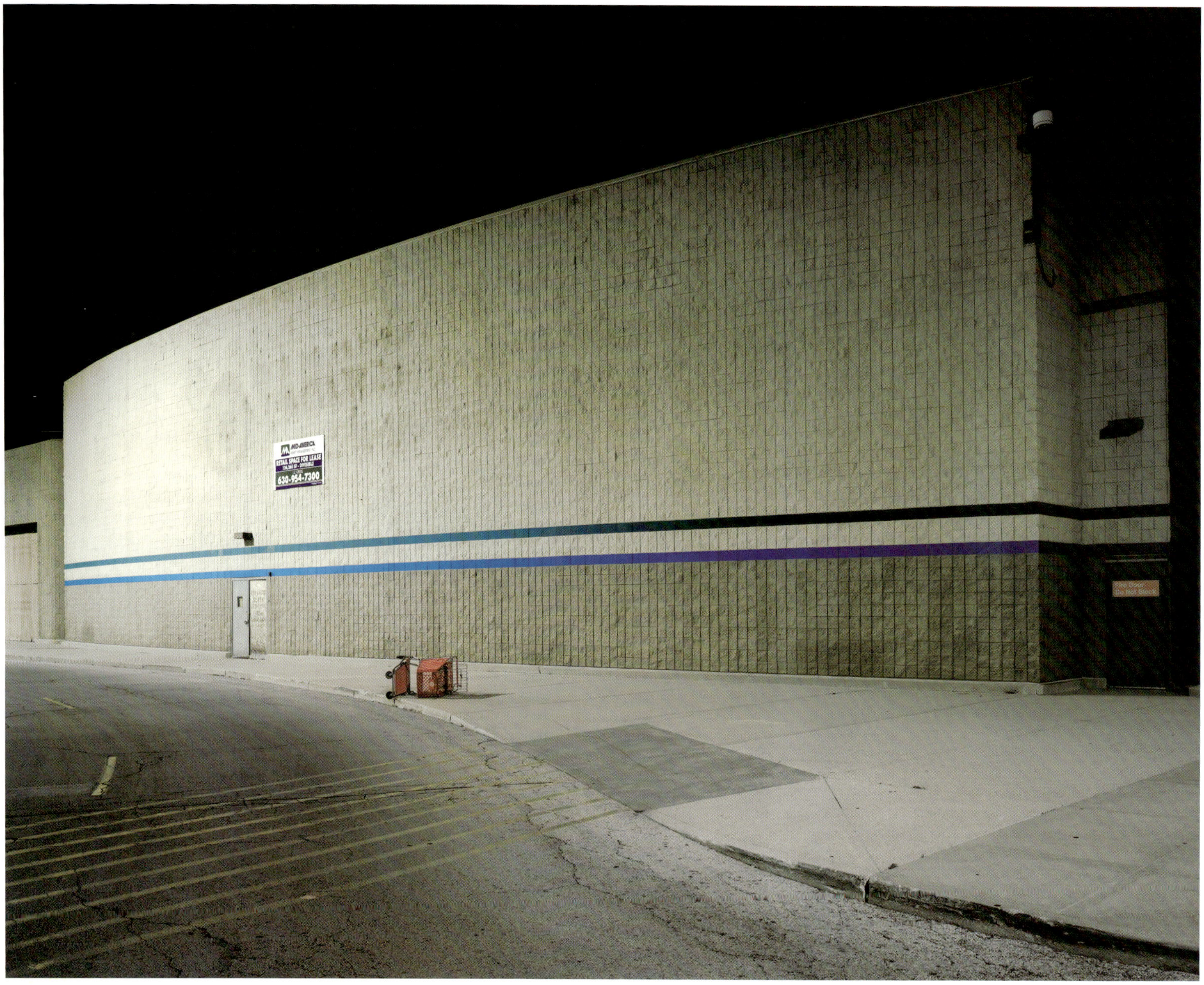

78.

79.

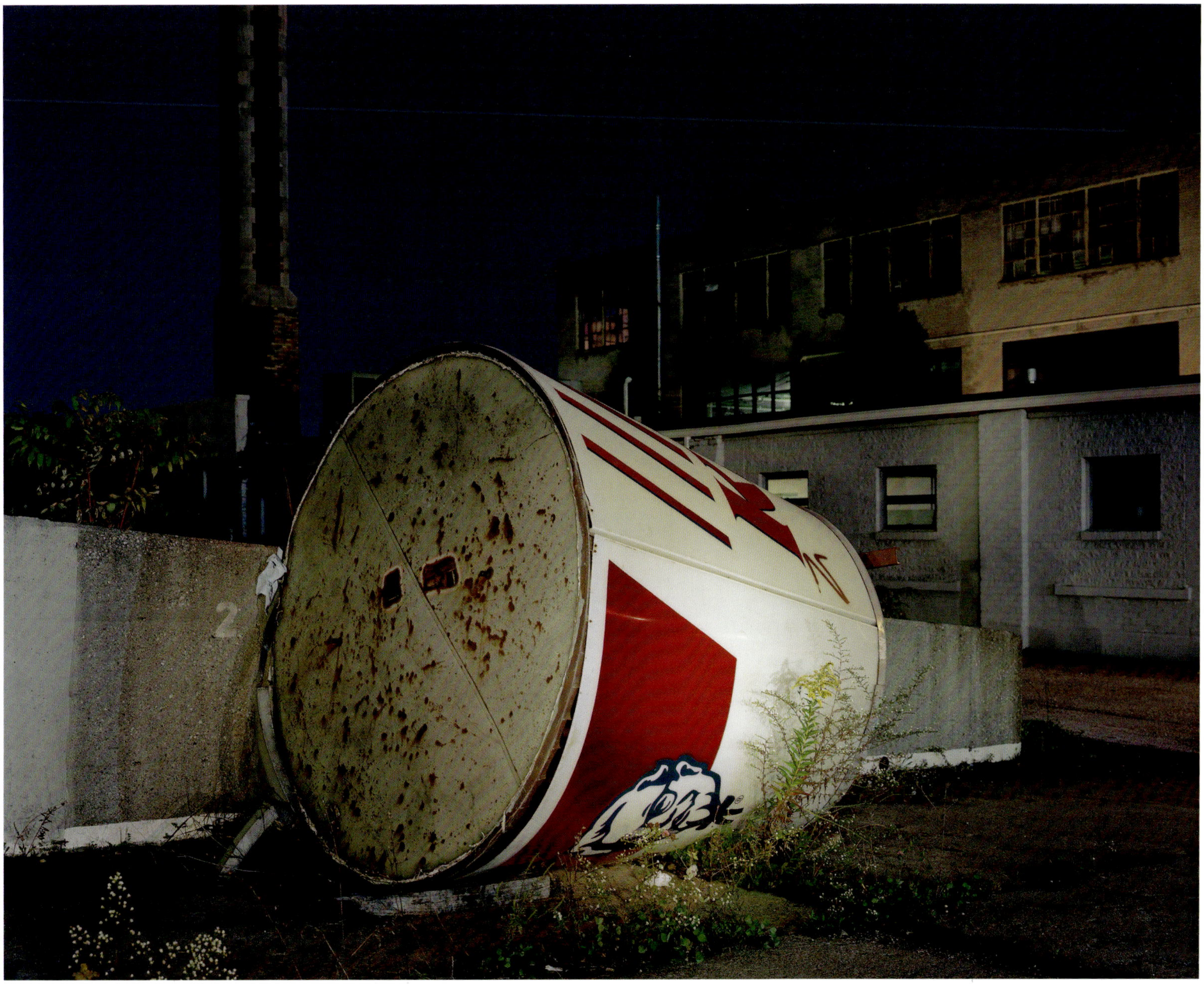

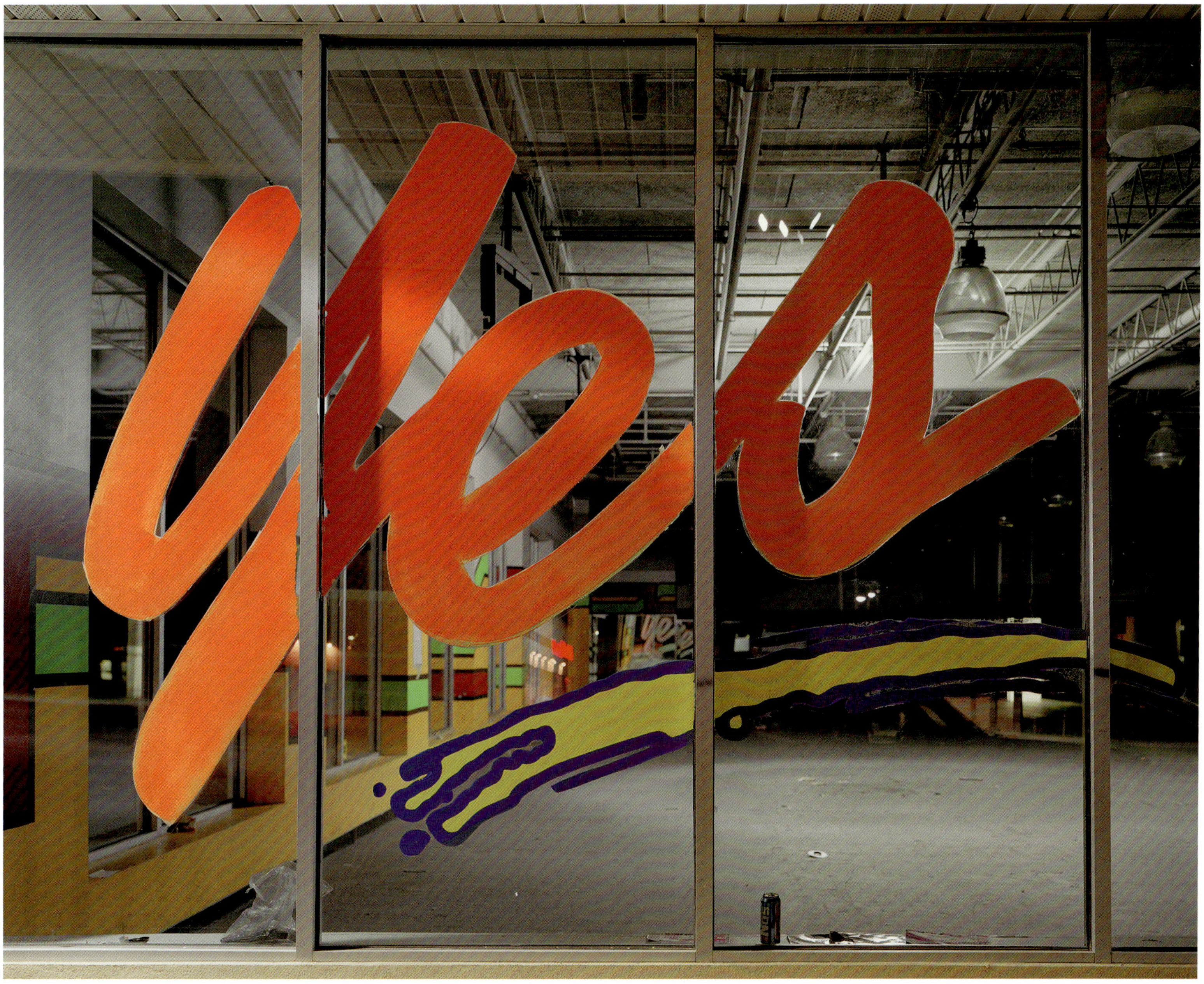
yes

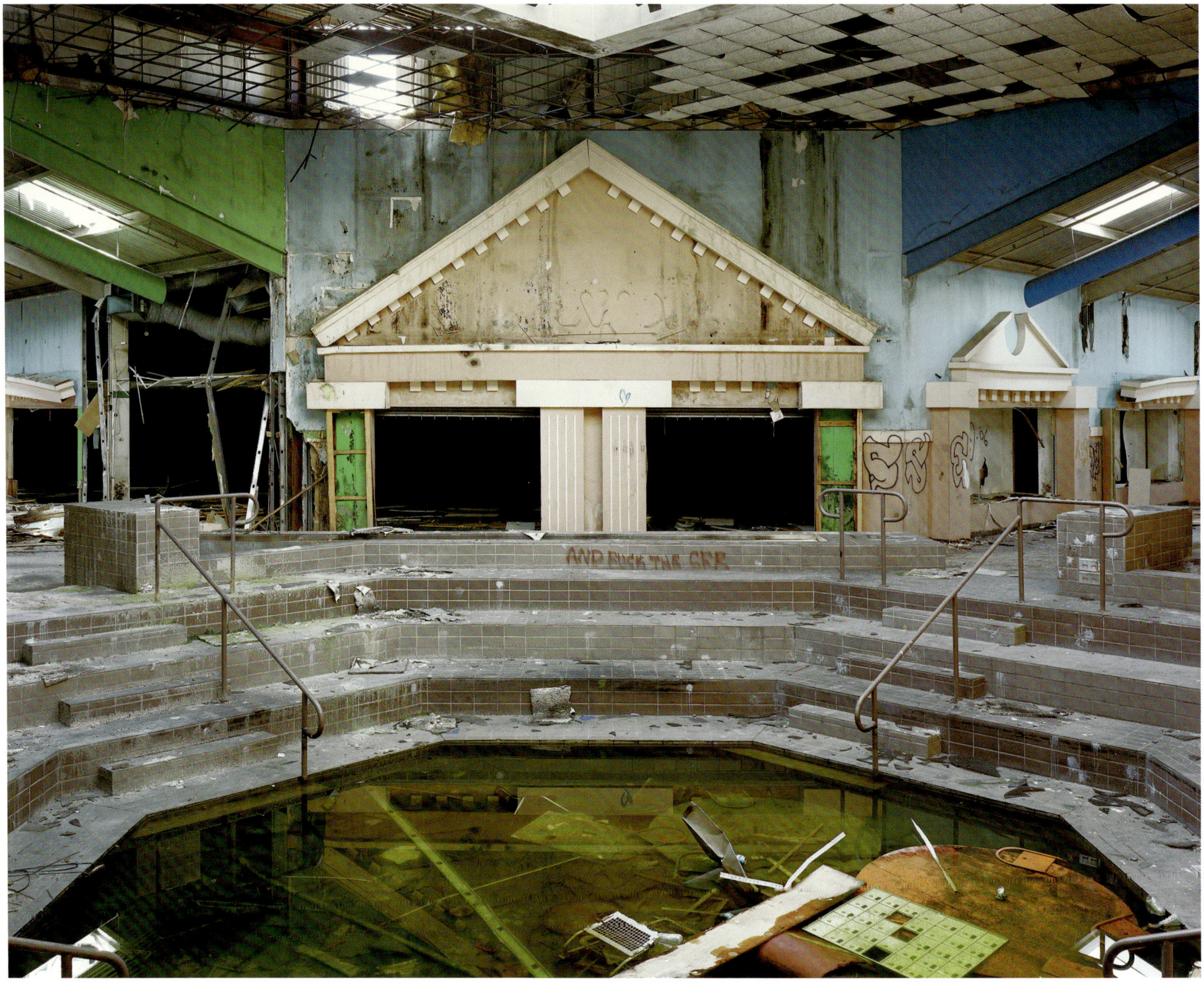

81.

82.

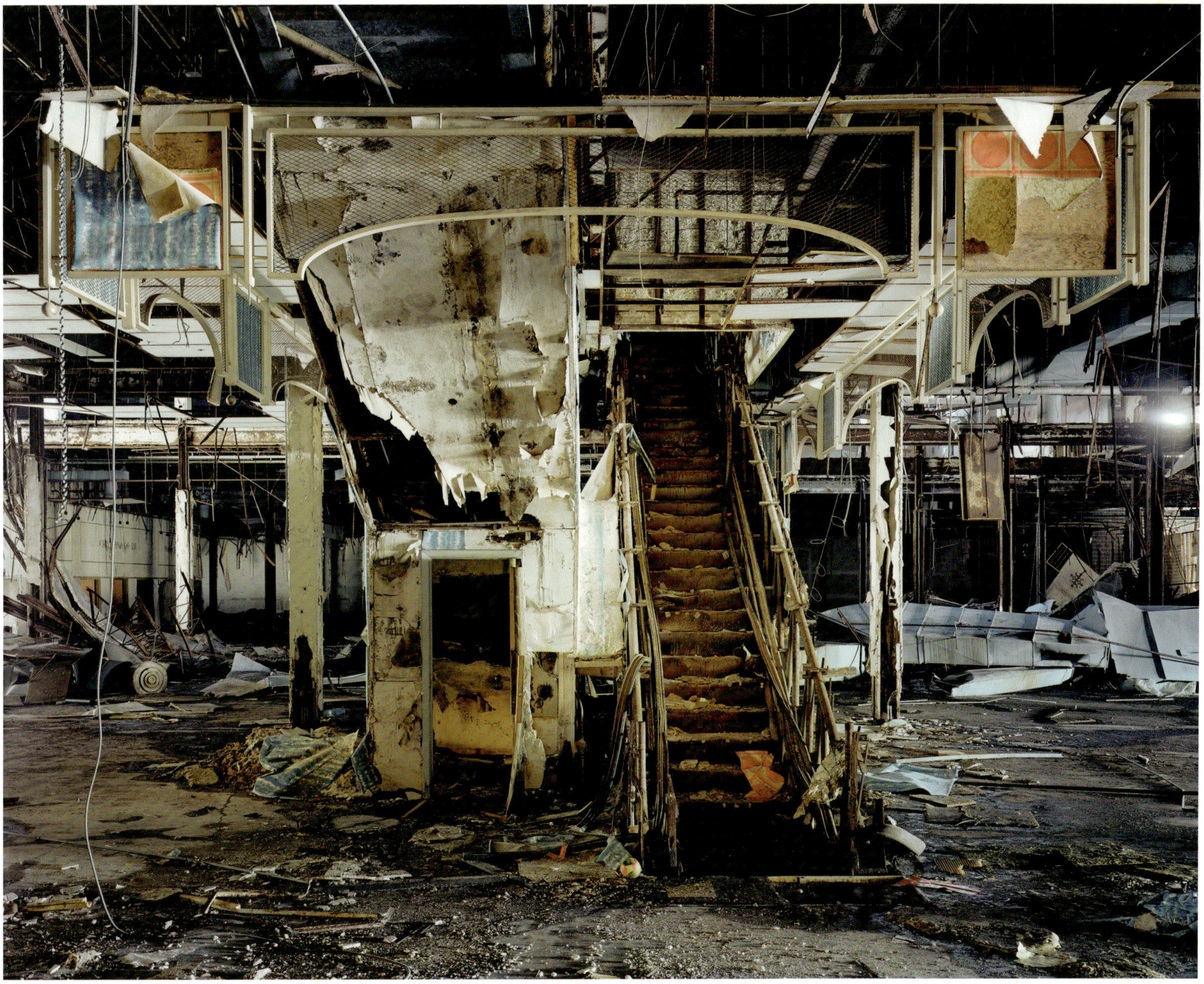

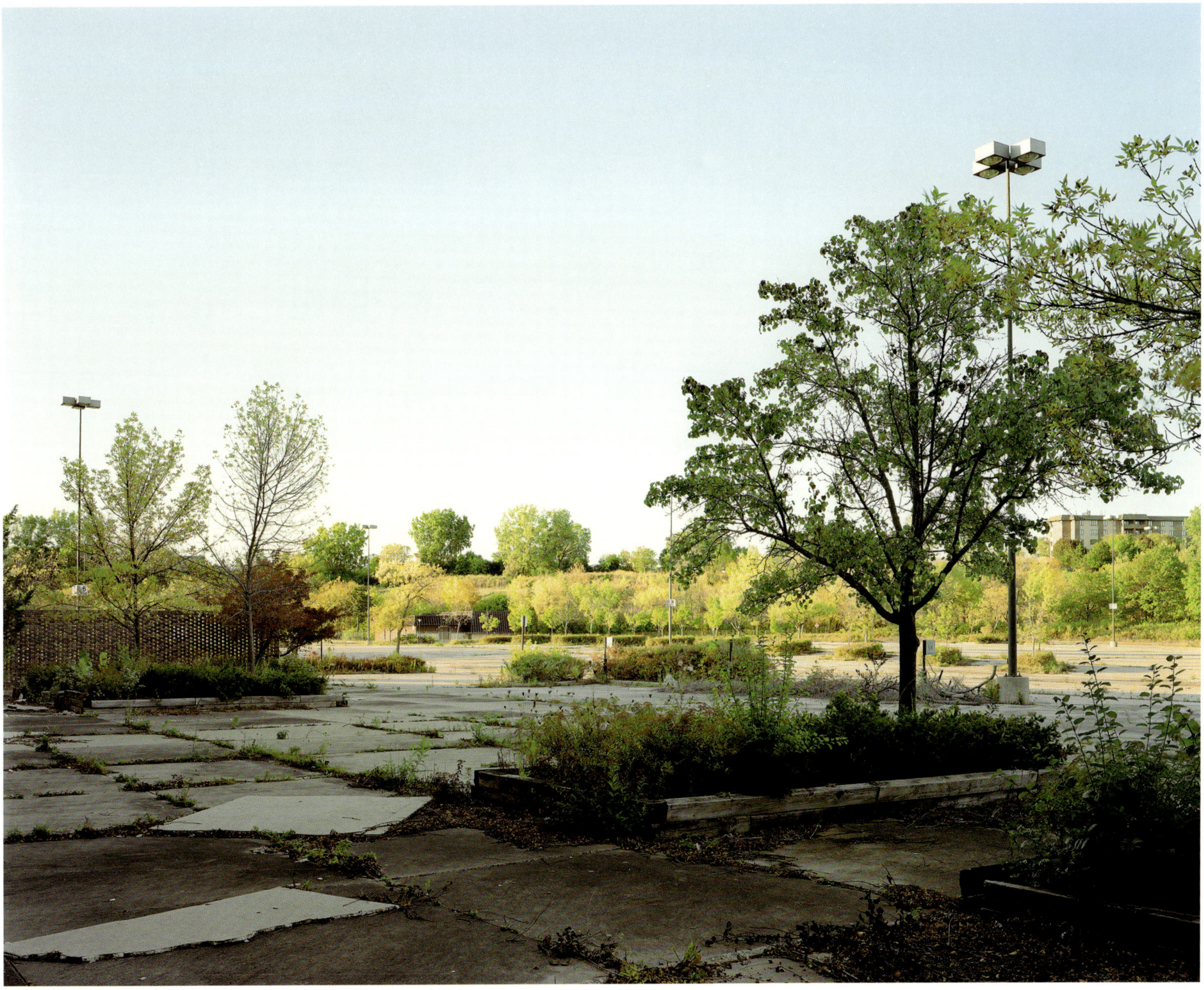

83.

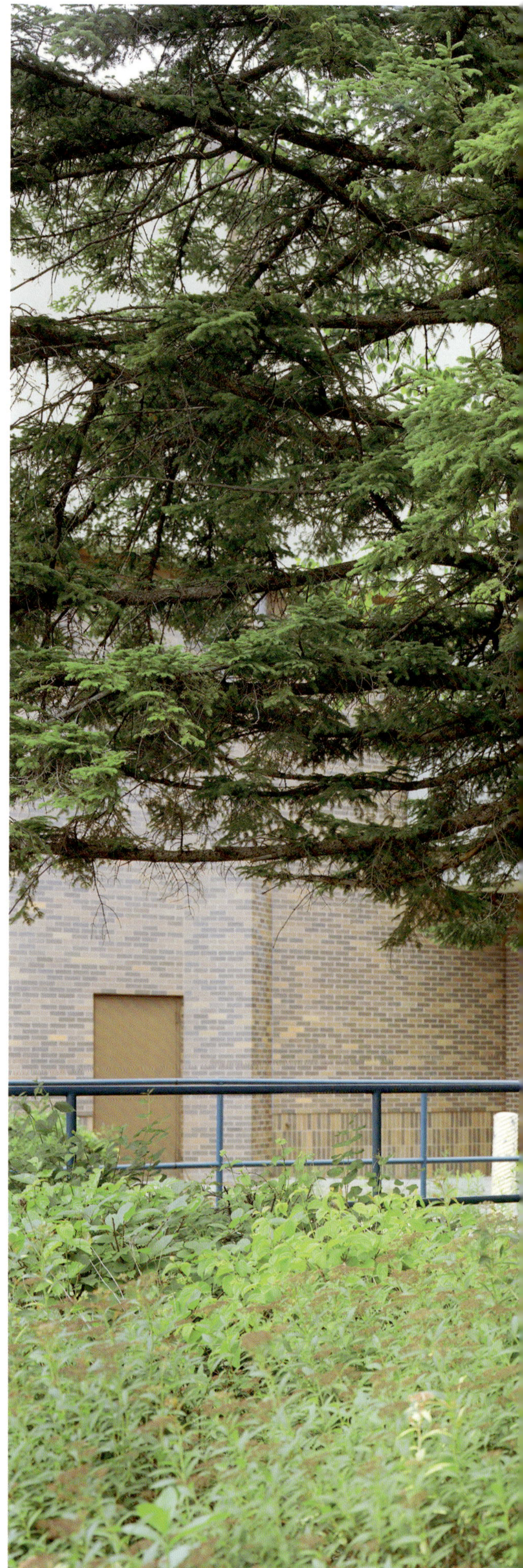

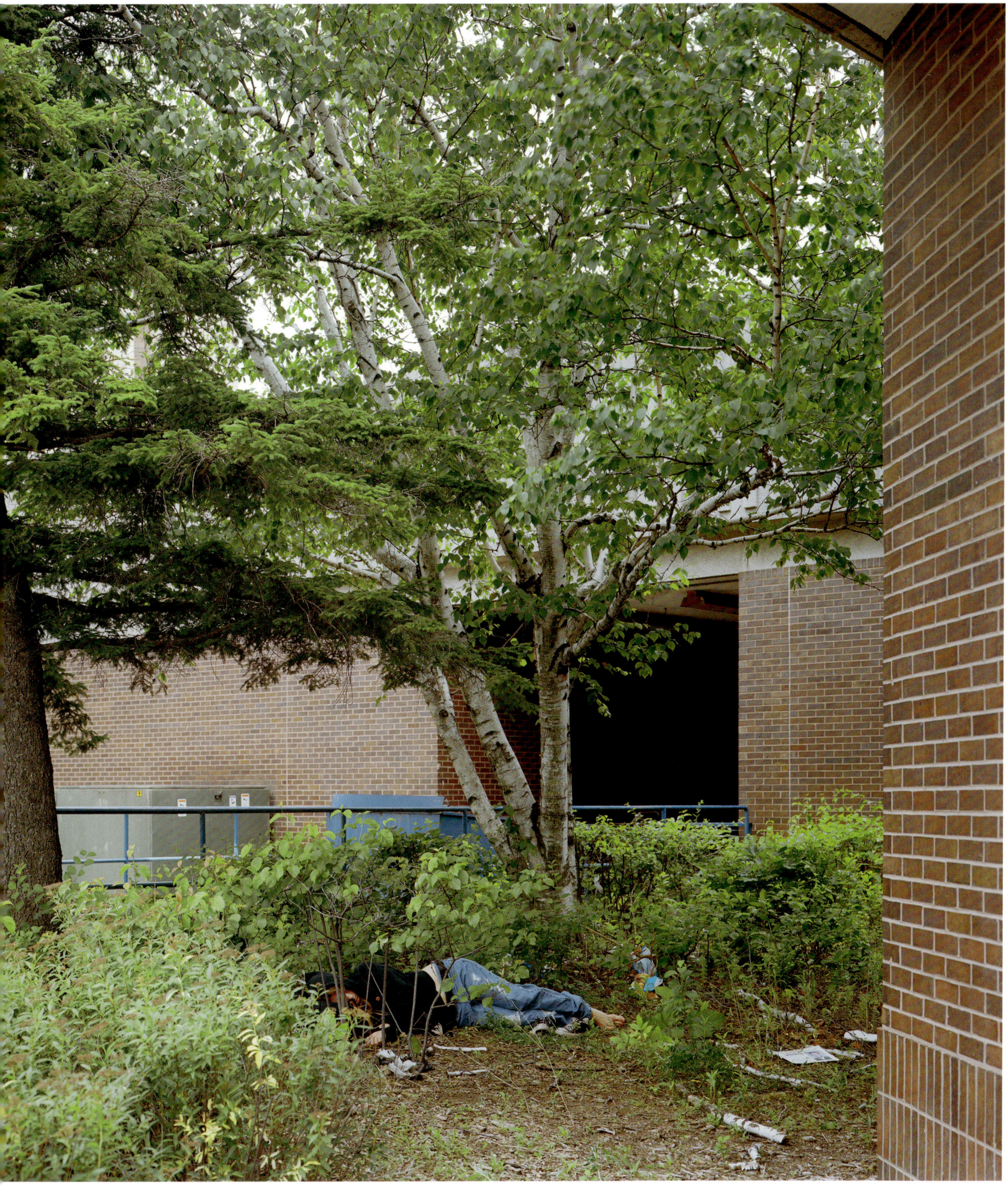

PLATE LIST

RETAIL

5. New York, NY, 2005 (frontispiece)
6. Granger, IN, 2003
7. Flushing, NY, 2004
8. Kenosha, WI, 2003
9. Cleveland, OH, 2003
10. Smithhaven, NY, 2003
11. Bloomington, MN, 2004
12. Gurnee, IL, 2003
13. Gurnee, IL, 2005
14. Lyndhurst, OH, 2004
15. Chicago, IL, 2002
16. Chicago, IL, 2007
17. Gurnee, IL, 2005
18. Las Vegas, NV, 2003
19. Chicago, IL, 2006
20. Miami, FL, 2006
21. Milwaukee, WI, 2006
22. Medford, NY, 2003
23. Gurnee, IL, 2005
24. Indianapolis, IN, 2004
25. Skokie, IL, 2007
26. Cleveland, OH, 2003
27. Chicago, IL, 2003
28. Black River Falls, WI, 2006
29. Chicago, IL, 2003
30. Chicago, IL, 2003
31. Chicago, IL, 2007

THRIFT

32. Untitled, 2007
33. Untitled, 2007
34. Untitled, 2006
35. Untitled, 2006
36. Untitled, 2007
37. Untitled, 2007
38. Untitled, 2005
39. Untitled, 2007
40. Untitled, 2006
41. Untitled, 2006
42. Untitled, 2007
43. Untitled, 2005
44. Untitled, 2006
45. Untitled, 2005
46. Untitled, 2006
47. Untitled, 2006
48. Untitled, 2007
49. Untitled, 2006
50. Untitled, 2006
51. Untitled, 2006
52. Untitled, 2007
53. Untitled, 2005

DARK STORES

54. Chicago Place Mall, 2008
55. Rolling Acres Mall, 2008
56. Dominick's, 2008
57. Canton Centre Mall, 2009
58. Sarah, Deerbrook Mall, 2010
59. Randall Park Mall, 2008
60. Saks Fifth Avenue, 2009
61. Pep Boys, 2009
62. Marshall Fields, 2009
63. Columbus City Center, 2009
64. Simon, Winrock Shopping Center, 2010
65. Toys "R" Us, 2009
66. Richland Mall, 2009 (after Stephen Shore, 1973)
67. Rolling Acres Mall 2, 2008
68. Klingman's Furniture, 2008
69. Six Flags Mall, 2009
70. Summer, Dixie Square Mall, 2008
71. Spring, Dixie Square Mall, 2009
72. Circuit City, 2008
73. Best Thrift, 2010
74. Circuit City, 2010
75. Future Comp USA, 2010
76. Fall, Dixie Square Mall, 2010
77. Winter, Dixie Square Mall, 2011
78. Target, 2008
79. Kentucky Fried Chicken, 2009
80. Powerhouse Gym, 2008
81. Belz Factory Outlet Mall, 2009
82. JC Penney, Dixie Square Mall, 2009
83. Northridge Mall, 2009
84. Rose, Northridge Mall, 2010

INTRODUCTION

1. Opening ceremonies, Goldblatt's Store, September 14, 1960
2. Mr. Thrifty Clown greets Jewel Store officials at Lake Meadows Shopping Center, November 10, 1954
3. Grand opening of the fiftieth Little Big Dollar Store, June 26, 1959
4. Christmas shopping crowd, Polk Brothers Store, December 1959

ESSAYS AND CV

85. Architect's rendering, Dixie Square Mall Center Court, from found 8-by-10-inch negative
86. Page from Economic Area Assessment, Dixie Square Mall Project, 1964
87. Billboard advertisement proposal, Grand Opening, Dixie Square Mall *Courtesy the collection of Jon Revelle*
88. Found photograph remnant, Dixie Square Mall
89. Letter to mall management regarding purse theft, 1966 *Courtesy the collection of Jon Revelle*
90. Price labels, Jewel Food Store, Dixie Square Mall, 1979
91. Zack, Zacharias, Zack, Matthew, Atrium with signage, Dixie Square Mall, 2010
92. City Life, refurbished retail signage, 2008–9 *Courtesy the collection of the Estate of Paul LeBaron Thiebaud*

The Copia project, presented here in *Is This Place Great Or What*, is composed of three series: Retail (2001–6), Thrift (2005–8), and Dark Stores (2008–11). During the course of this decade-long project, while trying to describe an extremely large and complicated set of issues via photography alone, I occasionally gave in to the inclination to collect and cultivate retail-based objects and ephemera (documents, signage, press photo negatives, etc.). Some of this ancillary material—all very much a part of this larger project—is presented at the front of this book. Another selection of items from the long-abandoned Dixie Square Mall in Harvey, Illinois, accompany the essay by Juliet B. Schor.

The Copia project began out of simple questions raised in response to the incredulous statements coming from the nation's politicians, equating shopping with patriotism. On October 26, 2001, the day he signed the Patriot Act into effect, George W. Bush asserted: "The vitality of our economy depends upon the willingness of Americans to spend . . ." So it seemed a simple enough question: "Were people in fact patriotic when shopping?" I simply had to see if this was indeed the case, so, as photographers are apt to do, I began to gather evidence by making pictures of the places where people shop. Slowly this project evolved into a decade-long investigation and obsession.

It could have been a simple series of photographs. There the entranced shoppers were, flags in hand, carts full, credit cards maxing, performing as ordained. Yet I could not accept that this equation was so simple. Having grown up in the suburbs of Long Island where malls and retail offered some form of respite from the banal, I had been there, too. I want things, too—this was not about photographing "the other." To attempt to surreptitiously make a photograph of buzzing and strutting shoppers was so technically problematic my only solution was to find an appropriate setting and simply wait. What revealed itself to me in those long hours under the fluorescent lights was that my method of looking was one more akin to anthropology than art. It also became clear that there was a long and complex history here, one not thoroughly examined.

From 2001 until roughly 2006 I made photographs across the country in big-box stores and malls. I looked specifically for homogenized spaces and in some cases traveled coast to coast to find out exactly how homogenized they were. This group of photographs called Retail presented more pathways toward other investigations than I had expected. I came to contemplate the effects of all this continually cheaper-by-the-dozen consumption and where it all might end after losing its sheen and the patina of the new.

From 2005 to 2008, I focused on the secondary life of consumer goods in thrift shops across the country because they seemed truly endemic as part of the dilemma of mass production of inexpensive products. In this series, Thrift, the subject of my portraits shifted from the shopper/user to the worker/sorter as they weekly faced the mounting pile. After spending three years in thrift shops staring at the tail end of the U.S. middle class I empathized with the workers, as the task of trying to visually conceptualize the gamut of donated items also left me feeling somewhat empty and insignificant.

It seemed, even then, obvious that an economy based on perpetually growing retail would be unsustainable. In May of 2008, in the face of the larger economic and banking catastrophes, tidal waves of new store closings began hitting communities almost daily. It was evident that something more significant was at hand. I wondered if we had reached a tipping point in which the big boxes and malls would lose their power over the consumer. My initial research found that the industry terms for closed retail spaces are dark stores, ghostboxes, and dead malls. In some instances some of the very spaces I had photographed in Retail were now sitting empty, with the signage removed, as if to mask their shame. This verbiage of drama and death over the space paled in comparison to the outcome on communities, unemployment, and the real estate market. In addition to the photographs I made, I found that the seemingly inconsequential objects left behind also gained gravity with new context of abandonment. I began adding those items to my collection: signage, documents, vintage press archive negatives, vintage credit cards, etc.

This attempt to describe an economic and cultural trajectory, set in motion in the twentieth century and how it evolved at the dawn of the twenty-first, has led me here, to a compilation of a record of the past decade of consumer culture.

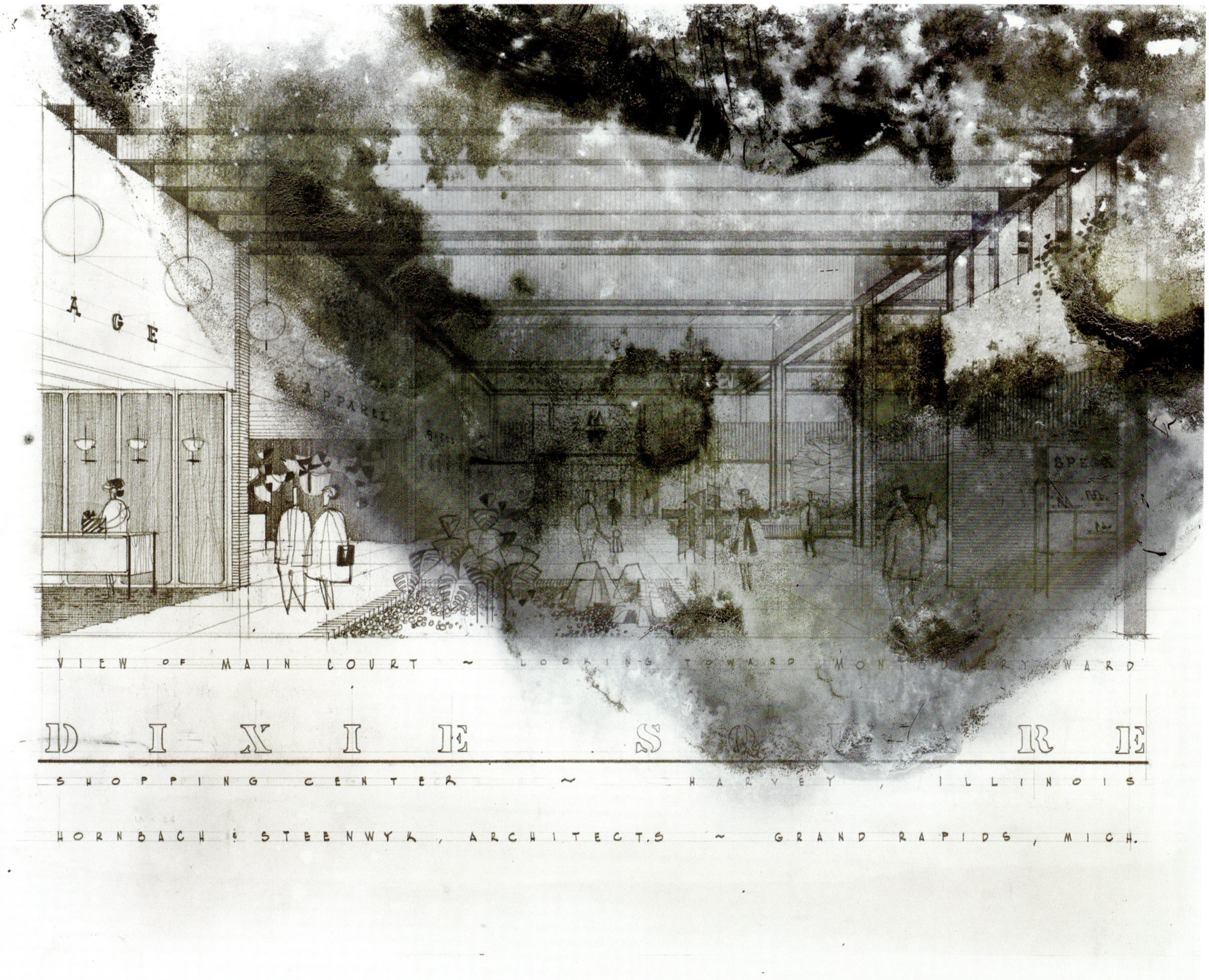
VIEW OF MAIN COURT ~ LOOKING TOWARD MONTGOMERY WARD
DIXIE SQUARE
SHOPPING CENTER ~ HARVEY, ILLINOIS
HORNBACH & STEENWYK, ARCHITECTS ~ GRAND RAPIDS, MICH.

85.

ROBERT MEYER CORPORATION

July 14, 1964 40-24
2

PEOPLE WITH BUYING POWER JUST MINUTES AWAY

EASY DRIVING DISTANCES TO DIXIE SQUARE

JULIET B. SCHOR

SHOPAPALOOZA: THE BOOM AND BUST OF THE RETAIL ECONOMY

American consumer culture, long thought to be as immutable a force of nature as exists, is suddenly unmoored. The consumer boom of the 1990s and 2000s came to a screeching halt in 2008, as the house of cards that was the global financial system collapsed. The U.S. economy tumbled shortly after, leaving consumers reeling. In the months that followed, people lost their jobs, their homes, their credit, and their pensions. The big-box stores, which only a year earlier had seemed like invincible category killers, began shuttering. Malls turned into ghost towns. Retail outlets, big and small alike, teetered on the edge. Dollar stores, once the province of the lowest segment of the market, began outcompeting Walmart and Target. The world of retail was turned upside down.

Nearly three years later no one really knows what the future holds for American consumers. Having been exported around the globe, the American style of life is suddenly looking shaky at home. Economic pundits still talk as if American consumers can resume their role as the engine of growth for the world economy, but this would require their taking on debt they don't want and can't afford. The conventional view assumes that manic shopping is built into the very DNA of Americans, but those formerly willing consumers have started asking questions about a culture whose celebrations of material excess coincided nonchalantly with growing poverty and ecological destruction. An expanding discourse about what makes people happy, whether growth is sustainable, and how community was lost is calling the shopping culture into question. As poverty persists and the planet's ecosystems implode, only time will tell whether 58-inch flat-screens, SUVs, and McMansions will continue to make sense.

THE BOOM YEARS

Most accounts of the consumer boom are morality tales. The conventional narrative is that Americans got greedy and ran up credit card debts to buy a lot of things that they couldn't afford and shouldn't have purchased. Whether it was housing, cars, or computers, the villains are ordinary consumers who engaged in unsustainable financial behavior. There is also a national mea culpa because the nation borrowed from abroad to pay for this spending. The consumer goods came from China, and instead of buying American goods with their export earnings, the Chinese collected their dollars and bought U.S. government debt.

Like most morality tales, this one is too simple. Consumers did buy a lot of stuff, and they, like the nation, used debt to do so. But focusing on character misses the powerful pressures and ecological imbalances that are at the core of the way the system now operates. Some of those pressures are well-known. Through the 1990s and 2000s, American society was becoming increasingly unequal. Income and wealth flowed to the top 20 percent of the population, and even within the top 20 percent, to the highest few percent. This was especially true after 2000. As in other gilded ages, inequality spurred conspicuous consumption and a pervasive sense that everyone was upscaling. The responses were both competitive and defensive. People feared being left behind, so they bought what others in their social circles were buying, whether computers, cell phones, or expensive extracurricular activities for their children. (Suddenly a volunteer summer in Costa Rica seemed necessary for college admission.) People renovated their kitchens and bathrooms because, well, everyone else was replacing that 1950s Formica with granite countertops and cherry cabinets. Yet while consumer norms were rising, incomes were stagnating for most families. Spending had to be paid for by longer hours of work and taking on debt.

At the same time, many of the things that people really needed, like health insurance, child care, and education were getting farther out of reach. The prices for these social and public goods were rising rapidly. The government did less and less to ensure high quality public goods, so affluent households began looking for private substitutes. Unable to afford those pricey big ticket services, the consolation prize for people of ordinary means was cheap goods at IKEA and Best Buy. These came courtesy of a global production system that was churning out enormous numbers of artificially underpriced commodities due to the shift of production to countries where labor is repressed and therefore cheap, and environmental regulations are lax. When workers did manage to demand more, the companies picked up shop and moved on to countries where labor and the environment are even more exploited. Throughout the commodity chain, the failure to include the true cost of carbon emissions in manufacturing and transport kept prices down.

Eventually, this system was producing wildly unsustainable outcomes. The story is best told by considering the case of apparel. Clothing is perhaps the most symbolically important commodity—and it led the way to consumer trends so extreme that collapse became a predictable outcome.

Clothing purchases skyrocketed through the 1990s and 2000s. My research reveals that in 1991, the average American bought 34.7 pieces of outwear and underwear—pants, shirts, coats, dresses, skirts, T-shirts, pajamas, bathing suits, and the like (not counting socks and hosiery). By 1998, that number had increased to 46 per year. By 2007, the last year of the boom, new purchases had increased to an unprecedented 68 per person per annum. That's a new item every 5.4 days.

Falling prices were a big part of why consumers began to purchase so many items. Fashion also played a role. What the industry calls "basics," the styles that stay the same year after year, became a shrinking part of the market. The fashion cycle also speeded up. Clothing producers increased the number of different styles that they offered in any given year. Retailers began moving stock through the selling floor more rapidly. Industry practices "trained" shoppers to look for new merchandise on every return trip to the mall. Suddenly Americans were building walk-in closets, buying containers to put the clothes in, and renting storage space.

They were also giving clothes away or throwing them out, at an unprecedented rate. Donations to Goodwill and other charities that take used clothing began to soar. Textiles increasingly ended up in the trash, and by 2007, the average American tossed 78 pounds of textiles into the household waste stream. A booming business in used textiles topped a billion a year as used items from the U.S. were exported to Africa, Asia, and Latin America. The more Americans bought, the more they discarded. Before long, used clothing was accumulating at a rate and scale that dwarfed all previous levels. Goodwill received so many donations that less than 10 percent ended up in their stores. By the end of the boom, it got hard to even give away clothes, because they were so ubiquitous. The nation was awash in used apparel.

Looked at in historical terms, this state of affairs is hard to fathom. For centuries, clothing was quite expensive. Used garments were also valuable. In fact, they were worth so much that historians report that even into the twentieth century in the West, used clothing often served as an informal, or secondary currency. A coat or suit, or other garment could be given to a trader in exchange for cash, or pawned with an eye to future redemption. The materials (wool, linen, or cotton) were expensive to produce, and a great deal of labor, often skilled, went into garment production. This is no longer the case. While new clothing can still command a price, used clothing is worth very little. Some thrift shops even sell it by the pound, like rice or beans, and at a price that's below what either of those historically cheap commodities cost.

And, it is ecological madness. The fact that apparel has been historically expensive

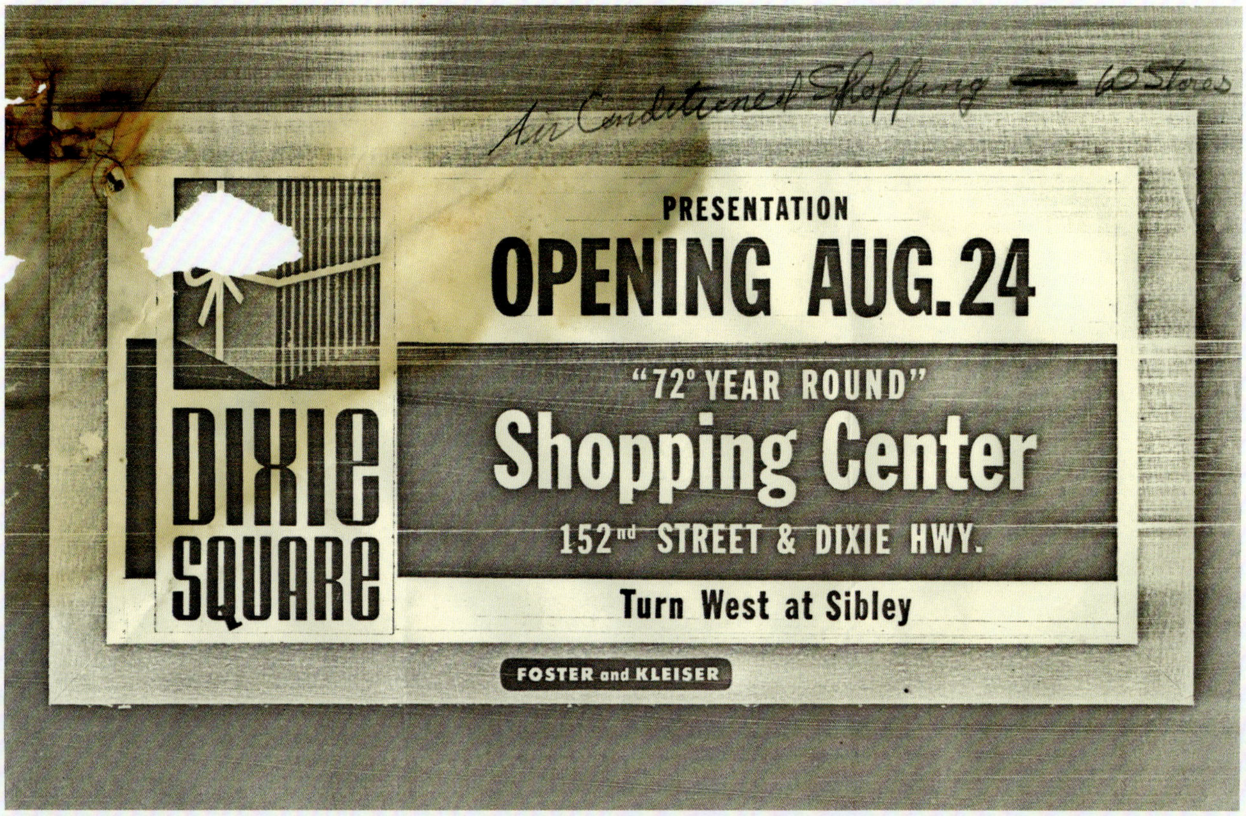
Air Conditioned Shopping 60 Stores
PRESENTATION
OPENING AUG. 24
"72° YEAR ROUND"
Shopping Center
152nd STREET & DIXIE HWY.
Turn West at Sibley
DIXIE SQUARE
FOSTER and KLEISER

87.

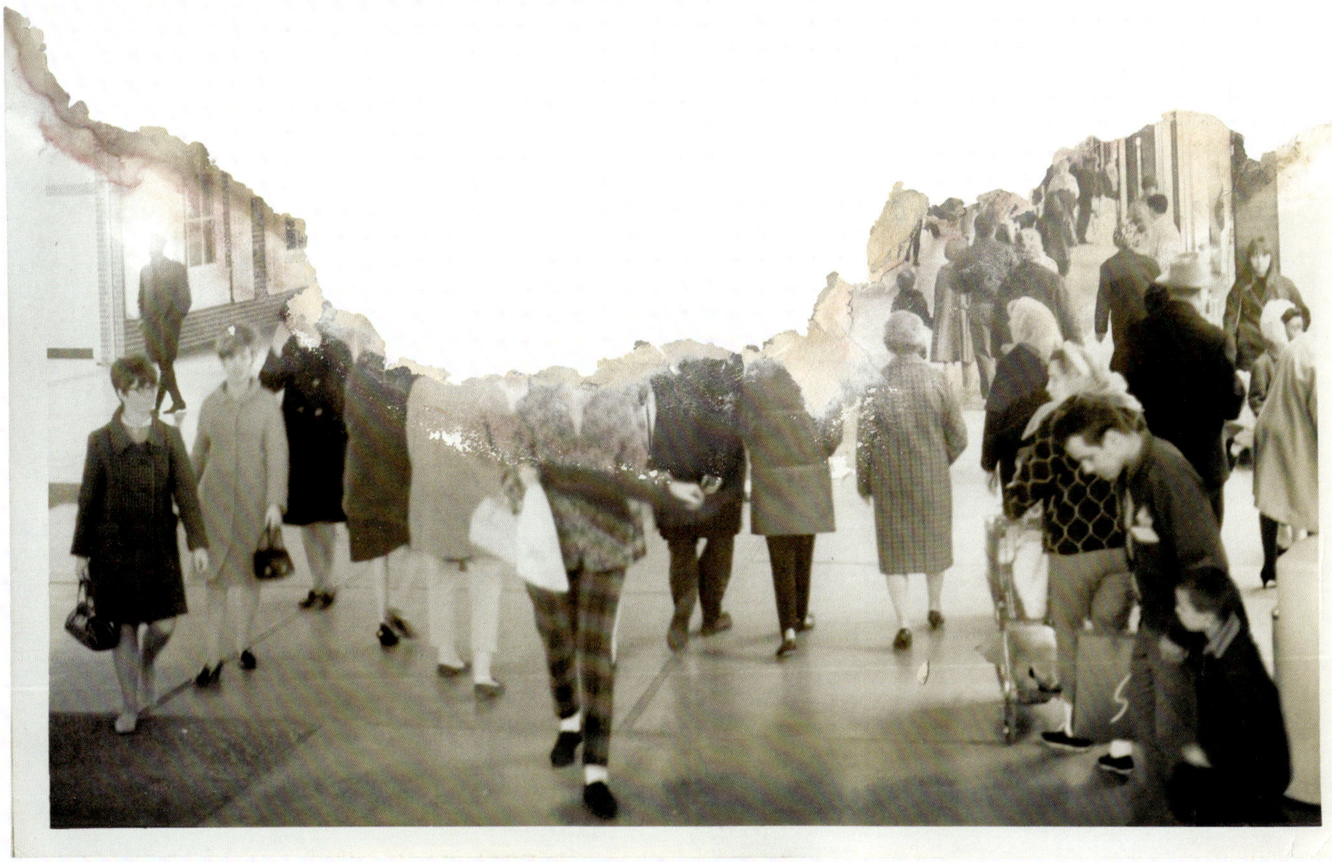

88.

is a reflection of its true costs in terms of human labor and biological resources, such as the land for raising sheep or growing cotton. The near-worthlessness of used apparel means that we have an economic system that creates incentives to waste nature. A rising fraction of what was being thrown out or given away was perfectly usable. Indeed, thrift store shoppers were increasingly likely to find items that had barely been worn, or even came with tags. The detritus of the apparel economy was still perfectly good in functional terms. But it had lost its social value, and as a result, its market price had fallen to near zero. And yet, its value in terms of meeting human needs was higher. And its true ecological costs were higher still. Global capitalism had turned the economics of apparel upside down with consequences that would ultimately prove to be unsustainable, not only for households and the economy, but for retailers and producers as well.

The apparel story has been repeated across the consumer sector. IKEA was the H&M of furnishings, and an important factor in why furniture consumption increased by 150 percent over the period of 1998 through 2007. Long a highly durable good that was passed down from generation to generation, furniture was suddenly cheap and disposable. People began replacing their couches, tables, and chairs because they wanted to, and sometimes because these cheap versions fell apart.

Consumer electronics? By the end of the boom, Americans were purchasing in the billions of new gadgets each year, with discard rates not far behind. According to my calculations consumers bought nearly 200 million cell phones annually, and even more vacuum cleaners. In the small electronics category, purchases reached into the billions.

Ceramics, glassware, sporting goods, knickknacks, jewelry, and most other products followed this pattern of substantial increases in the volume of purchases, and then, after a time, substantial increases in the rate of discard. It was as if all consumer goods were drawn into the vortex of fashion. The cycle of acquisition and discard speeded up across the consumer landscape.

Predictably, the upsurge in buying led in turn to the expansion of retail space. Big boxes expanded. More stores opened. Even as the Internet threatened to replace the bricks and mortar economy, the nation built more palaces of glittering chrome and glass. Visiting the mall became a leisure activity, a default option in a society where people worked too hard and were often too tired to do much else but shop. And as neighborhoods declined as places of social interaction, and time spent socializing fell, the symbolic and practical importance of shopping expanded. Opportunities for spending proliferated, from the boutique to Sam's Club. As the 2000s wore on, there seemed to be no end in sight to the great Shopapalooza.

The spatial trajectory of retailing parallels that of spending. In 1986, the United States had an estimated 15 square feet of shopping center space per person. By 2003 that number had increased by a third, to 20. International comparisons put this outsized level of selling space into perspective. The closest country is Canada, with 13 square feet. In Europe, the country with the most mall space is Sweden, but their 3 square feet per person is a mere seventh of the U.S. level. The mall boom was an especially American phenomenon.

THE CONSUMER AND THE COLLAPSE

For consumers, the 2008 meltdown was traumatic. Houses were foreclosed on. Eight million jobs were lost. Credit card debts went unpaid, and economic pain was everywhere. The retail sector collapsed. In contrast to Europe, where companies tried hard to keep workers on, and used work-sharing as a way to spread the pain, American employers used the recession to institute large-scale layoffs that were in excess of what the drop in sales required. It was hard to avoid the suspicion that companies were using the downturn as a way to continue outsourcing and shifting out of the U.S. labor market. In the first year of recovery U.S. companies created 2.4 million jobs, but only 1 million of them were inside the country.

The country had not experienced a downturn this painful since the 1930s. The fact that it was precipitated by a financial panic caused consumers to adopt a new frame of mind. The present was catastrophic and the future uncertain. So debt had become risky. The housing market was in freefall. No one knew when, or if, employment would rebound. It was, truly, a world turned upside down.

Survey data confirmed a shift among consumers. Attitudes about basic needs began to flip. Since the 1970s, there had been a steady trend toward more consumer goods being regarded as necessities, rather than luxuries. But now, the fraction of the population reporting that clothes dryers, microwaves, TVs, home air conditioning, and dishwashers were necessities dropped dramatically. In other surveys, people expressed newfound enthusiasm for saving. Journalists reported that people were cancelling a variety of luxury services, such as dog walkers. There was a boom in shoe repair and home haircuts. Consumers articulated strong intentions to pay down debt, which they did in droves, and to build up assets. Shopping and spending were suddenly out. Frugality and do-it-yourself were in.

There was also a new cultural attitude toward spending. Some researchers argued that people had shifted from an orientation of me and mine, toward a more communal sensibility. Spenders expressed remorse about the freewheeling boom years, in which they lived for the moment and without much thought for others. People paid attention to the widespread suffering. As they did, many of the things that they had accumulated seemed without worth, even profane. People began downsizing and decluttering and vowed to live within their means. There was a turning away from materialism, consumer excess, and hedonism. The narrative of the greedy consumer came not just from elites, but was picked up by ordinary people who engaged in self-critique and even soul-searching. We have sinned. Time to shop less.

The new frugality meant that the old way of putting people back to work—a debt-financed consumption binge—was unlikely. There were other approaches being advocated, such as a big push from the government for clean energy, or infrastructure, or education spending. But they were mostly ignored as the political discourse moved to the right. The wealthy got more tax breaks. The economy was stuck in neutral.

As time wore on, the problem of unemployment persisted and poverty grew. One in seven Americans ended up on food stamps. Twenty-five million Americans either were officially unemployed, or could only find part-time work. There were five unemployed people for every available position. Recovery, when it started, failed to produce anything like the number of jobs required to put people back to work.

Meanwhile, corporate profits were flush and Wall Street financiers used taxpayers' money to give themselves mega-bonuses. Enabled by growing corporate contributions, an increasingly ugly political discourse turned on immigrants, the unemployed, and public sector workers. Social spending came under increased attack. It seemed increasingly clear that the people who would pay for the economic crisis in years to come would be those least able to afford it—the poor, the middle class, the elderly, the disabled, immigrants, people of color, women, and the young. The rich were getting richer and more transnational. The U.S. economy was being abandoned. And as that happened, the consumer space was restructuring.

Whole malls were abandoned. The weaker retail chains went bust. From bookstores to household goods companies, bankruptcies led to closings and liquidations. Empty storefronts were everywhere, even in parts of the country where the economy wasn't that bad. While retail uncertainty hovered over the land, one thing was clear; the cycle of acquisition and discard had slowed down. People had become more conscious of value, price, and quality. They shopped more carefully and cautiously, buying less and keeping it longer. Thrift shop inventories fell, as donations declined and their middle class clientele grew. The thrifts, along with dollar stores, are examples of how better-off consumers have moved into territory that had formerly been reserved for poor and low-income people.

Around the nation, the wreckage of the consumer economy was evident. In areas that had experienced the cycle of overbuilding and foreclosure, neighborhoods were in various states of collapse. A similar process occurred in retailing. Some malls and big-box locations were abandoned outright. In others, closures and bankruptcies led to high rates of vacancies, with a creeping ghostliness as a result. While the process was most pronounced at the lower end of the retailing spectrum, even high-end malls were not immune.

THE CONVERSION OF RETAIL

These haunting images of empty shopping malls compel us to think about a different way forward. It's hard to avoid the conclusion that the U.S. retail sector is overbuilt. And this is especially true for malls. Even before the building boom the space devoted to malls was many times that of comparably wealthy countries.

Dec. 11, 1966

Administration Office
Dixie Square Shopping Center
154th & Dixie Highway
Harvey, Illinois

Gentlemen:

For many months I looked forward with great anticipation to shopping in your beautiful shopping center. My family and friends have heard rumors that "it wasn't safe to shop at Dixie Square" but we came to see it anyway.

On Dec. 7th, around noon, I came to do some Christmas shopping. About 30 feet from the Woolworth entrance, I was shoved from behind and my purse was snatched by a negro boy about 13 years of age. I pursued him in my high heels as far as possible, but he disappeared into one of the back yards adjoining your parking lot. There were several people around at the time but they would not lift a finger to help me. I can't help but feel that if there had been a security guard or plainclothesman in the lot, he would have heard my screams and would have been able to catch that boy and the gang he was with. As it is, he will probably keep on succeeding with his thievery.

I would like to commend one young man from Woolworths who was kind enough to call the police for me. This enabled me to remain with my car, which might have also been stolen if I had to leave it there. I lost car keys, house keys, driver's license, credit card, favorite, irreplacable pictures and important papers, besides my purse and $64.00. I lost peace of mind, which is worth most of all. To think of some criminals with all of my personal effects, is very unnerving.

My main purpose in writing is to say that I think it is dangerous to shop at your center and I will be afraid to ever park there again even in broad daylight, after my experience. Can't something be done to make Dixie a safer place to shop? I realize it is expensive to hire extra security people and see that trouble makers are brought to justice, but I believe it would be worth every penny. Otherwise, I think Dixie Square may be doomed to fail. An all out effort should be made by the people in charge, the bad reputation your center is getting should be changed while there is still time!

Very truly yours,

[illegible signature]

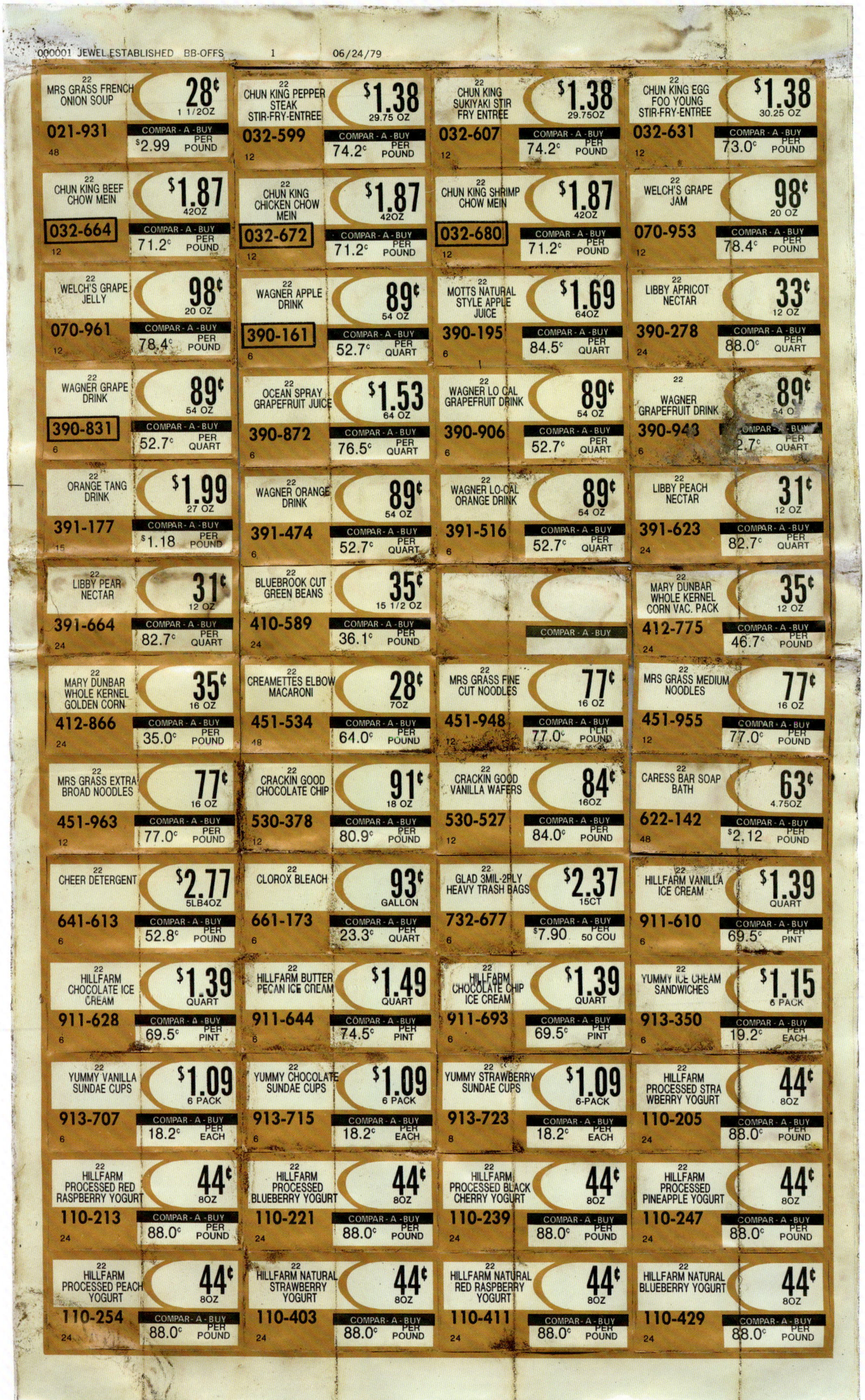
000001 JEWEL ESTABLISHED BB-OFFS 1 06/24/79

MRS GRASS FRENCH ONION SOUP 28¢ 1 1/2OZ 021-931 COMPAR-A-BUY $2.99 PER POUND 48
CHUN KING PEPPER STEAK STIR-FRY-ENTREE $1.38 29.75 OZ 032-599 COMPAR-A-BUY 74.2¢ PER POUND 12
CHUN KING SUKIYAKI STIR FRY ENTREE $1.38 29.75OZ 032-607 COMPAR-A-BUY 74.2¢ PER POUND 12
CHUN KING EGG FOO YOUNG STIR-FRY-ENTREE $1.38 30.25 OZ 032-631 COMPAR-A-BUY 73.0¢ PER POUND 12

CHUN KING BEEF CHOW MEIN $1.87 42OZ 032-664 COMPAR-A-BUY 71.2¢ PER POUND 12
CHUN KING CHICKEN CHOW MEIN $1.87 42OZ 032-672 COMPAR-A-BUY 71.2¢ PER POUND 12
CHUN KING SHRIMP CHOW MEIN $1.87 42OZ 032-680 COMPAR-A-BUY 71.2¢ PER POUND 12
WELCH'S GRAPE JAM 98¢ 20 OZ 070-953 COMPAR-A-BUY 78.4¢ PER POUND 12

WELCH'S GRAPE JELLY 98¢ 20 OZ 070-961 COMPAR-A-BUY 78.4¢ PER POUND 12
WAGNER APPLE DRINK 89¢ 54 OZ 390-161 COMPAR-A-BUY 52.7¢ PER QUART 6
MOTTS NATURAL STYLE APPLE JUICE $1.69 64OZ 390-195 COMPAR-A-BUY 84.5¢ PER QUART 6
LIBBY APRICOT NECTAR 33¢ 12 OZ 390-278 COMPAR-A-BUY 88.0¢ PER QUART 24

WAGNER GRAPE DRINK 89¢ 54 OZ 390-831 COMPAR-A-BUY 52.7¢ PER QUART 6
OCEAN SPRAY GRAPEFRUIT JUICE $1.53 64 OZ 390-872 COMPAR-A-BUY 76.5¢ PER QUART 6
WAGNER LO CAL GRAPEFRUIT DRINK 89¢ 54 OZ 390-906 COMPAR-A-BUY 52.7¢ PER QUART 6
WAGNER GRAPEFRUIT DRINK 89¢ 390-94 COMPAR-A-BUY PER QUART 6

ORANGE TANG DRINK $1.99 27 OZ 391-177 COMPAR-A-BUY $1.18 PER POUND 15
WAGNER ORANGE DRINK 89¢ 54 OZ 391-474 COMPAR-A-BUY 52.7¢ PER QUART 6
WAGNER LO-CAL ORANGE DRINK 89¢ 54 OZ 391-516 COMPAR-A-BUY 52.7¢ PER QUART 6
LIBBY PEACH NECTAR 31¢ 12 OZ 391-623 COMPAR-A-BUY 82.7¢ PER QUART 24

LIBBY PEAR NECTAR 31¢ 12 OZ 391-664 COMPAR-A-BUY 82.7¢ PER QUART 24
BLUEBROOK CUT GREEN BEANS 35¢ 15 1/2 OZ 410-589 COMPAR-A-BUY 36.1¢ PER POUND 24
COMPAR-A-BUY
MARY DUNBAR WHOLE KERNEL CORN VAC. PACK 35¢ 12 OZ 412-775 COMPAR-A-BUY 46.7¢ PER POUND 24

MARY DUNBAR WHOLE KERNEL GOLDEN CORN 35¢ 16 OZ 412-866 COMPAR-A-BUY 35.0¢ PER POUND 24
CREAMETTES ELBOW MACARONI 28¢ 7OZ 451-534 COMPAR-A-BUY 64.0¢ PER POUND 48
MRS GRASS FINE CUT NOODLES 77¢ 16 OZ 451-948 COMPAR-A-BUY 77.0¢ PER POUND 12
MRS GRASS MEDIUM NOODLES 77¢ 16 OZ 451-955 COMPAR-A-BUY 77.0¢ PER POUND 12

MRS GRASS EXTRA BROAD NOODLES 77¢ 16 OZ 451-963 COMPAR-A-BUY 77.0¢ PER POUND 12
CRACKIN GOOD CHOCOLATE CHIP 91¢ 18 OZ 530-378 COMPAR-A-BUY 80.9¢ PER POUND 12
CRACKIN GOOD VANILLA WAFERS 84¢ 16OZ 530-527 COMPAR-A-BUY 84.0¢ PER POUND 12
CARESS BAR SOAP BATH 63¢ 4.75OZ 622-142 COMPAR-A-BUY $2.12 PER POUND 48

CHEER DETERGENT $2.77 5LB4OZ 641-613 COMPAR-A-BUY 52.8¢ PER POUND 6
CLOROX BLEACH 93¢ GALLON 661-173 COMPAR-A-BUY 23.3¢ PER QUART 6
GLAD 3MIL-2PLY HEAVY TRASH BAGS $2.37 15CT 732-677 COMPAR-A-BUY $7.90 PER 50 COU
HILLFARM VANILLA ICE CREAM $1.39 QUART 911-610 COMPAR-A-BUY 69.5¢ PER PINT 6

HILLFARM CHOCOLATE ICE CREAM $1.39 QUART 911-628 COMPAR-A-BUY 69.5¢ PER PINT 6
HILLFARM BUTTER PECAN ICE CREAM $1.49 QUART 911-644 COMPAR-A-BUY 74.5¢ PER PINT 6
HILLFARM CHOCOLATE CHIP ICE CREAM $1.39 QUART 911-693 COMPAR-A-BUY 69.5¢ PER PINT 6
YUMMY ICE CREAM SANDWICHES $1.15 6 PACK 913-350 COMPAR-A-BUY 19.2¢ PER EACH 6

YUMMY VANILLA SUNDAE CUPS $1.09 6 PACK 913-707 COMPAR-A-BUY 18.2¢ PER EACH 6
YUMMY CHOCOLATE SUNDAE CUPS $1.09 6 PACK 913-715 COMPAR-A-BUY 18.2¢ PER EACH 6
YUMMY STRAWBERRY SUNDAE CUPS $1.09 6-PACK 913-723 COMPAR-A-BUY 18.2¢ PER EACH 8
HILLFARM PROCESSED STRA WBERRY YOGURT 44¢ 8OZ 110-205 COMPAR-A-BUY 88.0¢ PER POUND 24

HILLFARM PROCESSED RED RASPBERRY YOGURT 44¢ 8OZ 110-213 COMPAR-A-BUY 88.0¢ PER POUND 24
HILLFARM PROCESSED BLUEBERRY YOGURT 44¢ 8OZ 110-221 COMPAR-A-BUY 88.0¢ PER POUND 24
HILLFARM PROCESSED BLACK CHERRY YOGURT 44¢ 8OZ 110-239 COMPAR-A-BUY 88.0¢ PER POUND 24
HILLFARM PROCESSED PINEAPPLE YOGURT 44¢ 8OZ 110-247 COMPAR-A-BUY 88.0¢ PER POUND 24

HILLFARM PROCESSED PEACH YOGURT 44¢ 8OZ 110-254 COMPAR-A-BUY 88.0¢ PER POUND 24
HILLFARM NATURAL STRAWBERRY YOGURT 44¢ 8OZ 110-403 COMPAR-A-BUY 88.0¢ PER POUND 24
HILLFARM NATURAL RED RASPBERRY YOGURT 44¢ 8OZ 110-411 COMPAR-A-BUY 88.0¢ PER POUND 24
HILLFARM NATURAL BLUEBERRY YOGURT 44¢ 8OZ 110-429 COMPAR-A-BUY 88.0¢ PER POUND 24

Environmental realities also point to excess expansion. Gas prices are currently at $4.00 per gallon, a powerful disincentive to visit the remote locations that many big-box stores and malls occupy. The growing awareness of environmental degradation has also made people much more conscious of the wastefulness of mall culture. There are dangerous metals inside the gizmos at Best Buy. Clothing takes a heavy ecological toll, whether it's the cotton for the T-shirts, or the toxic dyes and finishes. There's an emerging culture of sustainability that recognizes we need to use less energy and fewer virgin resources and materials. In a world awash in stuff, this will require not just re-manufacturing, which is energy intensive, but exchanging, reselling, and trading the surfeit of goods that currently exist. This kind of activity is already well underway, kicked off by eBay and craigslist and joined by Freecycle, thredUP, and other more specialized markets for used goods. While retail spaces can be a part of these trends, they are mainly taking place over the Internet, through the mail, and in residential settings.

So the malls and big-box locations will have to convert to other uses. The economics of retail space dictate that. We are already seeing the future of that conversion, although it is slowed by long-term leases and unrealistic desires for a return to business-as-usual. But around the country retail space is not just turning over to different kinds of retailers such as short-term pop-up stores, thrifts, and flea markets. It is also being repurposed for social uses: schools, day care centers, churches, wellness centers, medical facilities, and libraries are setting up shop where Linens 'n Things, Borders, and Kmarts once operated. There's even a SPAM museum (for the meat, not its electronic progeny) in a former retail space. The linguistic lineage is so appropriate—big-box retailing is the spam of consumer culture.

The relocation of libraries and day care centers into retail spaces is a reminder that part of what kept people at the mall was a growing sense of disconnection and social breakdown. That's why part of how we will solve our problems is by reconnecting with each other and the land that Walmart paved over. We can hold onto our iPhones and computers longer, and put the money we save into our local economies. We can convert the parking lots into community vegetable gardens. We can use the empty stores to teach, and heal, and worship in. That's how we will remember that true wealth comes not from how many pieces of apparel hang in our closets, but from the health of our ecosystems, the time we have available for ourselves, and the quality of our relationships with one another.

Juliet B. Schor is professor of sociology at Boston College, a former Guggenheim Fellow, and the author of *The Overworked American*, *The Overspent American*, and most recently, *True Wealth: how and why millions of Americans are creating a time-rich, ecologically-light, small-scale, high-satisfaction economy.*

DAVID FRANKLIN, *DIRECTOR, THE CLEVELAND MUSEUM OF ART*

AFTERWORD

The Cleveland Museum of Art is honored to present the first major museum exhibition of Brian Ulrich's decade-long examination of the American consumer psyche. The museum is also delighted to be a copublisher with Aperture of the handsome accompanying book, *Is This Place Great Or What: Photographs by Brian Ulrich*.

The power of these engaging color photographs demand the viewer's full visual and emotional attention. Indeed, the CMA began, in 2007, to collect outstanding examples from this project. With insight and patience, Ulrich has created a remarkable body of work that is a revealing yet tender look at the complex issues associated with unbridled consumption at the beginning of the twenty-first century, the results of that excess, and the ongoing impact of the country's financial collapse in 2008. The museum is deeply appreciative of the support and encouragement of Fred and Laura Ruth Bidwell. Their passion for photography and dedication to encouraging individual photographers to achieve personal visions is both admirable and contagious. They have graciously lent their stunning collection of Ulrich photographs, and their foundation generously supported the show, its future display at other museums, and this publication.

After receiving a BFA in photography at the University of Akron, Ohio, Brian joined the Installation Department at the Cleveland Museum of Art in 1997. Following his four years as an Installation Technician, Ulrich went on to undertake his graduate studies at Columbia College Chicago and subsequently gained widespread recognition for his series Copia, through exhibitions, publications, and acquisitions. The Cleveland Museum of Art gladly welcomes Brian back to Cleveland.

The body of work highlighted in this book and exhibition, with an insightful essay by Juliet B. Schor and a revealing artist's statement, aims to meet head-on the reality of our consumer culture. Through extensive travel throughout the United States, Ulrich first documented in the series Retail, shoppers engrossed in navigating the abundance of goods found in the seemingly ubiquitous and vast malls and big-box stores. Then he turned his attention to the workers in the second series, Thrift, as they tried to bring order to the vast amounts of donated, discarded, and unwanted consumer products. Lastly, in Dark Stores the photographer explores the impact of the 2008 financial crisis with haunting architectural landscapes of abandoned buildings and empty parking lots that have become commonplace in towns across America.

Through these photographs and book, available for presentation by the efforts of the staff at the Cleveland Museum of Art and Aperture, we hope that you come to a better understanding of the impact of consumer culture on the landscape we inhabit: the interconnectedness of consumers, what they buy, and what they choose to leave behind. The show, *Brian Ulrich: Copia—Retail, Thrift, and Dark Stores, 2001–11*, will be on display from August 27, 2011, to January 16, 2012, featuring some sixty color photographs and is a welcome addition to the museum's program of contemporary exhibitions.

ACKNOWLEDGMENTS

Brian Ulrich's work is a part of the Cleveland Museum of Art's collection and exhibition program due in large part to the work of Tom Hinson, curator emeritus, who worked closely over the years with the artist, and with Fred and Laura Ruth Bidwell. *Brian Ulrich: Copia—Retail, Thrift, and Dark Stores, 2001–11* will make a statement on the current state of commerce and of the reflection of that in photography in the form of this book as well as the exhibition tour.

Deputy Director and Chief Curator Griffith Mann's support and leadership was welcomed, as was that of Heidi Strean, Director of Exhibitions, and Sheri Walter, Exhibition Coordinator.

A group of staff members from the Cleveland Museum of Art also deserve mention for the time and talent they devoted to the project: Jeffrey Strean and Jim Engelmann in Design for the exhibition design; August Napoli and the Development and External Affairs staff; Moyna Stanton, Jim George, and Joan Neubecker in Conservation; Mary Thomas, Terra Blue, and Alex Jung in Design; Mary Suzor and Kim Cook in Collections Management; Publications staff Jane Takac Panza, and Amy Sparks; and Robin Koch, Curatorial Assistant for Photography and Contemporary Art.

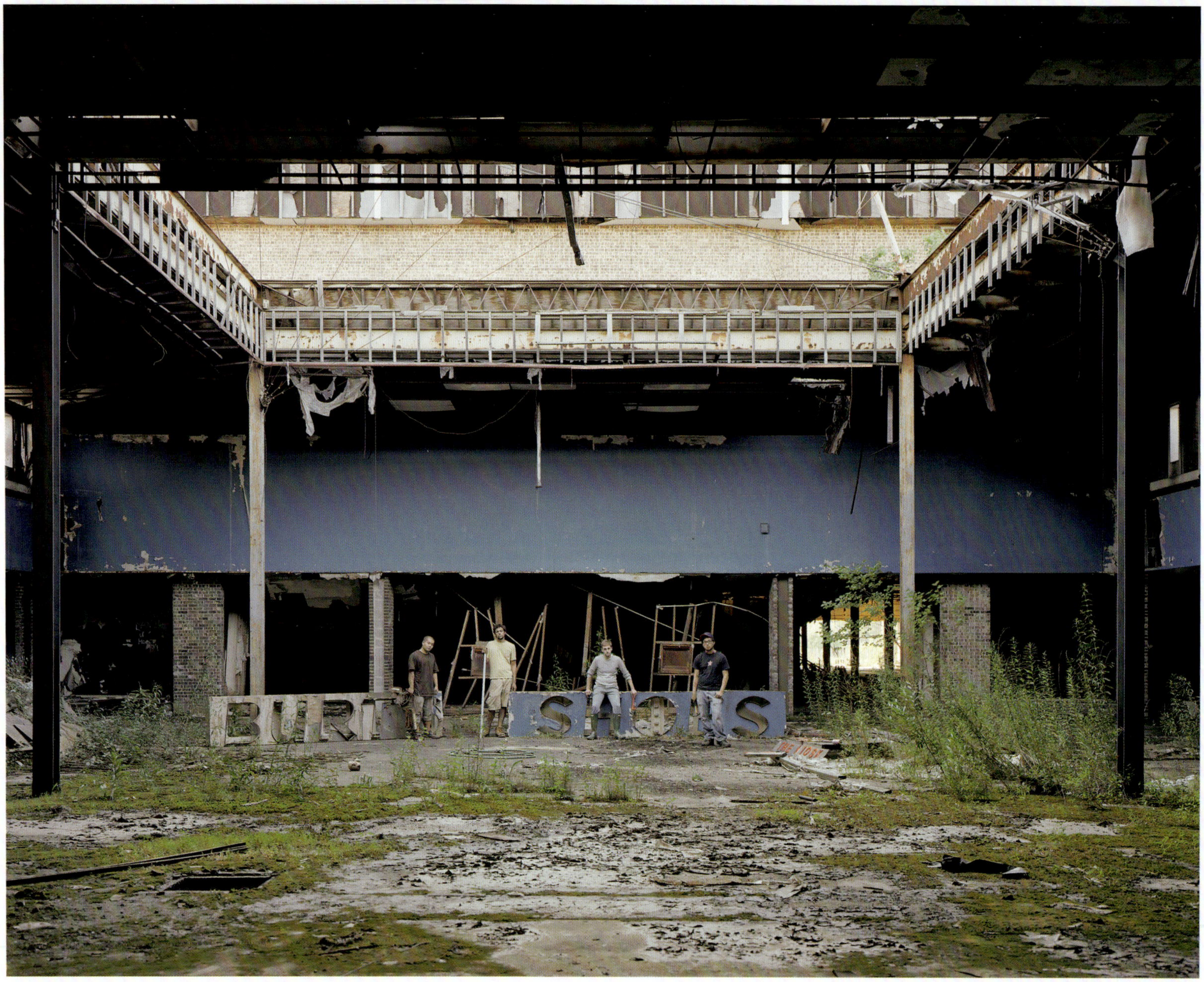

91.

BRIAN ULRICH

Born 1971, Northport, New York
Lives in Richmond, Virginia

EDUCATION

2004 MFA in photography, Columbia College Chicago
1996 BFA in photography, University of Akron, Ohio

SELECTED SOLO EXHIBITIONS

2011 *Brian Ulrich: Copia—Retail, Thrift, and Dark Stores, 2001–11*, Cleveland Museum of Art

2010 *Dark Stores, Ghostboxes and Dead Malls*, Galerie f5,6, Munich

2009 *Dark Stores*, Robert Koch Gallery, San Francisco
Retail and Dark Stores, CEPA Gallery, Buffalo, New York
Thrift and Dark Stores, Julie Saul Gallery, New York

2008 *Copia*, Nerman Museum of Contemporary Art, Overland Park, Kansas
Thrift, Quality Pictures, Portland, Oregon

2007 *notifbutwhen*, Mississippi State University, Mississippi State
Melodramas of Consumption, University of Illinois, Champaign
Copia, Julie Saul Gallery, New York
Copia, Museum of Contemporary Art, San Diego

2006 *Thrift*, Rhona Hoffman Gallery, Chicago
Copia, Robert Koch Gallery, San Francisco

2005 *UBS 12 x 12: New Artists/New Work: Brian Ulrich*, Museum of Contemporary Art, Chicago

2004 *Copia*, Peter Miller Gallery, Chicago

1999 *Produce, Protect, Project*, Millworks Gallery, Akron, Ohio

1996 *Harmony, Dissonance, Harmony*, Millworks Gallery, Akron, Ohio

SELECTED GROUP EXHIBITIONS

2011

American Psyche, Religāre Arts Initiative Gallery, New Delhi

2010

Open Season, Flanders Gallery, Raleigh, North Carolina
Pingyao International Photography Festival, Pingyao, China
Made in Chicago, Photographs from the Bank of America Merrill Lynch Collection, Mona Bismarck Foundation, Paris
Road to Nowhere, Fotofest Biennial, Houston
Ruptures and Continuities: Photography Made After 1960, Museum of Fine Arts, Houston
Instruments of Empire, Brian Ulrich and Amy Stein, Caption Gallery, Brooklyn
Versus, Hous Projects, New York

2009

Contemporary American Portrait Photography, Cleveland Museum of Art
North Carolina Museum of Art, Selections from the Permanent Collection, Raleigh
Summer Reading, Jen Bekman Gallery, New York
MP3 II, Museum of Contemporary Photography, Chicago
Worlds Away: New Suburban Landscapes, Yale School of Architecture, New Haven, Connecticut
Dystopia, Robert Koch Gallery, San Francisco

2008

Lost in the Supermarket, Armand Bartos Gallery, New York
Made in Chicago, Photographs from the Bank of America LaSalle Collection, Chicago Cultural Center
Revisiting America, Bond Street Gallery, Brooklyn
Worlds Away: New Suburban Landscapes, Carnegie Museum of Art, Pittsburgh
About Art: Jason Lazarus and Brian Ulrich, City Gallery, Chicago
Variable Capital, Bluecoat Arts Centre, Liverpool, United Kingdom
Worlds Away: New Suburban Landscapes, Walker Art Center, Minneapolis
Branded and On Display, Scottsdale Museum of Contemporary Art, Arizona

2007

Cornucopia: Documenting the Land of Plenty, Montserrat College of Art Gallery, Beverly, Massachusetts
Ad / Agency, Photographic Resource Center, Boston
Chicagraphy, Galerie f5,6, Munich
The New American Portrait, Jen Bekman Gallery, New York
Branded and On Display, Krannert Art Museum, Champaign, Illinois

2006

MP3: Kelli Connell, Justin Newhall, Brian Ulrich, Museum of Contemporary Photography, Chicago
Point of Purchase, Dumbo Arts Center, Brooklyn
tinyvices, Spencer Brownstone Gallery, New York

2005

Aus Amerika, Galerie Lichtblick, Cologne, Germany
Photocentric, Minnesota Center for Photography, Minneapolis
On the Scene: Jessica Rowe, Jason Salavon, and Brian Ulrich, Art Institute of Chicago
The New Chicagoans, Select Media Festival, Iron Studios, Chicago
Rencontres Internationales de la Photographie/Festival d'Arles, France
Contemporary American Photography, Internationale Fototage Mannheim/Ludwigshafen, Cologne, Germany
Other America, Exit Art, New York
Manufactured Self, Museum of Contemporary Photography, Chicago

2004

Frozen in Light, Zolla/Lieberman Gallery, Chicago
Unframed First Look, Sean Kelly Gallery, New York
FACT/FICTION, Creative Arts Workshop, New Haven, Connecticut

SELECTED COLLECTIONS

Akron Art Museum, Ohio
Art Institute of Chicago
Bank of America LaSalle Collection, Chicago
Bidwell Projects, Peninsula, Ohio
Cleveland Museum of Art
deCordova Museum and Sculpture Park, Lincoln, Massachusetts
J. Paul Getty Museum, Los Angeles
Larry Fields Collection, Chicago

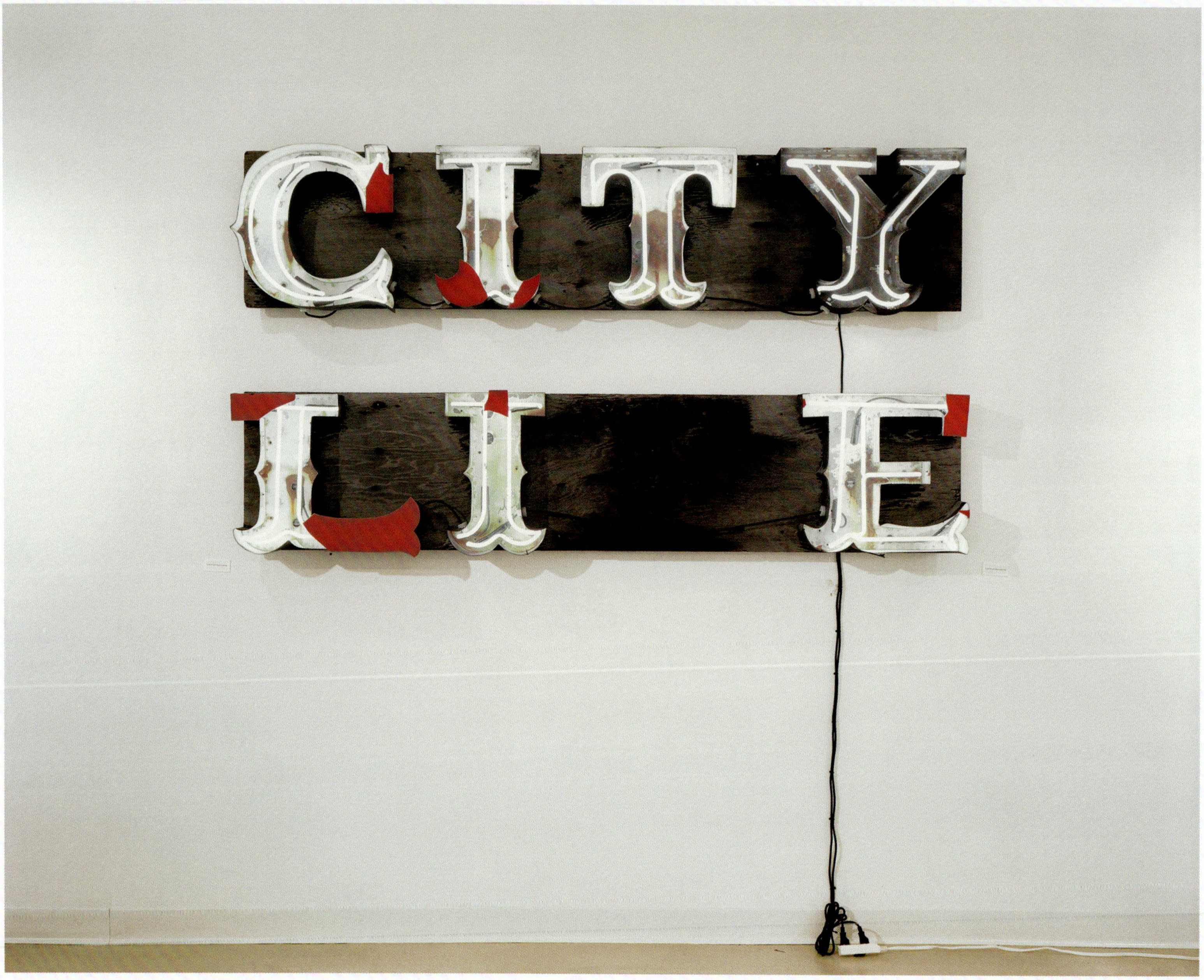

92.

Light Work, Syracuse, New York
Margulies Collection, Miami
Milwaukee Art Museum
Museum of Contemporary Art, San Diego
Museum of Contemporary Photography, Chicago
Museum of Fine Arts, Houston
New York Public Library
Nerman Museum of Contemporary Art, Overland Park, Kansas
North Carolina Museum of Art, Raleigh

SELECTED AWARDS, GRANTS, AND FELLOWSHIPS

2010 Artist-In-Residence, Light Work, Syracuse, New York

2009 John Simon Guggenheim Memorial Fellowship

2007 *Photo District News*'s "30 New and Emerging Photographers to Watch," nomination by Martin Parr
Illinois Arts Council Artist Fellowship, Chicago

2005 City of Chicago Department of Cultural Affairs Community Arts Assistance Grant

2003 Stuart and Iris Baum Grant, Chicago
Albert P. Weisman Scholarship, Columbia College Chicago

2002 Jack Jaffe Purchase Award, Chicago
Follett Fellowship, Columbia College Chicago

SELECTED BOOKS AND EXHIBITION CATALOGS

2011 *Is This Place Great Or What.* New York: Aperture; Cleveland Museum of Art.

2010 *Prix Pictet 2010–Growth.* New York: teNeues Publishing Group.
Fotofest 2010 Biennial Catalogue: Contemporary US Photography, Vol. 1. Houston: Fotofest; Amsterdam: Schilt Publishing.

2008 *Presumed Innocence: Photographic Perspectives of Children.* Lincoln, Massachusetts: deCordova Museum and Sculpture Park.
Campbell, David, and Mark Durden. *Variable Capital.* Liverpool, U.K.: Liverpool University Press.

2007 Halberg, Garth Risk. *A Field Guide to the North American Family.* Brooklyn: Mark Batty Publisher.
Hirsch, Robert. *Light and Lens: Photography in the Digital Age.* Waltham, Massachusetts: Focal Press.
Branded and On Display. Champaign, Illinois: Krannert Art Museum.

2006 *MP3: Midwest Photographers Project, "Copia"* New York: Aperture; Chicago: Museum of Contemporary Photography.
McQuade, Donald, and Christine McQuade. *Seeing & Writing 2.* New York: Bedford/St. Martin's.

2005 *Universal Experience: Art, Life, and the Tourist's Eye.* Chicago: Museum of Contemporary Art.

2004 *Sites* (6x6 Series). Chicago: Columbia College Chicago.

SELECTED PUBLICATIONS AND REVIEWS

Lowenstein, Roger. "Deleveraging." *New York Times Magazine*, July 18, 2010.
Dykstra, Jean. "Dispatches from the Brink." *Art in America*, June/July 2010, pp. 77–80.
Watriss, Wendy, and Andreas Muller-Pohle, eds. "Contemporary US Photography." *European Photography, No. 87*, June 2010.
"Requiem voor de mall." *Vrij Nederland*, January 2010, pp. 36–41.
Helfand, Glen. "Brian Ulrich." *Color Magazine*, January 2010, pp. 70–77.
"Shots of Reality." *Time Out Chicago*, August 20–26, 2009, pp. 12–13.
"The Story: Consumerism as Art." *American Public Media*, August 5, 2009.
"Everything Must Go." *Mother Jones* magazine, July/August, 2009, p. 15.
Aletti, Vince. "Thrift and Dark Stores." *New Yorker*, June 29, 2009.
"Closed for Business." *Chicago Tribune Magazine*, June 28, 2009, pp. 12–13.
Rexer, Lyle. "About the Cover." *Photograph* magazine, June 2009.
Walsh, Bryan. "Recycling the Suburbs." *Time Magazine*, March 23, 2009.
"Thrift." *Vice Magazine*, August 2008.
Lowenstein, Roger. "No More Free Bubble." *New York Times Magazine*, July 27, 2008.
Madrick, Jeffrey. "La Fin De L'Illusion." *Le Monde Magazine*, July 2008, pp. 66–70.
Colberg, Joerg. "Brian Ulrich—Copia." *YVI Magazine*, No. 2, June 2008.
Kaplan, Jeffrey. "The Gospel of Consumption." *Orion*, May/June, 2008.
"Brian Ulrich: Thrift." *La Republicca*, No. 601, June 2008.
Stoll Steven. "Fear of Fallowing." *Harper's Magazine*, March 2008, p. 88.
Melis, Wim. "Act of Faith." *Noorderlicht*, 2007.
Woodward, Richard B. "Brian Ulrich: The Tough Go Shopping." *ARTnews*, November 2007.
Genocchio, Benjamin. "The Walk (Silently) Among You: The Suburban Photographers." *New York Times*, September 30, 2007.
Time Magazine, August 2007.
Pollan, Michael. "You Are What You Grow." *New York Times Magazine*, April 22, 2007.
"30 Emerging Photographers." *Photo District News*, March 2007.
"Happiness." *Mother Jones* magazine, March/April 2007.
"Brian Ulrich." *New Yorker*, February 5, 2007.
"Brian Ulrich, Copia." *New York Times*, February 2, 2007.
Lu Jan, Patricia. "Ambient Parking Lot." *Harper's Magazine*, January 2007.
Arter, Alan. "Still materialism, even when the material is second-hand." *Chicago Tribune*, December 22, 2006.
Helfand, Glen. "Brian Ulrich, Robert Koch Gallery." *ArtForum*, October 2006.
Fischer, Zane. "MP3 Midwestern Photographers: The Midwest Photographers Publication Project." *Photo-Eye*, Winter 2006.
Swanson, Mary Virginia. "Publishing the Photographic Book." *Photo-Eye*, Winter 2006.
Faconti, Dana. "Photography Now." *Photography Quarterly*, No. 94, 2006.
"Consuming Passion." *Chicago Tribune Magazine*, February 5, 2006.
"Young, Gifted and Creative." *Chicago Tribune*, November 17, 2005.
Leica World, 2/2005, September 2005
"Lost in the Supermarket." *Chicago Journal*, March 17, 2005.
Photo District News EDU, Vol. 3, Issue 2, Fall 2004, pp. frontispiece, 6, 10.
Adbusters Magazine, 2004–2008.

This book and exhibition would not at all be possible without the generous vision of Frederick E. and Laura Ruth Bidwell. Their commitment to the arts subverts the consumer paradigm that this book describes. In addition, Tom Hinson, Lesley Martin, Jenny Goldberg, Andrew Sloat, Heidi Strean, Griffith Mann, Juliet Schor, and staff at the Cleveland Museum of Art and Aperture Foundation worked many hours distilling such voluminous work into a coherent publication. The John Simon Guggenheim Memorial Fellowship made much of the photographing possible, as did a grant from the Illinois Arts Council. Support came from passionate friends and mentors such as Dawoud Bey, Bob Thall, Michael Weinstein, Andrew Borowiec, Pat Bishop, Kelli Connell, Paul D'Amato, Barbara Kasten, Barbara DeGenevieve, Terry Evans, Peter Hales; and also my dearest peers: Jon Gitelson, Matthew Siber, Colleen Plumb, Ian Whitmore, Shannon Benine, Greg Stimac, Bryan Steiff, Daniel Shea, Anna Shteynshleyger, Brad Temkin, Scott Fortino, Jason Reblano, and Mary Farmilant. For guidance and comaderie: The North American and European Piece of Cake Collective, Amy Stein, Ofer Wolberger, Bill Sullivan, Justin James Reed, Cara Phillips, Alec Soth. The list could go on and on. . . .

I've also been quite lucky to have assistance and support while photographing, traveling, exploring, and producing work from Alice Wells, Cory Scozzari, Johnathan Swafford and June Sung, Mike Schwartz, Zack Forsyth, Zack Sabin, Kara Peters, Claire Demos, Jeffrey Brandsted, Kate Rogers, Sandy Carson, Stephen Dirado, Justin Newhall, Luke Burke, Chase Browder, Peter Baker, Cassandra Davis, Zacharias Abubecker, Matthew Avignone, Marc Falzon, Hani Eid, Harvey Smith, Sara Condo, Alison Malone, and Jon Revelle.

I am grateful to my galleries Julie Saul, Rhona Hoffman, Nicole Stanner, and Robert Koch and Ada Takahashi. Thanks as well to Rod Slemmons, Natasha Egan, Karen Irvine, Kate Bussard, David Travis, Lisa Hostetler, Barbara Tannenbaum, Joerg Colberg, Jeff Hoone, Hannah Frieser, and Mary Goodwin. I have also appreciated the patronage of Matti Bunzl and Billy Vaughn, Martin Margulies, Mike Hoeh, William Katzin and Katherine Solender, John and Jane Panza, Gary Greener and Bret McAllister, John Hass and Mary Francis Budig, Chris and Tracie Guthrie, Tom O'Neil, Allen Thomas Jr., Ellen Harris, George Lenz, Lawrence Nathan, and Jeffrey Cohen.

Thank you to my friends, Todd, Laurel, George; and family, Hans and Naomi, Frank and Anja, Ron and Colleen.

Finally, with all my love to my wife, Rachelle, and my daughter Aralie.

. . . .

Editor: Lesley A. Martin
Designer: Andrew Sloat
Production: Matthew Harvey

The staff for this book at Aperture Foundation includes: Chris Boot, *Executive Director*; Mary Colman St. John, *Chief Financial and Administrative Officer*; Jenny Goldberg, *Associate Editor*; Susan Ciccotti, *Senior Text Editor, Books*; Kellie McLaughlin, *Director of Sales and Marketing*; Linda Truesdale, *Director of Development*; Amelia Lang, Andrea Chlad, *Work Scholars*

Is This Place Great Or What is part of Aperture Foundation's First Book Initiative to publish new work by emerging artists.

Copublished with the Cleveland Museum of Art on the occasion of the exhibition, *Brian Ulrich: Copia—Retail, Thrift, and Dark Stores, 2001–11*, on view August 27, 2011, to January 16, 2011.

Organized by the Cleveland Museum of Art, the accompanying exhibition was made possible by the Fred and Laura Ruth Bidwell Foundation. The Cleveland Museum of Art is generously funded by Cuyahoga County residents through Cuyahoga Arts and Culture. The Ohio Arts Council helped fund this exhibition with state tax dollars to encourage economic growth, educational excellence, and cultural enrichment for all Ohioans.

THE CLEVELAND MUSEUM OF ART

First edition
Printed by Main Choice in China
10 9 8 7 6 5 4 3 2 1

Library of Congress Control Number: 2011927770
ISBN 978-1-59711-192-8

Aperture Foundation books are available in North America through:
D.A.P./Distributed Art Publishers
155 Sixth Avenue, 2nd Floor
New York, N.Y. 10013
Phone: (212) 627-1999
Fax: (212) 627-9484

Aperture Foundation books are distributed outside North America by:
Thames & Hudson
181A High Holborn
London WC1V 7QX
United Kingdom
Phone: + 44 20 7845 5000
Fax: + 44 20 7845 5055
Email: sales@thameshudson.co.uk

aperturefoundation

547 West 27th Street
New York, N.Y. 10001
www.aperture.org

CLOSE OUT

07/29/79

22

GENERAL MILLS
PEANUT BUTTER
COOKIE MIX

89¢

32OZ

253 211

12

COMPAR - A - BUY

44.5¢ PER POUND

CLOSE OUT

07/29/79

22

COLD POWER X-E
15¢ O/L

$1.59

49OZ

641 423

10

COMPAR - A - BUY

51.9¢ PER POUND

CLOSE OUT

COMPAR - A - BUY

CLOSE OUT

COMPAR - A - BUY

CLOSE OUT

CLOSE OUT

07/29/79

2

BETTY C
DBLE C
BTCH C

253 2

12

CLOSE OUT

CLOSE OUT

CLOSE OUT

CLOSE OUT